A SIMPLE GUIDE TO COMMON MUSHROOMS

Mushrooms of the Northwest

by Teresa Marrone and Drew Parker

Adventure Publications
Cambridge, Minnesota

Acknowledgments

Some of this material has appeared in ***Mushrooms of the Upper Midwest***, by Teresa Marrone and Kathy Yerich. It may have been edited for the Northwest.

Cover, book design and illustrations by Jonathan Norberg

Page layout by Teresa Marrone

Edited by Brett Ortler

Photo credits by photographer and page number:

All photos by Drew Parker unless noted.

Cover photo: Rainbow Chanterelle *(Cantharellus roseocanus)* by Drew Parker

Additional photo credits

Teresa Marrone: **9**, all 3. **10**, Conical, Flat, Bowl-shaped, Funnel-shaped. **11**, Irregular, Scalloped edge, Ribbed, Hygrophanous (all 3). **12**, Volva. **13**, Skirt-like ring, Ring zone. **14**, Attached gills. **15**, Cross-veins, Jagged gills, Bolete tubes, Very fine pores, Larger pores, Angular pores. **17**, Spore print. **26**, Hollow interiors. **27**, Gray form of yellow morels. **121**, Cross veins. **162**, Faded specimens. **163**, Shrimp Russula. **203**, *T. pubescens*.

Walt Sturgeon: **58**, Deadly Galerina. **59**, Velvet Foot. **95**, Bearded Milk Cap. **173**, Slippery Jack.

MushroomObserver.org: See pages 274–275.

Others: **7**, BGSmith/Shutterstock.com. **111**, *L. riparius:* Fred Stevens/ Mykoweb.com. **121**, Hairs at base: Kathy Yerich.

10 9 8 7 6 5

Mushrooms of the Northwest

Published by Adventure Publications, an imprint of AdventureKEEN
310 Garfield Street South
Cambridge, Minnesota 55008
(800) 678-7006
www.adventurepublications.net

Printed in China
ISBN 978-1-59193-792-0 (pbk.); ISBN 978-1-59193-793-7 (ebook)

Table of Contents

About This Book

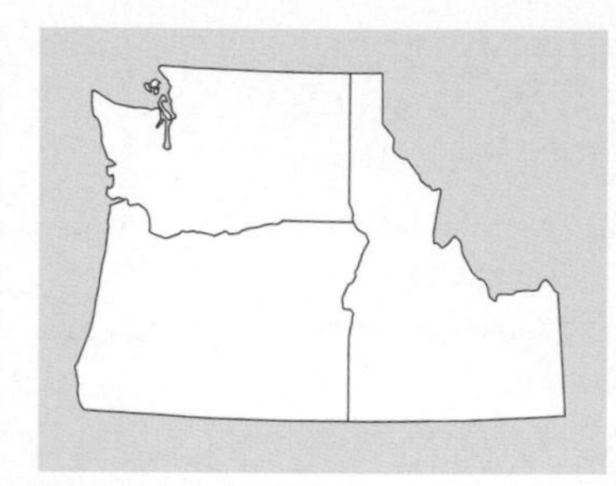

This book includes Washington, Oregon and Idaho.

This book was written with the beginning mushroom enthusiast in mind. It is a pocket-size field guide featuring hundreds of the most common species in the Northwest, with clear pictures and additional comparisons for each species. Many "beginner" books feature just the top eminently edible and deadly toxic varieties, while leaving out the hundreds—maybe thousands—of other species that grow in the area. Some books are generalized and may present descriptions and photos of mushrooms that don't grow in our area, the Northwest. Given the sheer number of mushroom species in the Northwest alone, one book cannot cover every species you are likely to find … especially not one you'd care to carry into the field!

Our hope is that this book will both spark your interest about mushrooms and provide you with the means to learn more. A list of useful resources is included at the end of this book, as is a list of some mushroom terms you may encounter in those and other resources. First and foremost, we have arranged the entries in this book by what they look like, or their ***morphology***. Many of the genus and species names that originally placed a mushroom in a certain family were assigned by experts because of the mushroom's physical appearance, and many other books arrange species based on their scientific names, grouping members of a genus together. But it is hard to look up a mushroom in a book by its name when you don't have a clue what it is yet.

Many misidentifications start with a hopeful guess that guides you to a book entry that, while incorrect, may have numerous features that seem to match the specimen you have found. The temptation is strong to "force" the description to fit what you have in hand. This can be a dangerous path to travel when attempting to identify wild mushrooms; a mistaken identification may prove harmful or, in the worst case, even fatal if a misidentified mushroom is eaten because the reader attempted to make the specimen "fit" the description given in a book. **For this reason, we strongly advise that novice mushroom enthusiasts consult multiple reliable references or, better still, a local authority who can verify the identity of the mushroom in question before it is eaten.**

Remember, too, that when attempting to compare features of mushrooms in various references or when discussing them with other enthusiasts, the scientific name (which is always in Latin) must be used. The colorful, sometimes descriptive and often humorous common names of mushrooms are fun but can vary by region and are not a truly reliable way to label a species. Using the Latin genus and species name, referred to as ***taxonomy***, is the standard and most respected way of referring to a specific variety. However, without a microscope it is often impossible to determine the difference between species with similar appearances. Even some scientists have been overheard in the field referring to a drab specimen simply as an LBM ("little brown mushroom").

To make things more complicated, as more species are discovered and scientists have the ability to study them in more depth with microscopic examination, mating studies and DNA sequencing, authorities are finding that many of the mushrooms that were given their Latin name hundreds of years ago may belong to a different genus than that to which they were originally assigned. In fact, some of the names remain in constant flux, creating so much confusion that at any one time a specific mushroom could be referred to by multiple names, depending on your source. Again, we've attempted to list as many species as possible while keeping this a pocket-size book. We've also used single quotes around names (such as *Russula 'densifolia'*) used for species which appear in, say, Europe but not in North America; this means that specimens found in North America are very similar but not exactly the same as their European counterparts, but a new name has not yet been published.

There is also a complete index starting on pg. 282 referencing both common and Latin names, and you'll see that we have included both on the ID pages.

No person is born with the knowledge to identify mushrooms; it must be learned from books, teachers and other sources, as well as a lot of time spent in the field. We have been greatly aided in our decades-long studies by numerous people who generously shared their expertise with us. In writing this book we have also consulted many excellent books and other sources; a list of the best is included in Helpful Resources and Bibliography, starting on pg. 272.

We would like to thank Kathy Yerich, co-author (with Teresa Marrone) of *Mushrooms of the Upper Midwest*. That book is the first in this series of mushroom identification guides, and the basic structure of *Mushrooms of the Northwest* is based on the Upper Midwest book. Some of the text in the Northwest book is picked up or adapted from the Upper Midwest book, and we gratefully acknowledge Kathy's contributions.

What Is a Mushroom?

Mycology is the study of mushrooms. In very general terms, mushrooms and macro fungi are the fruiting bodies of organisms from the fungi kingdom. Indeed, many references refer to the aboveground portion of a fungal organism as a ***fruitbody***, although the word ***mushroom*** is far more common in everyday use. Mushrooms are not plants, because unlike plants they do not use sunlight to photosynthesize their food. More like animals, they use enzymes to break down what they consume. In their role as decomposers of organic material, fungi are essential to life on earth, because without them, the world would be buried in its own debris. In the forest, fungi break down dead or dying organic matter and render it into soil, making it usable for new growth.

The ***mycelium*** (root-like filaments) of the organism may spread for miles underground, or inhabit an entire tree. The part that we see (and harvest, if we so choose) is comparable to the fruit we pick from a tree; the tree—and the mycelium—remains to bear fruit the following season. Like fruits, mushrooms can also assist in reproduction; just as an apple produces seeds that can grow into a new tree, mushrooms produce microscopic ***spores*** that are dispersed by wind, insects or other vectors, allowing the larger organism to spread into new areas. Of course, that is a very simple description. There are thousands of species of fungi with complicated life cycles and growth patterns. Learning some basic mycological terms and understanding how mushrooms grow and reproduce will help you understand some of what you'll encounter, but because of the staggering amount of diversity you'll run into, it is more important to learn **how** to decipher what you are seeing.

How to Look at Mushrooms

The main goal of an identification book is to teach the reader how to identify, name and understand more about something. With mushrooms, the sheer number of possibilities makes them a challenging but fascinating subject. Besides the large number of different species, there is an amazing variety of characteristics among those species. Additionally, some of the features are tactile or even sensory elements, like smell or taste, which can be described in a book but should really be experienced firsthand. Other features are too small to be seen without a microscope. This book will cover only criteria visible to the naked eye or through a magnifying glass or loupe (called a ***hand lens*** in this book), or observable by the senses. Removing microscopic features from our view leaves no shortage of traits that can be observed to positively identify a species. These traits provide a wealth of interesting content for a book, but firsthand experience in the field is even more fascinating! So, what we are really sharing in this book is **how to look at a mushroom**. Reading about different traits and studying the images refines our ability to notice them.

Store bought white button mushroom and brown cremini (or crimini) are varieties of the same species. Portabella mushrooms are mature cremini. All three are *Agaricus bisporus*.

Modern digital photography captures details that may not be readily noticed by the naked eye, making it easier to spot subtle ID features. Multiple photos can be taken and reviewed at home, perhaps even shared on blogs and social media sites, creating an almost instant digital field record. Many universities, mycological societies and individuals have created virtual field guides with amazing photos and descriptions (see a list of recommended websites on p. 272), but as noted, the best learning experience is a trip to the woods with an experienced teacher.

The practice of taking notes and making drawings to highlight features of the specimens you've found is an old exercise but a good way to become aware of important details. Dr. Michael Kuo's wonderful book, *100 Edible Mushrooms* (see p. 273), recommends trying this with store-bought mushrooms. He suggests studying button mushrooms and portabellas to observe and compare the features of different stages of growth and different varieties of the same species. Some mushrooms have similar features at different stages of growth, beginning their life as a smaller version of the mature mushroom. Other mushrooms, however, change quite drastically as they grow, going through stages that would be described quite differently. Weather also has a huge effect on the growth, development and size of a mushroom. That is why it is important to look at not only the entire mushroom, but also multiple specimens, if possible. Most proper identification depends on evaluating many distinct features, some of which occur only at certain stages of growth, during specific types of weather or with other various factors. Due to all the factors noted, your mushroom may not look exactly like the ones in the photos.

In this book, we have listed the key identification features for each species in **green**. One of those key elements, which you'll see listed even before the description on the page, is habitat. When you see a mushroom, get used to looking around you. What type of terrain is there? What other plants or trees are nearby? What is your mushroom really growing on? Sometimes, it may look like a mushroom is growing from the soil when in reality it is growing from a buried piece of wood or an underground tree root. Many species are ***saprobes***, mushrooms that get their nutrients from decaying or dead organic matter, whether from a specific type of tree or other vegetation. Some species are ***parasites***, attacking living plants and insects. Other mushrooms grow from the soil in association with certain trees, in a symbiotic relationship that is called ***mycorrhiza***. Getting to know your trees is a good way to look for certain species of mushrooms.

Learning the parts of a mushroom will help you examine them more closely. Many books take a scientific approach to terminology; this book will not. The diagram below gives an overall view of the parts of a mushroom we'll be mentioning in the upcoming descriptions. Rather than list all of the possible variations of those parts, let's start looking at some pictures and save the terminology and definitions for the Glossary at the back of this book. Some of the features you'll need to consider are easier to distinguish in a picture, so we've included closeup photos on the next pages that clearly show these elements.

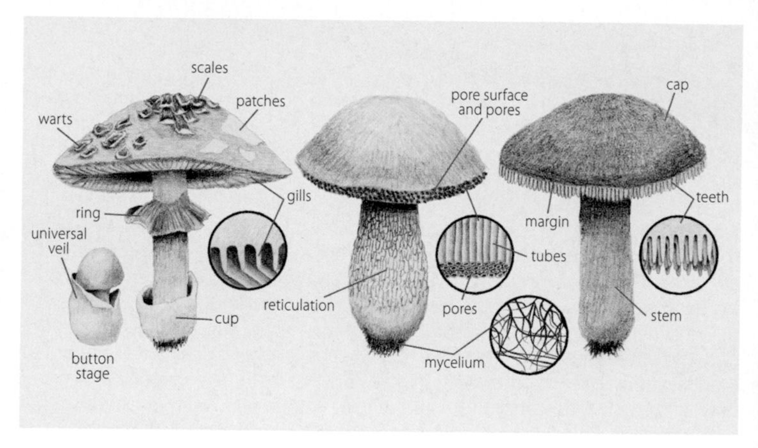

GROWTH STAGES

This discussion focuses on mushrooms—fruiting bodies, actually—that have a distinct cap and stem, resembling familiar store-bought species. Some types of mushrooms take different forms; shelf mushrooms, for example, have no distinct stem, puffballs have neither a traditional stem nor a cap in the common sense of the word, and others, such as coral fungi, are simply structured differently.

Young mushrooms arise from the ***mycelium***, root-like fungal filaments that are underground or growing in another substrate such as rotting wood. Most emerge from the substrate as a ***pinhead***, a small rounded bit of tissue that grows rapidly, soon becoming recognizable as what we call a mushroom. The photos below show the mushroom *Chlorophyllum molybdites* (a species not known from the Northwest but related to the Shaggy Parasols on pg. 86) over the course of four days. Many cap-and-stem mushrooms don't develop this quickly, but the stages are similar. (Some mushrooms, such as Amanitas and Volvariellas, are encased in a ***universal veil***, a thin membrane that encircles the entire developing mushroom; see pg. 60 for photos that show the early growth stages of an Amanita.)

In the photo below at left, the mushroom has emerged from the ground; the cap and stem are distinct and recognizable. At this point, the cap is about 1½ inches wide. The next day, the cap has expanded dramatically to about 4½ inches wide. The photo at right shows the fully expanded cap, which is now about 7½ inches wide. The cap is almost completely flat, with just a slight curve on top, and the darkened gills are visible underneath.

Different species mature at different rates and in different ways. Development is also affected by the weather; mushrooms tend to mature quickly during periods of warm, wet weather and more slowly when it is cool and dry.

CAPS

The cap is generally the first thing that is seen, and its features such as shape, color, size and texture are a good starting point for identification.

As shown on the previous page, the cap's **shape** can change dramatically over the life of a mushroom. The size increases as well; this is particularly dramatic on mushrooms that have the traditional cap-and-stem shape, but caps become larger on other shapes such as shelf mushrooms. Here's a look at some of the common cap shapes.

In the ***button stage***—when the specimen has recently emerged from the ground—most caps are ***spherical*** or ***egg-shaped***. As the mushroom grows, the cap expands and begins to open up like an umbrella. Common shapes are shown at right and below.

In addition to the shape of the cap, its **texture** must be considered. Some textures are obvious; the egg-shaped cap above is ***patchy*** (covered with small, slightly raised patches), while the elongated example is ***shaggy*** (covered with scales that curl or create an irregular, highly textured surface). The conical example above is ***smooth***; however, a smooth cap may feel dry, velvety or slimy, and the best way to know is to touch the cap.

Irregular/ wavy edge

Scalloped edge

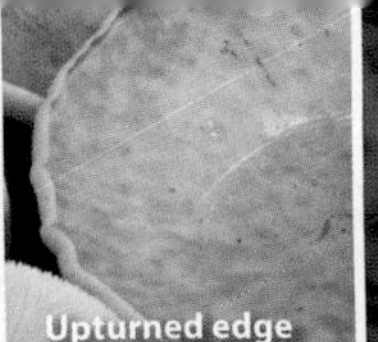
Upturned edge

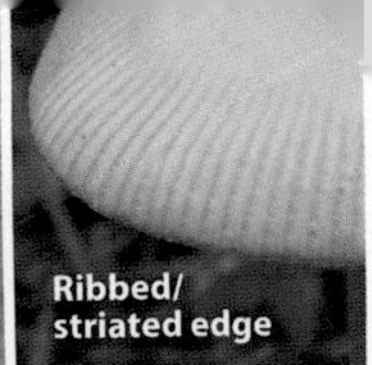
Ribbed/ striated edge

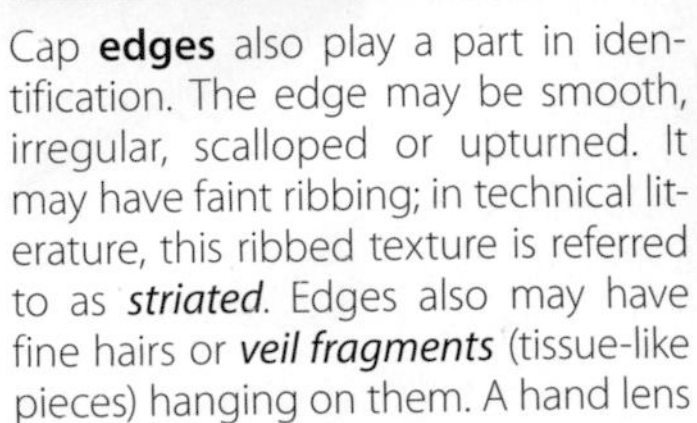

Cap **edges** also play a part in identification. The edge may be smooth, irregular, scalloped or upturned. It may have faint ribbing; in technical literature, this ribbed texture is referred to as ***striated***. Edges also may have fine hairs or ***veil fragments*** (tissue-like pieces) hanging on them. A hand lens is sometimes needed to observe these characteristics.

Hairs on edge

Veil fragments on edge

The **color** of the cap may be uniform over the entire surface, but it may also have variations that may be subtle or very obvious. Some are mottled or streaky; others appear to have faint stripes, bands or rings. The center may be a different color than the outer edges; many mushrooms also fade or darken over time. It's not uncommon to have a mushroom change color substantially after it is picked; a digital photo taken before the specimen is picked can be helpful in later identification.

Sometimes, cap colors change on the same specimens depending on the weather. The photo sequence below shows the same group of mushrooms over a three-day period during which the weather changed from rainy to dry and back to rainy (a few of the individuals fell over or were removed from photo to photo). A mushroom whose cap changes color in response to moisture is referred to as ***hygrophanous***; if you can observe specimens over the course of a few days, this can be a diagnostic characteristic. Hygrophanous genera include *Agrocybe*, *Galerina*, *Panaeolus*, *Psathyrella* and *Psilocybe*.

Day 1: Wet

Day 2: Dry

Day 3: Wet

STEMS

After you've inspected the cap, take a look at the stem underneath it. It's a good idea to study the stem a bit before picking the mushroom, as there are several things you should look for.

Mycelium

Study the base of the stem to look for ***mycelium***, root-like fungal filaments that look like fine threads, cotton or a fuzzy coating. The color, texture and quantity of the mycelium (if present) provide a clue to the mushroom's identity. Mycelium may be also found on any substrate that provides a growing medium for mushrooms: soil, decaying wood, live trees—even soggy carpet!

Volva

Next, look for any sign of a ***volva***, a fragile, cup-like structure that surrounds the stem base on Amanitas and Volvariellas. You may need to dig around carefully in the dirt at the base of the stem to find the volva, but if you do find one, you're well on your way to identifying the mushroom, since very few types of mushrooms have them. The volva is a remnant of a universal veil; see pgs. 60–61 for more information about this.

Club-shaped base

Bulbous base

Look at the shape, length and thickness of the stem. It may be fairly even in thickness from top to bottom, or it might taper at the top, becoming thicker towards the base. Many can be said to have a ***club-shaped*** base; this resembles the shape of a baseball bat or may be slightly wider, but generally the taper is smooth. A ***bulbous*** base is also broader at the bottom, but the swelling is generally more abrupt and the stem appears to bulge at the base.

Now it is time to pick the mushroom, making sure to get the bottom of the stem, and turn it over. Note whether the stem is centered on the cap, or if it is off-center (mycologists call this positioning ***eccentric***). What do you see under the cap? There may be ***gills***, thin blade-like structures that run radially (like spokes of a wheel) between the cap edge and the stem. Instead of gills, some mushrooms have ***pores*** that look like a very fine sponge. A few, such as Chanterelles (pgs. 42–44), have neither gills nor pores. Gills and pores are discussed in detail on pgs. 14–15.

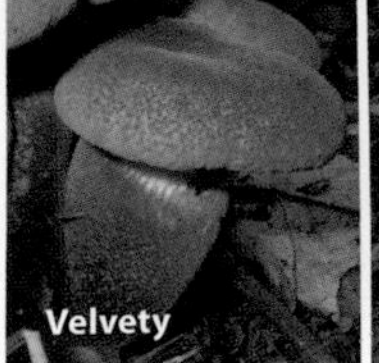
Velvety

Scaly

Ridged/grooved

Patterned/ reticulated

Like the cap, the stem may be smooth and fairly featureless, or it may be highly textured. Some of the common textures are illustrated above. Textures can be crucial to identifying your mushroom, so study them carefully; a hand lens may be helpful in some cases. If the stem appears smooth, touch it and note whether it is velvety, slimy or dry.

Partial veil

You may notice a ring on the upper part of the stem. This is a remnant of the ***partial veil***, a thin tissue that covers the developing gills or pores on some mushroom species (this is not the same thing as the universal veil mentioned at left and discussed in more detail on pgs. 60–61). If you look at a common button mushroom from the grocery store, you'll see a partial veil on small specimens. As the mushroom grows, the cap expands and opens up, tearing the veil away from the cap and allowing the spores to disperse from the gills or pores. The veil remains attached to the stem. It may persist as a ***ring*** or it may deteriorate, leaving behind a ***ring zone***, a sticky band that is often colored by falling spores; sometimes it disintegrates completely, leaving no trace. The photos above illustrate these features. Note that pieces of the veil may also remain attached to the cap edge, as shown in the photo of veil fragments on pg. 11.

Skirt-like ring

Simple ring

Ring zone

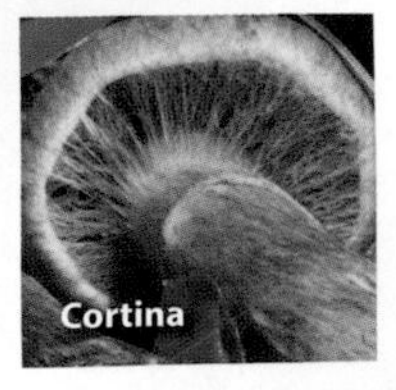
Cortina

Some species have veils that are extremely thin and cobweb-like; this type of veil is called a ***cortina***, and it is found on *Cortinarius* species as well as several others. Because the cortina is so insubstantial, it does not leave a classic ring; at most, a faint ring zone remains behind on the stem.

UNDER THE CAP

Some of the most important mushroom features are found under the cap. On cap-and-stem or shelf mushrooms, this area produces ***spores***, microscopic particles that function like seeds to help the mushroom reproduce.

Gills

Many mushrooms, including common grocery-store mushrooms (*Agaricus bisporus*), have ***gills***, thin blade-like structures (referred to as ***lamellae*** by mycologists) that grow like the spokes of a wheel between the cap edge and the stem. Spores are produced on the flat faces of the gills and are forcibly ejected when they are mature. The spore color often affects the color of the gills; if you look at a young button mushroom from the grocery store, you'll notice that the gills are pinkish, but on mature specimens the gills have turned chocolate-brown from the spores. (Indeed, you may often find a dusting of brownish spores on the tray underneath portabella caps.) When collecting wild mushrooms, it's always a good idea to make a spore print as described on pg. 17; this is the best way to determine the color of the mature spores, which is often key to properly identifying your find.

When you're holding a gilled mushroom you've picked, look closely at the way that the gills are attached to the stem. Mycologists use numerous terms to describe a wide variety of attachment methods; the differences between some of them are so subtle that it's difficult for the layperson to detect them. In this book, we're going to focus on those attachments that are easy to see with the eye, or perhaps with use of a hand lens. Other attachment methods can be included broadly in the four described here.

Attached gills are just what they sound like: the gills are attached to the stem. ***Decurrent gills*** are attached gills that run down the stem, slightly or a fair distance, rather than ending abruptly. ***Free gills*** stop short of the stem; when viewed from above, it looks like there is a miniature racetrack around the stem. ***Notched gills*** are attached gills with a slight notch at the point of attachment. It's helpful to cut the mushroom in half from top to bottom to get a clearer view of the attachment.

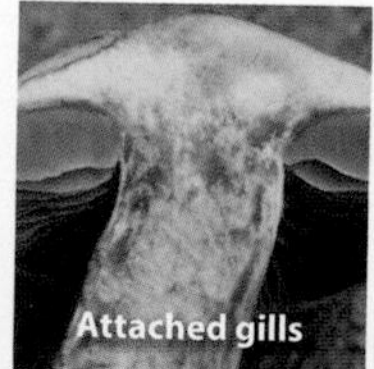
Attached gills

Decurrent gills

Free gills

Notched gills

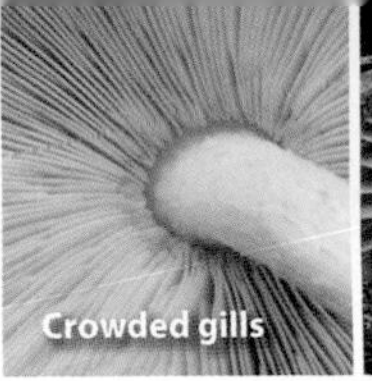
Crowded gills

Widely spaced

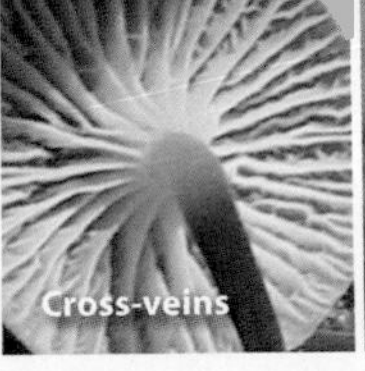
Cross-veins

Jagged gills

The spacing of the gills is an important identification point. From tight to loose, spacing is described in this book as crowded, closely spaced, moderately widely spaced, or widely spaced. They may be as straight as a knife blade, wavy or curved, as shown in the photo of decurrent gills on the facing page. Sometimes there are short ***cross-veins***, small ridges that connect the gills in a net-like fashion; a hand lens is often needed to see these. Some gills have a jagged texture on the edge; others are forked near the edge of the cap. The color of the gills is an important identifying factor; also note that some species have gills that are a different color along the thin edge. And as previously noted, gills often change color over time as spores collect on them.

Pores

Rather than gills, some mushrooms have ***pores***, created by a sponge-like layer of very thin tubes attached to the underside of the cap. The spores develop inside the tubes, then drop down through the open bottom ends of the tubes when they are mature. ***Boletes*** are the most well-known of the cap and-stem mushrooms that bear pores. The pore layer of a bolete can be peeled away from the cap as a fairly cohesive unit; this differentiates it from the pore layer on ***polypores***, short-stalked or shelf-like mushrooms that grow on wood.

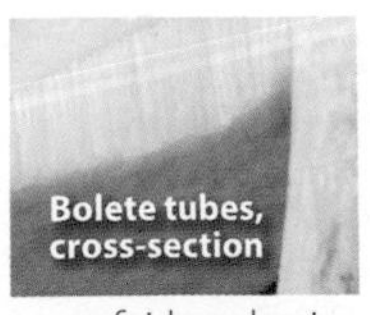
Bolete tubes, cross-section

Like gills, pore surfaces are various colors. The pores may be extremely tiny or fine, appearing almost like a solid, featureless layer unless studied through a hand lens; they may also be large and coarse enough to see easily with the naked eye. Pores may be rounded, angular or hexagonal. Many species have pores that ***bruise***, or change color when handled, cut or damaged.

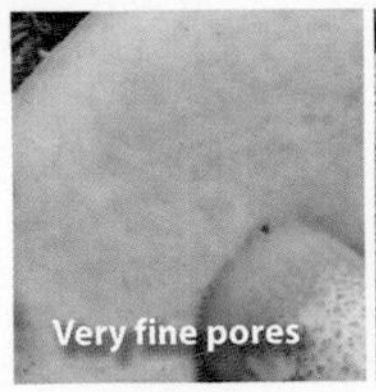
Very fine pores

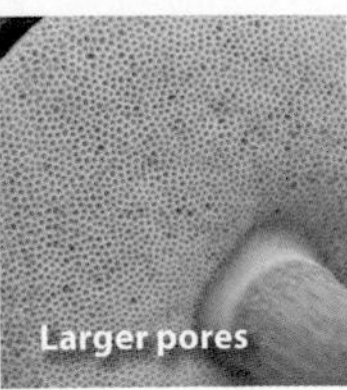
Larger pores

Angular pores

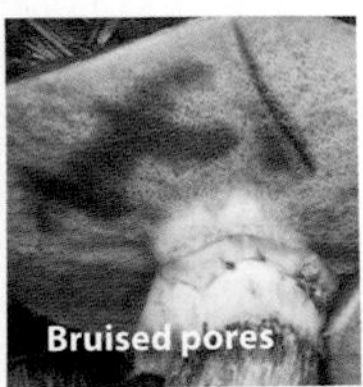
Bruised pores

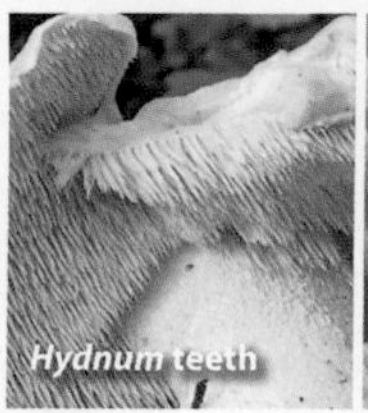
Hydnum teeth

Hericium teeth

Teeth

Rather than gills or pores, some mushrooms have ***teeth***, spine-like structures on which the spores develop. Members of the *Hydnum* genus (pgs. 52–53) and the *Hydnellum* genus (pg. 258) look like standard mushrooms when viewed from above, but they have short teeth on their undersides. *Hericium* species (pgs. 50–51), on the other hand, seem to be composed of nothing but long, dangling teeth.

Folds

These spore-bearing structures look like gills at a quick glance, but further inspection reveals that they are not separate, individual structures like true gills; they are merely thin, raised veins that are part of the mushroom body. Chanterelles (pgs. 42–44) are the best example of this, and the folds are not the only features that differentiate them from lookalikes. They do not have a distinct cap and separate stem; rather, the entire mushroom is a single item that is somewhat trumpet-shaped. Pig's Ear Gomphus (pg. 270) is another mushroom in this book that has spore-bearing folds rather than gills.

Chanterelle folds

Other spore-bearing structures

The mushroom world is complex, and the examples above are only part of the story of how mushrooms spread their spores. Morels (pgs. 26–30) carry their spores on pits between external ridges. Puffballs (pgs. 48–49, 230, 232) are solid sphere-like mushrooms with spores located in the interior flesh; when the spores ripen, the mushroom becomes shrunken and will burst open when lightly touched, scattering its spores. Other mushrooms are shaped like cups, coral or shapes that are too numerous to list here; each shape of mushroom has its own unique way of dispersing its spores. If you gently blow onto the top of a cup mushroom, you are usually rewarded with a small cloud of ejected spores.

SPORE PRINTS

As noted on pg. 14, the color of the spores is often a major clue to the identity of a mushroom, and we're including information about spore color for every species discussed in this book. Sometimes, a mushroom that is still standing in the woods or field has deposited spores on surrounding vegetation, logs or other mushrooms; in cases like this, you can determine the spore color without any further action. At right is a photo of a Velvety Milk Cap (pg. 136) that has deposited its cream-colored spores on the top of another milk cap that is below it.

Most of the time, however, you'll have to make your own spore print at home. It's easy to do and fun to see the results. The spore deposit may be white, black, or nearly any color of the rainbow. White prints won't show up well on white paper, and black prints won't show up on black paper, so the best way to make a print is to use a piece of paper that is half white and half-black; it's easy to run sheets of paper on a laser printer that have a large black field covering half of the paper. Or a wide black marker can be used to darken a portion of white paper.

You'll need a completely developed but still-fresh mushroom; specimens that are too young or too old probably won't produce spores. It should not have any trace of a partial veil over the gills. Cut off the stem so it is just a stub that fits inside the cap; scissors often work better than a knife. Place your black-and-white paper on a table where it can sit undisturbed. Carefully place the mushroom with the spore-producing surface down, positioning it so half of it is over the white paper and half is over the black area. Cover it with a bowl or glass and let it sit for several hours, or overnight. Carefully remove the bowl, then the mushroom cap; with any luck, you'll have something that looks like the example at left.

The benefit of the two-colored paper is obvious. The spore print shown here is whitish to pale cream-colored; it shows up well on the black part of the paper, and just a slight trace of it can be seen on the white part of the paper.

Eating Mushrooms

Identifying mushrooms from a book is a good way to begin learning about them, but when edibility is your goal you must be extremely careful. It is recommended to obtain a firsthand, positive ID from an expert before eating any mushroom, as many of the toxic varieties look similar to the edible ones and could make you very ill, or even kill you! Join a local mycological society (see information in the Helpful Resources section on pg. 272), or hook up with an experienced forager who is familiar with local species.

Even after you have positively identified a good edible, always try just a small portion the first time to assess your body's tolerance to it. Never eat more than one new species at a time the first time you try it, because if you combine several and have problems, you won't know which mushroom was the culprit. Don't assume that because others can enjoy a particular species, it will be OK for you, too; a friend who is an amazing outdoorsman recently shared his unfortunate discovery that even though he loves the taste of morels, he found that eating them made him nauseous. Also remember that **wild mushrooms should never be eaten raw**.

It is tempting to look for a simple rule or test that tells you whether an unknown mushroom is edible, but unfortunately no such rule exists. Taking the time to learn how to identify each species by its unique characteristics (even though some may be hard to see) is the only appropriate method. Also read Top Edibles and Top Toxics on pg. 23 for additional guidance.

Some mushroom folklore to ignore

- If a mushroom was eaten by animals or insects, it isn't poisonous.
- If you cook a mushroom with a silver utensil or coin in the pot and the metal doesn't turn black, the mushroom isn't poisonous.
- If a mushroom smells and tastes good, it isn't poisonous.
- If a mushroom peels easily, it isn't poisonous.
- Brightly colored mushrooms are the only poisonous ones.
- Pickling or boiling eliminates toxins from poisonous mushrooms.
- Rice will turn red if cooked with poisonous mushrooms.

Digging Deeper into Mycology

Physical features that can be observed with the eye (possibly aided by a hand lens) are enough to identify some mushrooms positively. Many other mushrooms, however, are difficult or impossible to identify unless the spores (the reproductive units) are studied microscopically. Mycologists classify mushrooms into groups (called ***phyla***) based on how the spores are dispersed. Two major groups are described briefly below: basidiomycetes and ascomycetes.

Most mushrooms in this book fall into the ***basidiomycetes*** group, which includes all mushrooms with gills or pores and others such as puffballs. The spores are carried on the surface of club-shaped appendages called ***basidia***. The surface of the gills on gilled mushrooms, and the insides of pore tubes on boletes and polypores, are covered with basidia. Each basidium (the singular form of basidia) holds several spores on tiny prongs at the end of the appendage. By the time the tiny spores are on the mycologist's slide, however, they have often been ejected from the basidium, so this appendage is not visible in most microscopic views of the spores.

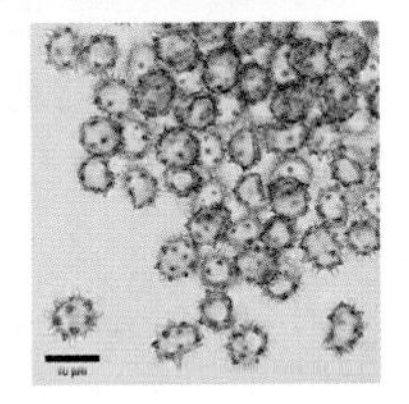

Ascomycetes are also called sac fungi because the spores are contained in a sac-like container called an ***ascus***. These sacs are carried on the spore-bearing surface of non-gilled and non-pored mushrooms, including morels, cup fungi and others. When the spores are ripe, the end of the sac opens to eject the spores. The number and shape of spores in each ascus may vary, although many asci (the plural form of ascus) contain eight spores. As with basidiomycetes, the spores have often been ejected out of the ascus before they are collected for analysis; however, mycologists sometimes shave off a section of the mushroom before the spores are ejected, in order to observe the asci (shown in the detail at left).

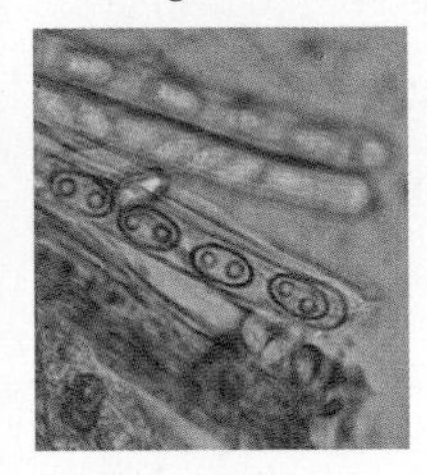

This discussion may seem highly technical to the novice; however, it is actually an extremely simplified overview. Mycologists who study mushrooms microscopically use terms that are baffling to the novice when describing the shape and other characteristics of the spores. Should you wish to learn more, check with your local mycological society or a university; some mycological societies offer periodic seminars on studying mushrooms microscopically.

Terrain and Climate

The three states covered in this book encompass an area roughly 700 miles wide by slightly less than 500 miles from north to south. The region is extremely geographically diverse, ranging from coastal lowlands along the west side, to the heart of the northern Rockies on the east. In between there are several north/south trending mountain ranges, principally the Cascade Range, which includes several glacier-capped volcanoes that dominate the landscape. Between the Cascades and the Rockies in Washington and northern Oregon is a wide semi-arid to arid region known as the Columbia Plateau. It boasts a highly varied topography of shrub-steppe and grassland, low mountains, and water-carved canyons underlain by volcanic rock. Southeastern Oregon and much of southern Idaho are also arid to semi-arid regions. Elevations for the three-state area range from sea level to over 14,000 feet.

One of the greatest forces shaping the climate of the region is the moist air that flows off the Pacific Ocean from the west, bringing substantial precipitation to the coastal lowlands and the western slopes of the mountain ranges, and leaving the Columbia Plateau in a much drier, rain shadow. The western slopes of the Columbia and Rocky Mountain Ranges to the east maintain the same moisture pattern, though to a lesser degree. Most of the precipitation occurs from fall through spring, peaking in the winter months. Summers are mostly dry. Within the area west of the Cascade crest, annual precipitation totals of 60 inches to well over 100 inches are not unusual. This rainfall sustains large swathes of temperate rainforest where winters are mild and summers relatively cool compared to Inland areas east of the Cascades, where temperature swings are much greater. Precipitation in the Columbia Plateau mostly range from 5 to 25 inches; in the mountains of eastern Washington and central and northern Idaho, 30 to around 60 inches annually is typical.

Overall, conifer forests predominate by far, particularly in the mountainous areas, though deciduous species such as cottonwood, aspen, birch, alder, maple and others often grow among them either intermingled or in small stands. In the mild, wet, maritime climate west of the Cascades, oaks, and the evergreen madrone can also be found. In the mountains, the forest composition changes gradually from lower-elevation species such as western red cedar, Douglas fir, and western hemlock, to higher-elevation species like Engelmann spruce, subalpine fir, and western white pine.

In the Northwest, the best mushroom collection times vary, depending on where one lives. Mushroom season in general centers on spring and fall when it is normally warm enough and wet enough for them to fruit, but it is hardly that simple in a landscape this diverse. West of the Cascades in the coastal lowlands, the fall mushroom season is very long, extending into winter, especially so in southern Oregon where the winter months can be one of the more productive times of year to search for mushrooms. If you live in the mountains or anywhere in the interior, the fall season can be short, sometimes depressingly so, lasting from the first fall rains until freeze out. Typically there is a surge of mushroom fruiting in the spring as temperatures warm and moisture is abundant. Spring collecting can be extended well into the summer by exploring higher elevations as spring conditions advance into the mountains. Heavy winter snowpacks in the Northwest allow for our unique "snowbank" fungi, comprised of species that fruit at or near the edges of melting snow banks as they recede over the summer.

The fungi have adapted to all but the most extreme environments of our region, and can be found even in more arid landscapes under the right conditions; however, species have individual preferences for when and where they fruit. It is essential to keep this in mind when seeking out and identifying the macrofungi of the Northwest.

How to Use This Book

As noted in the Introduction, this is an abbreviated field guide designed for ease of use by a layperson—one who is not intimately familiar with mushrooms in the field or on the written page. It focuses on mushroom features that can be seen without the aid of a microscope, so it is organized a bit differently than other field guides you may have seen.

Many books organize the entries based on an alphabetical listing of the ***genus***, which might be thought of as the mushroom's "last name." That is followed by an alphabetical sub-listing of the exact ***species***, the mushroom's "first name" that makes it different from other members of its genus. This listing is referred to as the mushroom's ***scientific name***, and it is always in Latin. This is a much more reliable system than using "common names" which change depending on the language being spoken; indeed, common names can change from one state to another, making them unreliable.

The Meadow Mushroom (pg. 84), for example, is also referred to as Field Mushroom, Pink Bottom and Champignon, but its scientific name is listed as *Agaricus campestris* in all references, regardless of language. *Agaricus* is the genus name; *campestris* is the species name. This tells us that this mushroom is closely related to, say, *Agaricus hondensis*, often referred to as the Felt-Ringed Agaricus. However, while *Agaricus campestris* is a choice edible with a white cap, *Agaricus hondensis* is toxic, with a cap that often has a heavy layer of pinkish-brown to dark brown scales. Thus, within the same genus, you may have a listing for a white mushroom followed by a brown one. As another example, caps of *Russula* species range from red to green to yellow. If you know what you're looking for, the scientific organization is easy to follow, but if you're not sure what genus your mushroom belongs to, it's difficult to know where to start looking.

Some mushrooms are delicious edibles, while others are dangerously toxic—even deadly. As discussed above, these distinctions do not follow genus classifications. Before you take to the field in search of edibles, it is helpful to know which mushrooms are safe even for beginners, but it is also imperative to become familiar with the deadliest mushrooms so you know what to avoid. This book starts with two sections that offer expanded coverage on the Top Edibles and Top Toxics in our area. The rest of the book is like a catalog of mushrooms, organized by their shape and other visible features.

In this book, mushrooms are grouped by basic categories, and within each of those categories they are grouped by color. Thus, if you find a mushroom that has a distinct cap and stem, and it has gills under the cap, you would go to the section entitled Cap & Stem with Gills, starting on pg. 76 (refer to the listing of Basic Categories on pgs. 24–25). Colors within the section are organized from light to dark, as much as possible. So if your cap-and-stem mushroom is yellowish, go to pg. 98, where the first of the yellowish cap-and-stem mushrooms is listed. Compare your specimen to the photos and pay particular attention to the details listed. With luck, you'll find a description that matches your specimen, but if not, use the scientific name of the closest match to search more complete references. Also remember to check the Top Edibles and Top Toxics sections, as well as the abbreviated Others of Note sections found at the end of each category.

TOP EDIBLES AND TOP TOXICS

These special sections highlight two categories of mushrooms you should be very familiar with before collecting anything for the table. First up is a selection of some of the top edibles in our region, chosen not only for edibility but also because these are easy to identify without fear of collecting a toxic species. Following that are the top toxic mushrooms in our area. Some are **deadly**; all will make you very sick if you ingest them. Study them until you can easily recognize them in the field. Remember that it is always best to have an experienced mushroom forager with you when you first learn about edibles—or about toxic species.

Top Edibles starts on pg. 26; Top Toxics starts on pg. 56. Each section includes expanded coverage of highlighted species, along with descriptions of lookalikes to watch out for. Some of the lookalike descriptions include references to other pages in this book; others include photos of species that aren't discussed elsewhere in the book. At the bottom of each of the lookalike photos, you'll find a band that provides information about edibility. A green band indicates that the lookalike is edible. A red band indicates that the lookalike is toxic, while a pinkish band indicates that while it may not be extremely toxic, the lookalike should not be considered edible.

White Beech Mushrooms

EDIBLE

Scaly Vase Chanterelle

NOT RECOMMENDED

Deadly Galerina

TOXIC

Basic Categories

Here are the basic categories used in this book, along with the page range for each section. Notes next to each category give a brief description and also list species that are covered in the Top Edibles or Top Toxics sections. The bands next to the photos indicate the color used for each section.

CAP & STEM WITH GILLS (PGS. 76–169)

Traditional cap-and-stem shape with gills underneath the cap.

In the Edibles section: Inky Caps, Matsutake
In the Toxics section: Deadly Galerina, Amanitas, Brown Roll-Rim, Deadly Parasol, Poison Pie

CAP & STEM WITH PORES (PGS. 170–193)

Traditional cap-and-stem shape with pores underneath the cap.

In the Edibles section: King Bolete
In the Toxics section: Toxic Boletes

ATYPICAL CAPS (PGS. 194–197)

Mushrooms that have stems but do not have a traditional cap with gills or pores.

In the Edibles section: Morels, Chanterelles
In the Toxics section: False Morels: Gyromitras

SHELF WITH PORES (PGS. 198–219)

Typically growing on trees or wood as a shelf or cluster with pores underneath; lacking a distinct stem.

In the Edibles section: Chicken Mushrooms

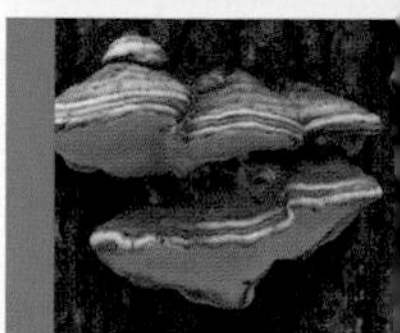

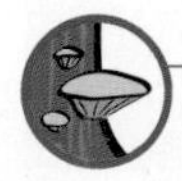

SHELF WITH GILLS (PGS. 220–225)

Typically growing on trees or wood as a shelf or cluster with gills underneath; lacking a distinct stem.

In the Edibles section: Oyster Mushrooms

SHELF/OTHER (PGS. 226–227)

Typically growing on trees or wood as a shelf or cluster with neither pores nor gills underneath; lacking a distinct stem.

SPHERICAL MUSHROOMS (PGS. 228–235)

Rounded or ball-like mushrooms that lack a distinct stem.

In the Edibles section: Giant Puffball

CUP-SHAPED MUSHROOMS (PGS. 236–243)

Mushrooms with no distinct stem whose body consists of a cup-like or flattened structure.

CORAL AND CLUB FUNGI (PGS. 244–253)

Irregularly shaped mushrooms that look like branches, soft sticks or sea coral; generally small in stature but often growing in large groups.

MISCELLANEOUS MUSHROOMS (PGS. 254–271)

Mushrooms whose shapes fit no other category.

In the Edibles section: Cauliflower Mushroom, Lion's Mane, Hedgehog Mushroom, Lobster Mushroom

Morels (several)

Morchella spp.

Morels are one of the most sought-after wild mushrooms in the United States. Because of varied habitat zones, our area enjoys a longer Morel season than other parts of the country, and many of the later-season Morels sold across the country are shipped from Oregon and Washington.

Like many other mushrooms, Morels are subject to debate about how many species there are and what they should be called; ongoing DNA studies are redefining traditional concepts and discarding long-standing species names. At the simplest, "classic" Morels can be divided into two main categories: Yellow Morels and Black Morels. However, several Morels in our area have physical characteristics that put them in the Black Morel group, but their coloration is different than that of the classic Black Morels. Half-Free Morels are another "true Morel," but they have some significant differences in appearance.

Hollow interiors (Yellow Morels)

HABITAT: Most Morels are found around trees, including living, dying and dead; some fruit only in areas that have been burned. A few species are found primarily in landscaped areas and disturbed sites. Morels typically grow singly or scattered but may also be found in small clusters.

DESCRIPTION: Morels have **pitted caps** that appear **honeycombed**. Caps may be conical, egg-shaped, elongated or nearly spherical. Stems have a smooth or granular texture; they are often crumbly or brittle, and there is no ring. Stems are whitish, cream-colored or yellowish. They may have a round profile in cross-section, or may be flattened or irregular; they often appear creased or folded, particularly at the base, which may be slightly wider than the rest of the stem. When sliced lengthwise, both cap and stem are **completely hollow** (photo at left) with

green = key identification feature

no trace of cottony material inside. The cap and stem are seamlessly connected so that the hollow space inside is a **single, continuous cavity**. On Black Morels, there is a slight but distinct **rim at the base of the cap** (sometimes called a groove). Half-Free Morels have a **short skirt around the lower half of the cap**, but they ***do not have a full, loose skirt that dangles from the top of the stem.***

YELLOW MORELS have ridges and pits that are **irregularly arranged**; ridges are typically paler than the pits. The American Yellow Morel (*M. americana*; also listed as *M. esculentoides*) is the Yellow Morel most often found in our area, and is the most common Morel in the United States. Caps are typically egg-shaped, often bluntly pointed at the top. A gray form is often found at the start of the season; in addition to being dark, these early-season Morels are often smaller than the yellow form that follows, making them difficult to spot. Ridges of older specimens are **yellowish to whitish**; pits are **brownish-yellow**, sometimes nearly black. Stems often appear pleated or folded, particularly at the base. Total height is typically 3 to 6 inches, but late-season specimens may be a foot tall or more, and are often referred to as Bigfoot Morels. In our area, American Yellow Morels are found near **cottonwoods and other hardwoods**, especially those growing in **river bottoms**. They also fruit near **apple and ash in urban areas**.

BLACK MORELS have a **ladder-like pattern**, with strong vertical ridges bisected by numerous short horizontal ridges. Ridges are often darker than the pits, but this is not a consistent characteristic.

- Several Black Morels in our area have the ladder-like pattern and rim at the base of the cap, but their coloration may make identification challenging.
- Snyder's Morel (*M. snyderi*) is one of the most common Black Morels in our area. Its caps are conical; the ridges are **yellowish-brown on young**

Western Blond

Black-Foot Morel

specimens, similar to the coloration of a Yellow Morel. The ridges darken over time, starting from the bottom of the cap; ridges on mature specimens are **grayish-brown to blackish**, and the pits are paler. Stems are often **ridged** and have **numerous pockets**. Total height is typically 3 to 5½ inches. Snyder's Morels are found in spring near **conifers**; they often grow in clusters. • Western Blond (*M. tridentina*; also listed as *M. frustrata* and sometimes referred to simply as Blond Morel) is another Black Morel with pale coloration. It is **yellowish to tan overall**, and does not darken with maturity. Caps are oblong to conical; total height is typically 3 to 5½ inches. It is uncommon in our area, and is found in both conifer and hardwood forests. • Black-Foot Morels (*M. tomentosa*) are **gray to almost black overall when young**. Ridges on the cap are thick, flattened and very close together on immature specimens, with a velvety or fuzzy texture. As the Morel grows, the ridges spread apart and become thinner. Mature specimens are **yellowish-brown, pale tan or grayish overall**, sometimes becoming nearly white in sunny areas. At maturity, caps may be oblong, conical or irregularly egg-shaped; stems are lightly hairy to smooth. Total height is typically 2 to 4¾ inches. Black-Foot Morels are one of the "burn Morels" that are found in conifer forests that have burned the year previously; they may continue to fruit in decreasing numbers for several years. They are found at moderate to high elevations and fruit from spring through late summer.

Young Black-Foot Morel

M. eximia group

Natural Black Morel

Northwest Landscape Morel

Immature NW Landscape Morel

- There are three other morel species found in burn zones **the spring following a fire** that are visually indistinguishable from one another; these are referred to here as the ***M. eximia* group** (including *M. sextelata* and *M. exuberans*). These come in a wide size range, and may be up to 6 inches or more tall. Caps are conical to rounded, with pits that are elongated vertically, often with **blackening edges**. Colors are quite variable, ranging from cream to fawn, brownish-pink, greenish-brown, and yellowish-gray to nearly black. They fruit following the Natural Black Morels and fade as the Black-Foot Morels begin to fruit.

- The **Natural Black Morel** (*M. brunnea*) is a classic example of a Black Morel. Ridges are **dark brown to black**; pits are **yellowish-brown**. Caps are conical; total height is typically 2 to 3½ inches talll. Found in early spring near **hardwoods**, including madrone and oak; uncommon.

- The **Northwest Landscape Morel** (*M. importuna*) is very common in our area. It is found in **landscaped spots** including gardens, planters and sites with wood chips. The laddering on its cap is **very regular**, at times appearing net-like. Ridges on very young specimens are **thick, flattened and very close together**, exposing little of the pits; they are grayish to brownish and may be velvety. The ridges spread apart and become thinner with maturity; they are brownish-black to black, with brownish pits between them. Caps are usually conical or oblong; some may be egg-like. Total height may be nearly 8 inches.

HALF-FREE MORELS (*M. populiphila*) are true, edible Morels that have a **small cap** perched atop a stem that may be up to 6 inches tall. The **bottom half of the cap is free from the stem**; when the mushroom is halved vertically, the top half of the cap is **part of the same hollow chamber** as the stem, while the bottom half of the cap hangs free like a **short skirt-like extension**.

SPORE PRINT: Creamy, whitish or yellowish; spore prints are seldom taken.

SEASON: Early spring through summer.

OTHER NAMES: Sponge Mushroom, Land Fish, Merkel, Molly Moocher.

COMPARE: Several mushrooms with wrinkled or pitted caps may appear in the woods during spring. • **Verpas** often fruit earlier than Morels and can still be found during the Morel season. Two forms exist. *Verpa conica* has a cap that is smooth; the cap of *V. bohemica* is wrinkled or pitted. With both forms, the cap is attached to the stem **only at the top**; the sides **hang completely free** from the stem, which is at least **partially stuffed** with a cottony material. Verpas can cause intestinal distress and are best considered inedible. • Several *Gyromitra* species (often called False Morels; pgs. 56–57) share the spring woods with Morels. Their caps appear **wrinkled, folded or brain-like** rather than pitted, and the interiors are **stuffed with pockmarked flesh** rather than being hollow. Colors range from reddish to tan or brownish; stems are whitish or yellowish. Most are regarded as **toxic**; none should be eaten.

NOTES: All true Morels are edible ***when cooked***, although Northwest Landscape Morels and Half-Free Morels are considered less desirable. Some people may have a reaction to one variety or another, so small quantities should be eaten at first. Morel allergies have also been reported, and may develop over time.

King Bolete

Boletus edulis

As the name King Bolete suggests, *Boletus edulis* is one of the most sought-after wild mushrooms. This is the mushroom that Europeans call the Porcini or Cep—and many experts believe that the true European *Boletus edulis* is not found in North America. Instead, there are most likely many different species across the country that many people simply refer to as *Boletus edulis* due to their similarities and popularity as a good edible.

From above, this brown-capped mushroom looks like a typical cap-with-stem shape, but turning it over reveals a **spongy pore surface**. This is composed of a series of tubes (see photo on pg. 15) that hold the spores. It is the feature that most strongly defines the group of mushrooms called, in general, ***Boletes***, a term used to refer to many cap-and-stem mushrooms with pores.

HABITAT: King Boletes grow from the soil, singly or in loose groups, in association with trees; they are generally found under conifers but may appear under hardwoods including birch.

DESCRIPTION: This **large, stout** mushroom has a **fleshy**, yellowish-brown to reddish-brown cap, anywhere from 3 to 10 inches wide; caps are smooth to slightly wrinkled, and the edges are usually paler. Caps are dry, becoming slightly sticky in wet weather. Immature caps are rounded and may seem small in relation to the swollen stem, which tends to be short and bulbous on young specimens. Stems lengthen with age and may be up to 7 inches tall and 1 to 3 inches thick; they become more slender with age but often remain bulbous at the base. Young, fresh specimens have stems that are **white or cream-colored**, and typically **brownish** at the top; the entire stem may turn somewhat brownish with age. Stems are

Spring King

B. fibrillosus

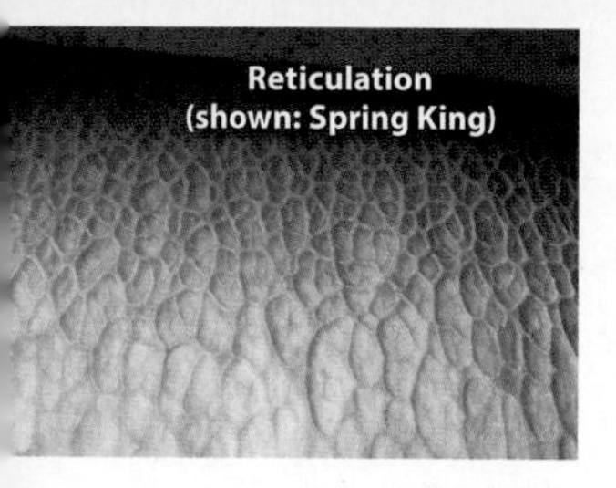
Reticulation (shown: Spring King)

adorned with surface **reticulation** (mesh-like texture) that is dull white on young specimens, often darkening slightly with age. The reticulation is always present at the top of the stem and may cover most or all of the stem. There is no ring. The interior of the stem is solid and white; although it is a little firmer than the cap, the stem is valued just as much for edibility. The pore surface is **white** and very finely textured when young; the pores are stuffed, making the surface appear **nearly solid**. With age the pores turn dingy yellowish, olive-yellow or brown. The interior flesh of the cap is white, with a firm texture. When cut or damaged, the flesh of the cap and stem **does not change color**; bruised pores may darken slightly. (In comparison, the flesh and pore surfaces of many other Boletes stain or discolor very noticeably when cut, scraped or bruised; some **toxic** varieties, shown on pgs. 66–69, turn blue when bruised.)

SPORE PRINT: The King Bolete has an **olive-brown** spore print.

SEASON: Late spring through late fall, depending on elevation (and rainfall).

OTHER NAMES: Porcini, Cep, Penny Bun, Steinpilz; *B. edulis* var. *edulis*.

COMPARE: Several other Boletes that are often considered to be part of a *Boletus edulis* complex are found in our area; all are edible. Visual comparisons to the King are detailed below; other differences are microscopic.

- Caps of **Spring King** (*B. rex-veris*; also listed as *B. pinophilus*) are usually **reddish-brown**, ranging from pale to dark; they may be tan to yellowish-brown when they develop under surface litter. The cap surface is sometimes lumpy-looking; young specimens may have a fine whitish bloom. Stems are cream-colored,

White King Bolete

The Queen

tinged reddish-brown at the top. The top half of the stem has fine whitish reticulation; the lower portion is typically bald but may sometimes be reticulate. The pore surface is whitish, darkening with age like that of the King Bolete; pores near the cap edge are often somewhat flattened, and may be cinnamon-brown. Spring King fruits in **mountainous areas near conifers in the spring**.

- *B. fibrillosus* is smaller than King Bolete, typically 3 to 6 inches wide and 4 to 6 inches tall; compared to other Boletes, its stems often look disproportionately long. It has **velvety, wrinkled** caps that are **dark brown to chestnut brown**. Stems are pale yellowish at the top, whitish at the base, and brownish elsewhere, sometimes appearing quite dark; reticulation is often present overall, but sometimes only in the upper part. The base of the stem is often sharply tapered. The pore surface is **pale yellow** on young specimens, darkening with age. *B. fibrillosus* is found primarily in **coastal forests**, near **conifers**.
- White King Bolete (*B. barrowsii*) is very similar in appearance and size to the King, but it is **whitish to grayish-buff overall** and its cap often has a suede-like texture. It associates with Ponderosa pine, fir and spruce; one variant has been found under oaks and basswood (also known as linden).
- Young specimens of Queen Bolete (*B. regineus*; also listed as *B. aereus*) have **dark brown to nearly black** caps that have a whitish bloom and are often pitted; with age, caps become paler and smooth. Other characteristics are similar to the King. The Queen is found primarily in **coastal areas, under oak and madrone**; it is also found in the Cascades, in association with conifers.

NOTES: Both the cap and stem of the King Bolete are edible and choice. It dries well, and drying intensifies its nutty flavor. Boletes should be cut into evenly thick slices before cooking or drying; this ensures that all pieces cook at the same rate and also allows you to check for insect larvae. The bugs will often beat you to this tasty find.

Inky Caps (several)

Coprinoid group

This group of related mushrooms is common in both urban and woodland settings. While they're not as highly regarded for the table as some others in this section, they are easy to identify and a good choice for beginners.

HABITAT: Inky Caps are saprobes, mushrooms that get their nutrients from decaying organic matter. They often appear in large clusters but also grow in scattered groupings.

DESCRIPTION: The most obvious feature of Inky Caps is that the gills of mature specimens dissolve, partially or completely, turning into an **inky black fluid** (photo at left). All species discussed here have a partial veil covering the gills of young specimens, and some have a universal veil; the resulting ring on the stem may be present for only a short time, often disappearing as the specimen matures. Caps of young specimens are rounded, but the edges soon flare and turn upward; as the cap opens up from the bottom, the gills and cap begin to deliquesce (dissolve) to release the spores. Gills are crowded or very closely spaced and white on young specimens; they soon turn gray or purplish-brown before turning **black** as they dissolve. Stems are **whitish and hollow**. Other features which separate the various *Coprinoid* species are microscopic.

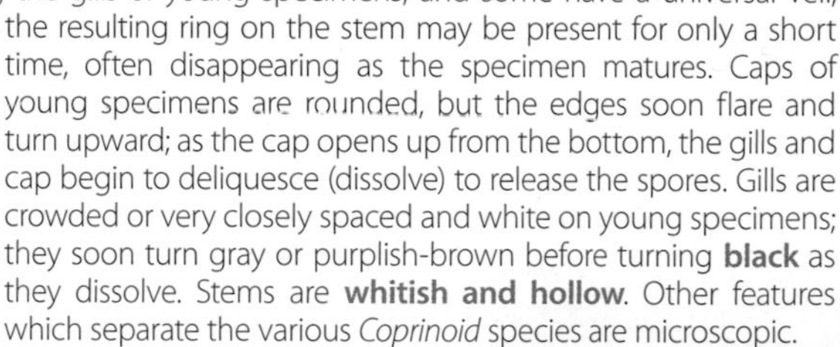

- Shaggy Manes (*Coprinus comatus*) are found in grassy areas, on wood chips, on disturbed ground and in areas with compacted soil. Caps of young specimens are shaped like an **elongated oval** and may be nearly **6 inches tall**, although they are usually shorter. They are whitish and covered with **small, elongated, shaggy scales that curl upward**; the very top of the cap is generally smooth and somewhat darker in color. Stems are 3 to 8 inches tall; when cut in half vertically, a **string-like filament** can be seen on the inside, hanging down from the top of the cap into the stem.

Shaggy Manes

green = key identification feature

Alcohol Inky

Mica Cap

- **Alcohol Inky** or Tippler's Bane (*Coprinopsis atramentaria*) fruits on decaying roots and buried woody debris, often at the base of stumps and dead trees; they also appear in cultivated areas. They generally fruit in **tight, dense clusters**. Young specimens have **egg-shaped to conical caps** up to 2 inches wide and tall; they are **pewter-gray or grayish-brown**. The surface is **silky** except at the center, which is **finely scaly** and often darker in color; **faint** grooves run upward from the edge of the cap. Stems are 3 to 5½ inches tall.

SPORE PRINT: Blackish to brownish-black.

SEASON: Alcohol Inkies and Shaggy Manes are most common in the fall but also occur in cool weather conditions in spring and summer.

OTHER NAMES: Inkies; Shaggy Mane is sometimes called Lawyer's Wig. Alcohol Inky is also listed as *Coprinus atramentarius*.

COMPARE: Several related mushrooms are easy to distinguish from the top edible Inky Caps. • **Mica Caps** (*Coprinellus micaceus*; edible) have **tawny**, conical caps that are **finely ribbed**, with no hairs, scales or patches; young caps are covered with **salt-like granules**. • **Wooly Inky Cap** (*Coprinopsis lagopus* or *Coprinus lagopus*; inedible) is generally 2 inches tall or less; caps are finely ribbed. Young caps are **gray and covered with pale hairs**. With age, caps **turn inside out** rather than dissolving.

Wooly Inky Caps

NOTES: Collect Inky Caps for the table before the gills darken. They deteriorate very quickly after picking and must be cooked without delay. Alcohol Inky **causes severe illness if consumed within several days of drinking alcohol** (either before or after the mushrooms are eaten). Some compare the reaction to the worst hangover imaginable, or even worse.

ON LIVE OR DEAD TREES AND LOGS

LATE SPRING THROUGH FALL

Chicken Mushrooms

Laetiporus conifericola, L. gilbertsonii

Unlike other edible mushrooms that seem to use natural camouflage to hide from the eager forager, the Chicken Mushroom announces its presence loudly. Its bright colors, large size and frequently elevated location make it easy to spot from a fair distance.

HABITAT: Found in association with live, dead or dying trees. The appearance of Chicken Mushrooms on a living tree is a signal that the tree has been attacked by the mushroom's parasitic mycelium (root-like fungal filaments), which can sometimes be seen as whitish fibers in cracks in the wood. The fungus causes butt rot of the host tree.

DESCRIPTION: Two *Laetiporus* species are found in our area. Both grow as a **grouping of thick, stemless fan-shaped caps** that are typically arranged in **tight, overlapping shelf-like layers**. Individual caps may be up to 10 inches wide but are generally smaller. Caps are some shade of **orange to yellow-orange**, with a fair amount of variation among different groupings of the same species; they often look subtly banded, with zones of varying shades. They are smooth to wrinkled and may be leathery but are **not hairy**. Edges may be rounded or scalloped and are generally quite wavy. The underside of each cap is covered with **tiny pores**. Older specimens are pale, becoming whitish when very old.

L. conifericola

L. gilbertsonii

green = key identification feature

- *L. conifericola* is the most common Chicken Mushroom in our area. It fruits directly on **coniferous wood**; it often grows on standing trees but is also found on stumps and downed wood. The pore surface is **sulphur-yellow**.
- *L. gilbertsonii* appears nearly identical to *L. sulphureus*, but it fruits on **hardwoods**, particularly oak and members of the *Prunus* genus (in California, it also appears on Eucalyptus trees). Its pore surface is typically **pale yellow to lemon-yellow**; other differences between the two species are microscopic. *L. gilbertsonii* is less common in our area than *L. conifericola*.

SPORE PRINT: White.

SEASON: Late spring through fall.

OTHER NAMES: Chicken of the Woods, Sulphur Shelf. The *Laetiporus* species in our area were originally listed as *L. sulphureus*, but that name more properly refers to species found east of the Rocky Mountains.

COMPARE: *Climacocystis borealis* are soft-bodied, fleshy polypores whose top surfaces are **hairy** and orangish tan to dingy whitish. The lower surface is covered with **irregularly shaped** whitish to dull yellowish pores that may project outward in a tooth-like fashion; pores of older specimens are often **maze-like**. It has no stems, but is attached to the host trees with a **stem-like neck**. This saprobe feeds on conifers, both living and dead; it is most common in the fall. It is bitter and inedible. • The inedible **Mock Oyster** (pg. 225) is a fan-shaped, stemless orange mushroom that fruits on rotting deciduous and coniferous trees. It has **orange gills** rather than pores; caps are up to 3¼ inches wide and **hairy**. It often grows in clusters but may be scattered. It is noted for its **foul odor**, and is sometimes referred to as the Smelly Oyster.

Climacocystis borealis
NOT RECOMMENDED

NOTES: Chicken Mushrooms have a meaty, chicken-like texture. Young growth on the cap edge is tender, but the older center portion becomes tough and requires stewing; many eat only the tender edges. Chicken Mushrooms, particularly older specimens, may cause digestive upset in some people.

Oyster Mushrooms (several)

Pleurotus spp.

Two *Pleurotus* species in our area are now considered variations of the "classic" Oyster Mushroom, *Pleurotus ostreatus*, which is a European species that does grow in parts of the United States but apparently not in our area. All are fragrant and choice edibles that are easy to identify. Oyster Mushrooms are saprobes that hasten decomposition of the wood on which they grow.

HABITAT: Oyster Mushrooms always **grow from wood** and are found on living trees, dying trees, or dead trees, stumps and logs; they also may grow on buried roots, appearing to grow from the soil.

DESCRIPTION: Oyster Mushooms are shelf-like, typically growing in overlapping clusters on living and dead wood. Caps are fan-shaped or semicircular if growing against a standing tree trunk but may be circular if the specimen is growing upright from a fallen log or from buried roots. Edges are often wavy, scalloped or irregular. The cap is **smooth and hairless** above and is **fairly meaty**, especially where the stem and cap

P. pulmonarius

green = key identification feature

meet. Stems may be short and stubby, or virtually nonexistent; when present and not covered with gills, they are usually downy near the base. They are attached to the cap **at one side or off-center**; there is **no ring**. Gills are closely spaced and **run down the stem**, or may simply taper down to a stem-like stub. Fresh specimens have an **anise-like** odor. The Oyster Mushrooms discussed here are similar in so many ways that it may be difficult to determine exactly which species you have found. Below are some traits that may be helpful; microscopic examination is necessary for absolute certainty. Happily, they are all edible, so exact species identification is not required when collecting for the table.

P. populinus (on live black cottonwood)

P. ostreatus (in Montana)

- Pale Oyster (*P. pulmonarius*; also referred to as the Summer Oyster) has caps that may be whitish, ivory-colored, tan or pinkish-brown. Individual caps are typically less than 3½ inches wide; they may be more oblong (lung-shaped) than caps of the other Oysters. Gills are white, becoming cream-colored with age. Pale Oysters are most common on the wood of **coniferous** trees but may also fruit on hardwoods. They are present from late spring through late summer, and are often found at mid-level elevations.
- Aspen Oyster (*P. populinus*) is similar in size and coloration to *P. pulmonarius*, but it fruits on the wood of trees in the *Populus* genus; in our area, it appears most frequently on **aspens and cottonwoods**. Gills are more widely spaced than the other Oysters described here. It is found from late spring into late fall.
- "Classic" Oyster Mushrooms (*P. ostreatus*) have caps that are up to **8 inches** across; they are often darker in color than Pale and Aspen Oysters, sometimes **dark brown to bluish-gray**. Classic Oysters are found in California and other nearby states, but have not been verified in our area.

SPORE PRINT: **White** to buff-colored; spores of Pale Oyster and *P. ostreatus* may have a **lilac or warm gray** tinge which is lacking in spores of Aspen Oyster.

SEASON: Late spring through late fall, depending on species.

Veiled Oyster

White Beech Mushrooms

EDIBLE

COMPARE: Numerous mushrooms in our area have some resemblance to classic Oyster Mushrooms. Some are edible; others are not recommended.

- The **Veiled Oyster** (*P. dryinus*) has a **distinct, stocky stem** up to 4 inches long that is **covered with fuzz** on the lower half. Caps are up to 5 inches across and white to cream-colored, turning **yellowish** when bruised; the surface is **scaly or hairy**. Gills are colored like the cap. There is a **partial veil** over the gills of young specimens, which breaks apart as the cap expands with age, leaving **remnants on the cap edge** and a **thin ring** on the stem; the ring disappears with age. Veiled Oysters grow from summer into early winter on the wood of living and dead oak and other deciduous trees. They have a citrus odor. They are edible but not as choice as the other Oysters.
- **White Beech Mushrooms** (*Hypsizygus tessulatus*) have a **distinct, thick stem** up to 8 inches long; the gills **do not run down the stem**. Caps are up to 5 inches wide and whitish to pinkish-cream; the surface is **subtly marbled** with darker areas that resemble **water spots**. White Beech Mushrooms are found on logs and stumps of broadleaf trees from late summer to late fall. They are edible when young, although they may be bitter and somewhat tough.
- **Green Oyster** (*Sarcomyxa serotina*; also listed as *Panellus serotinus*) are shaped like classic Oyster Mushrooms and grow in layered clusters, but their caps are **olive-green to olive-gray** and up to 6 inches wide; they are **sticky** when wet. Stems are stub-like to absent. Gills are **yellowish-white to orangish**; spores are **yellowish**. They fruit on hardwoods from fall into winter, and are sometimes called Late Oyster. They are edible but not considered desirable.
- **Angel Wings** (*Pleurocybella porrigens*) look very similar to Pale Oysters, but the caps are so thin that they are **partially translucent**. Caps are generally 3½ inches wide or less; there is no stem. Angel Wings are found from late summer through fall on dead **conifer wood**. Many sources list Angel Wings as edible,

but the North American Mycological Association reports that more than a dozen deaths in 2004 were attributed to ingestion of this mushroom in Japan; it is best to regard it as inedible.

- Stalkless Paxillus (*Tapinella panuoides*; also listed as *Paxillus panuoides*) grows on **conifers**. Caps are up to 4 inches wide and shell-shaped, often with scalloped edges; there is no stem. The surface is **tan to orangish-brown**; it is downy when young. Gills are yellowish. They have **cross-veins** and are **wavy**, appearing **corrugated**; they may be forked. Its spore print is **yellowish to yellowish-brown**. It is inedible.
- Gills of *Lentinellus* species (pg. 220) have **serrated edges**; caps are **fuzzy or hairy** and up to 4 inches across. Lentinellus are too bitter or acrid to be edible.

NOTES: Oyster Mushrooms can be cultivated fairly easily and are available in grow-it-yourself kits. White Beech Mushrooms can also be grown at home; the cultivated variety is sold as Shimeji.

Chanterelles (several)

Cantharellus spp.

At first glance, Chanterelles appear to be gilled mushrooms. Closer inspection reveals that what appears to be gills are actually **blunt-edged folds or ribs**. The folds dent when pressed with a blunt object, and can be teased from the cap in small sheets containing numerous folds. In comparison, true gills have sharp, **knife-like edges**; individual gills break or collapse when pressed with a blunt object and don't peel away easily.

HABITAT: Chanterelles grow **from the soil**, singly or in loose groups. Most are mycorrhizal; those in our area associate with conifers.

DESCRIPTION: Most Chanterelles have distinct, **gill-like folds** under the cap. The folds are often forked near the cap edge and **continue down the stem** for a short distance; the folds often feel waxy, and there is a network of fine veins between the folds. Stems are fairly sturdy and have no rings. Caps of young specimens are rounded with a depressed center. With age, caps spread and flatten out, developing **wavy edges**; mature caps often form a shallow, funnel-like bowl. Caps of the four Chanterelles listed on pg. 43 average about 4 inches wide at maturity. Most have a **fruity, apricot-like** odor that is stronger on dried specimens.

Golden Chanterelle

green = key identification feature

White Chanterelle

Rainbow Chanterelle

- The **Golden Chanterelle** (*Cantharellus formosus*) is the most common Chanterelle in our area. It is typically **orangish-yellow to warm buff overall**, sometimes rosy-buff; colors are brighter in damp weather and paler when the specimens are growing in the shade. Caps often appear finely scaly, particularly in dry weather. Stems are up to 4 inches tall and **slender**, often becoming narrower at the base. Spores are yellowish-white to pale yellow.
- **White Chanterelles** (*Cantharellus subalbidus*) are **cream-colored to ivory overall** when young, developing orangish tones as they age; old or dried-out specimens are dark orangish to rust-colored. Stems are **stocky** and less than 3 inches tall. Spores are white. Most common in coastal and montane forests.
- Caps of **Rainbow Chanterelle** (*Cantharellus roseocanus*; also listed as *Cantharellus cibarius* var. *roseocanus*) are pale yellowish-pink to orangish-yellow. Young specimens have a **pinkish bloom** over the cap; edges are typically **pinkish**. The folds under the cap are pale to **bright orangish-yellow**. Stems may be paler than the folds; they are typically short and stocky. Spores are orangish-yellow. Most common in old-growth coastal to montane forests.
- ***Cantharellus cascadensis*** was first identified in 2003. Caps are bright to deep yellow, fading to white in the center; gills are typically paler than those of the Golden Chanterelle. Stems are **stocky** and usually less than 2 inches tall, often with a club-shaped base. Spores are white to yellowish-white; its odor is less fruity than the others listed here. It is found east of the Cascades.

SPORE PRINT: Varies; see individual descriptions above.

SEASON: Chanterelles in our area fruit in summer into late fall.

OTHER NAMES: Golden Chanterelle is also called Pacific Golden Chanterelle or Yellow Chanterelle. Older sources refer to yellowish Chanterelles as *Cantharellus cibarius*, but mycologists believe that this European species doesn't appear in

Trumpet Chanterelle
EDIBLE

Scaly Vase Chanterelle
NOT RECOMMENDED

North America; it has been divided into numerous new species based on microscopic and DNA evidence.

False Chanterelle
NOT RECOMMENDED

COMPARE: Trumpet Chanterelle (*Craterellus 'tubaeformis;'* also called Yellowfoot) is less than **3 inches wide and 4 inches tall**. The **brownish-yellow to brownish** caps are dimpled in the center when young. Folds are pinkish, yellowish or grayish. Stems are yellowish-orange and often flattened or grooved. They typically fruit in bogs and other damp areas. • Black Trumpet (*Craterellus cornucopioides*; edible) has **blackish trumpet-shaped caps with a deep, hollow center**. Stems are **smooth** and colored like the cap or paler. They are rare in our area, fruiting under conifers and hardwoods. • Scaly Vase Chanterelle (*Turbinellus floccosus*; also listed as *Gomphus floccosus*) is up to 8 inches tall. It has **incurved scales** on the top surface; the base is **wrinkled or ribbed overall**. It can cause digestive problems and should be considered inedible. • False Chanterelle (*Hygrophoropsis aurantiaca*) is up to 4 inches wide and nearly as tall. Unlike true Chanterelles, it has **gills rather than folds** under its orangish-yellow to brownish cap. Stems are generally colored like the cap with some variations in color. Gills are orange; they are generally **brighter** than the cap and fork repeatedly. They are found on wood chips and rotting debris under conifers. False Chanterelle should be regarded as inedible.

NOTES: Chanterelles are considered a choice edible; most have a mildly peppery flavor. They often grow in large quantities and are easy to spot due to their color.

Cauliflower Mushroom

Sparassis radicata

Although the name suggests a vegetable, these unusual mushrooms look more like a rounded pile of whitish egg noodles. They are a choice edible.

HABITAT: Cauliflower Mushrooms are saprobes that fruit singly from the soil, at the base of living coniferous trees and stumps.

DESCRIPTION: This large, branching mushroom is easy to recognize. It is composed of a mass of tightly packed **flattened, curly petal-like branches** growing from a rooting base; the entire body is whitish to cream-colored. Very large examples may be up to 2 feet across, but most are much smaller. This mushroom doesn't have gills or teeth but a **smooth surface** on one side of the curly branches to release its spores.

SPORE PRINT: Whitish to cream-colored.

SEASON: Summer through fall.

OTHER NAMES: Formerly listed as *S. crispa*, which has been proven to be a different species from Europe.

COMPARE: Crested Coral (pg. 246) grows as a mass of flattened, whitish branches, but the tips of the branches are **toothed** and the branched fruiting body is less than 2 inches across; it resembles **coral**.

NOTES: When gathering for the table, cut the branches off near the base, leaving the remnant in the ground where it may produce again the following year. These culinary prizes require careful cleaning before cooking. Soak the branches in mild saltwater to remove debris and unwanted critters, then cook thoroughly. When cooked, their flavor and texture is often compared to buttered noodles.

Matsutake

Tricholoma murrillianum

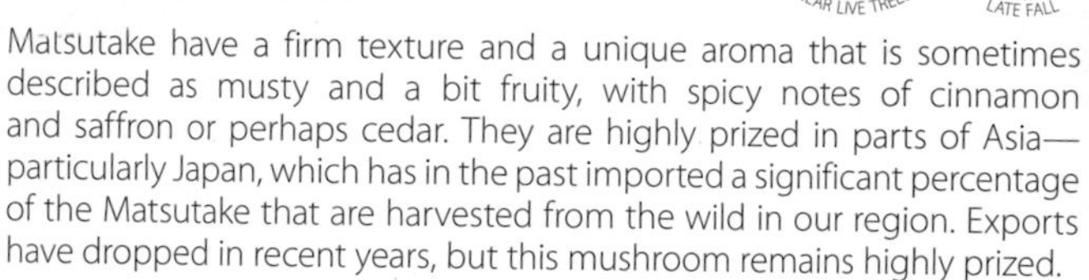

Matsutake have a firm texture and a unique aroma that is sometimes described as musty and a bit fruity, with spicy notes of cinnamon and saffron or perhaps cedar. They are highly prized in parts of Asia—particularly Japan, which has in the past imported a significant percentage of the Matsutake that are harvested from the wild in our region. Exports have dropped in recent years, but this mushroom remains highly prized.

HABITAT: These mycorrhizal mushrooms are found scattered or in groups near a wide range of conifers; they also fruit near huckleberry shrubs, rhododendron and madrone, and in sandy or poor soil in coastal areas.

DESCRIPTION: Matsutake are **large, sturdy** mushrooms; caps of mature specimens are often 7 inches wide, sometimes larger. Young, unopened "buttons" are the most valuable form on the Asian market; they are **peg-like**, with small, rounded caps bound to the stems by the thick veil that covers the immature gills. Caps become convex to flattened; the veil remnants sheathe the lower part of the stem, terminating in a **prominent, flaring ring** towards the top of the stem. Caps are **whitish to cream-colored** when young, developing orangish to pale brown stains and patches of fine fibers. Gills are crowded and attached to the stem, sometimes notched; they are white, developing orangish spots with age. Stems are 2 to 6 inches tall and one-third as wide. They are whitish with **brownish scales or fibers** below the ring; bases are frequently

green = key identification feature

tapered. Matsutake have a **firm, resilient texture** that is sometimes described as tough or bouncy; the flesh **peels in shreds**, much like string cheese.

SPORE PRINT: White.

SEASON: Summer through late fall.

OTHER NAMES: White Matsutake, Western Matsutake. *T. murrillianum* has long been listed as *T. magnivelare*, a name that is now generally used for Matsutake found in eastern North America. Matsutake in general are also called Pine Mushrooms. Older references may refer to Matsutake as *Armillaria ponderosa*.

COMPARE: Brown Matsutake (*T. caligatum*) are **smaller**, less than 5 inches wide and 3 inches tall. The fibers on the caps are more prominent, giving the mushrooms a **more brownish appearance**. Brown Matsutake are less common in our area than the white Matsutake, but their spicy aroma and flavor are similar and they typically lack the bitterness often reported for *T. caligatum* in the eastern U. S. and Europe. • Caps of Imperial Cat (*Catathelasma imperiale*) may be up to **15 inches** wide. The **gills run down the stem**, and the ring on the stem is typically **doubled**. It has a **grain-like** odor; it is edible but not as favored as Matsutake. Swollen-Stalked Cat (*C. ventricosum*) is similar but a bit smaller; caps are **paler**, and more **gray** than brown, and its stems may be swollen in the middle. • Smith's Amanita (pg. 63; **toxic**) is more delicate, with a **more brittle texture** and stems that **lack brownish scales**. The stem ring may be poorly developed or lacking, and the stem base is **bulbous and tapering**, with ragged, concentric rings. Smith's Amanita lacks Matsutake's distinct, spicy odor.

NOTES: Matsutake may fruit in the same area for years. Experienced foragers look for humps in conifer duff that indicate the presence of a buried Matsutake.

Brown Matsutake

Imperial Cat

Giant Puffball

Calvatia booniana, Calbovista subsculpta

If you want to feed wild mushrooms to a crowd, a single specimen of one of these might do the job. (But first, please read the Notes on the facing page for some cautions before eating—or serving—Giant Puffballs.)

HABITAT: These two species have very different habitat requirements; please see information in the individual species accounts below.

DESCRIPTION: Like all Puffballs, these consist of a fleshy spore mass that is surrounded by a thickened skin. Spore masses of the species discussed here are firm and white on young, edible specimens, turning yellow before ripening to a powdery brownish mass that explodes into the air, scattering the spores, when the skin splits or is broken (be careful not to inhale the spore cloud; it can cause respiratory distress).

- Western Giant Puffball (*Calvatia booniana*) may be **almost 2 feet** across at the widest point, although it is usually smaller. It may be roughly spherical, but more often is **flattened** and irregular. The surface is dry, smooth and whitish at first, turning grayish and breaking up into **large polygonal patches** that may be flat or slightly raised. Eventually the surface becomes tan to brownish, splitting to release the powdery olive-brown spores. Western Giant Puffball is found in **montane meadows**, or in **high desert areas** under sagebrush and juniper. Individual specimens are scattered but often grow in a large fairy ring.
- Sculptured Puffball (*Calbovista subsculpta*) is much smaller, typically

Western Giant Puffball

green = key identification feature

Calbovista subsculpta

5 inches across or less. It is generally more **spherical**, but may be softly folded towards the base. The surface is whitish to pale yellowish-brown and covered with 3- to 6-sided **projecting pyramid-shaped warts** that are up to ¼ inch tall and may be flat-topped or pointed; the tops of the pyramids are generally darker than the rest of the skin. With age the surface becomes olive-brown and splits open to release the powdery purplish-brown spores. It is found at mid- to high-elevation zones where it fruits singly, scattered or in small clusters in **open conifer woods, forest edges** or **areas with rocky soil**, including paths and dirt roads.

SPORE PRINT: Olive-brown or purplish-brown.

SEASON: Early summer through fall.

OTHER NAMES: *Calbovista subsculpta* is also called Warted Giant Puffball.

COMPARE: ***Calvatia sculpta*** is also called Sculptured Puffball, and is about the same size as *Calbovista subsculpta*. However, it is somewhat **pear-shaped**, and its warts are **up to 1 inch** tall, with **narrow tips** that may be curved; it sometimes resembles a multi-pointed star ornament. Found in conifer forests at high altitude. • Young examples of **Purple-Spored Puffball** (*Calvatia cyathiformis*) are spherical and generally less than 6 inches across; the skin is **thin** and whitish. As the specimen matures, the sphere develops a **neck-like base** that is typically narrower than the sphere; the skin becomes **brownish and scaly**. The sphere disintegrates after releasing its spores, which are **purple**, but the base remains attached to the ground, looking like a rough-surfaced purplish cup. Purple-Spored Puffball is found in prairielands and near-desert areas, where it fruits in grassy locations such as pastures.

NOTES: All the Puffballs listed here are edible when they are young and the flesh is **pure, featureless white throughout**. Cut the mushroom in half from top to bottom and look at the flesh inside. If there is any trace of yellow, or any shadowy shapes within, the specimen is too mature to eat, or it may be another species. Be particularly cautious with small specimens, as they can be mistaken for a number of cap-and-stem species in the button stage, including **deadly** Amanitas (pgs. 60–65), **toxic** Earthballs (pg. 228) or the egg stage of Stinkhorns (pg. 197). Puffballs may have a laxative effect on some people.

ON LIVING, DYING OR DEAD TREES; FALLEN LOGS

SUMMER THROUGH FALL

Lion's Mane (several)

Hericium spp.

The name Lion's Mane is used as a catch-all for various species in the *Hericium* genus. These beautiful mushrooms are a delight to come upon in the woods. They often grow in large clusters, so you may be lucky enough to bring home an abundant harvest for the table.

HABITAT: Lion's Mane are saprobes that help decompose dead trees, frequently appearing on stumps and downed logs; they may also act as parasites, fruiting from wounds on living trees. Bear's Head is found exclusively on **dead conifers**. American Tooth fruits on both hardwoods and conifers, while the others discussed here are found only on hardwoods.

DESCRIPTION: With its unique structure and overall appearance, this mushroom is easy to recognize. Rather than a cap or shelf, it is a **large, whitish fruitbody with hanging or projecting spines** that are the spore-producing structures; the fruitbody is branched in all species here except Bearded Tooth. These species are comprised of soft, flexible whitish flesh that becomes darker when bruised or with age. Four *Hericium* species are found in our region. All are edible and delicious.

Bear's Head

- Bear's Head (*H. abietis*) is the most common in our area, and also the largest; the branched fruitbody may be nearly **30 inches** across. Its spines **hang like clusters of small icicles** from the branch tips; spines are typically ⅓ inch long or less, but may be up to an inch long. The entire mass is whitish but may be tinged with salmon or yellowish-brown tones. It bruises yellowish to orangish; older specimens are orangish-brown.

- Comb Tooth (*H. coralloides*) has an **open structure** of primary branches, each of which branch repeatedly. Clusters of short, rounded teeth cover the branches; teeth are evenly distributed along the branches, resembling a **short-toothed comb**. The entire mass is up to 14 inches wide and about half as high. It is pure white when young, becoming yellowish-tan to buff with maturity.
- Bearded Tooth (*H. erinaceus*; also called Pom Pom) is **unbranched**; the **long, icicle-shaped teeth** grow densely packed from the base and hang down in a parallel arrangement, resembling a waterfall. The teeth are up to **2 inches** long. Bearded Tooth is up to 12 inches wide and tall; it often grows in pairs.
- American Tooth (*H. americanum*) is uncommon in our area; it is primarily found in the eastern U.S. It is similar in appearance and size to Comb Tooth, but has **fewer branches** and appears **less open**.

SPORE PRINT: White.

SEASON: Summer through fall.

OTHER NAMES: *H. coralloides* was formerly listed as *H. ramosum*; in this nomenclatural scheme, *H. americanum* was listed as *H. coralloides*.

COMPARE: Crested Coral (pg. 246) grows from the ground as a mass of **flattened, whitish branches with toothed tips**; the fruiting body is less than 2 inches across

NOTES: Bearded Tooth is sometimes considered the most prized variety, but all Hericium are lovely when sliced and cooked, with a flavor and texture that is sometimes compared to lobster. Gather them for cooking when they are young and fresh; older specimens may be sour or bitter tasting. Bearded Tooth is commonly cultivated, dried and sold in Asian grocery stores as Monkey Head Mushrooms. Hericium are also reported to have medicinal properties.

FROM THE SOIL NEAR LIVE TREES

LATE SUMMER THROUGH FALL

Hedgehog Mushroom

Hydnum repandum, H. umbilicatum

At first glance, these mushrooms look like many other cap-and-stem species. A glance underneath the cap reveals the difference: instead of gills or pores, the underside of the cap is covered with **spines or teeth**. Two related species are found in our area; both are edible and delicious.

HABITAT: Hedgehogs are mycorrhizal, growing from the ground near living trees; they fruit singly and in groups.

DESCRIPTION: Two closely related mushrooms are commonly called Hedgehogs. Both have a **bristly-looking surface** under the caps, consisting of spore-bearing spines or teeth.

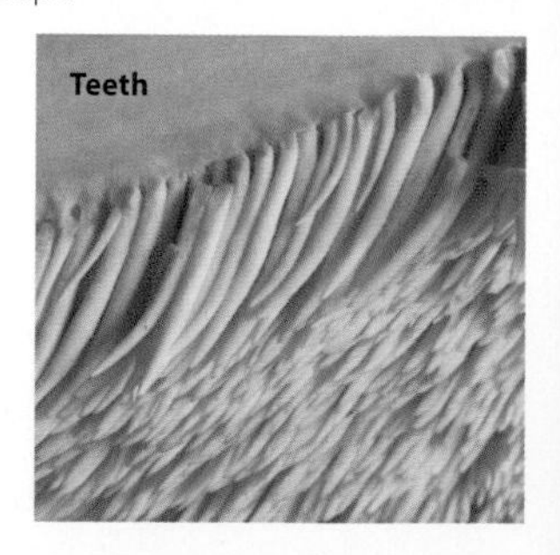

- *H. repandum* is the larger of the two, with **cream to tan to apricot** caps that usually are 2 to **7 inches** wide. The edge of the cap is rolled under when young, becoming flattened

green = key identification feature

and more lobed and wavy as it grows, a bit like Chanterelles (pgs. 42–44). The **thick, whitish** stem is often **off-center** and is less than 4 inches tall; the whitish to cream-colored teeth may run partway down it. The stem and teeth **bruise orangish-brown** when handled, and the whitish interior flesh may discolor yellow to orangish when cut. There is also a white variety, *H. repandum* var. *album*, which has flesh that shows orange staining when cut. *H. repandum* occurs with both conifers and hardwoods.

- *H. umbilicatum* is much smaller and is found in duff under conifers. Its cap is less than 2 inches wide and may have subtle concentric rings; the center is often **sunken**, giving it the common name of Depressed Hedgehog or Belly Button Mushroom. The stem is less than 3 inches tall; it is thinner and **more centrally located** than that of *H. repandum*. The teeth are whitish, whitish-orange or pale yellowish-brown. Other differences are microscopic.

H. umbilicatum

SPORE PRINT: White to cream-colored.

SEASON: Late summer through fall.

OTHER NAMES: Sweet Tooth, Wood Hedgehog. Older references place Hedgehogs in the *Dentinum* genus, using *D. repandum* and *D. umbilicatum*.

COMPARE: The inedible Orange Hydnellum (pg. 258) is usually found under conifers. Its caps are tough, bumpy and **clustered** and often fused; they are orange to brownish with a pale edge. Its **grayish to brownish teeth**, stocky **reddish-brown** stem that is less than 3 inches tall and **brown** spore print easily distinguish it from the edible Hedgehogs.

NOTES: A favorite and easily identified edible, Hedgehogs are closely related to Chanterelles and are often found in the same locations and at the same time. Hedgehogs have a lightly fruity aroma and peppery taste and unlike many good edibles, they are seldom attacked by insects.

Lobster Mushroom

Hypomyces lactifluorum

If you're in an area with lots of Short-Stemmed Russula (pg. 152), keep an eye out for flashes of bright orange in the woods—you might find Lobster Mushrooms, a unique edible.

HABITAT: Grows **from the ground** singly, scattered or in loose groups, primarily in coniferous forests. It is a parasite of *Russula* (and possibly *Lactarius*) species, so it is found near fruiting bodies of those mushrooms. It is often partially buried in soil or conifer duff.

DESCRIPTION: This unmistakable mushroom is **bright orangish-red**, like a cooked lobster shell; it also may smell somewhat fishy. Its firm, colorful shell is created when the *Hypomyces* parasite infects the fruitbody of the host mushroom; some mycologists believe that only white *Russula* and *Lactarius* species are parasitized by *H. lactifluorum*, with *R. brevipes* (Short-Stemmed Russula; pg. 152) being the most common by far. The distinct cap and stem of the host species become a misshapen body with a hard, **minutely pimpled** orangish-red surface. **Subtle gill-like folds** are evident on most specimens; others appear like featureless, misshapen blobs. The white spores may cover the entire surface of

green = key identification feature

Minutely pimpled surface

the mushroom as well as the surrounding dirt or plants. Lobsters are notoriously dirty, but the white flesh is so firm that they can be scrubbed clean without damage. Older specimens turn darker red to bright magenta or purplish and become soft inside.

SPORE PRINT: White.

SEASON: Late summer through fall.

OTHER NAMES: Orange Mushroom Pimple.

COMPARE: Green Mushroom Pimple (*H. luteovirens*) is very similar and is also caused by a parasitic mold that attacks the gills and stem of *Russula* or *Lactarius* species, but the pimply surface is **yellow** on very young specimens, becoming **yellowish-green** before darkening to nearly black with age. It is far less common in our area; it is reportedly edible, although most sources advise against eating it. • Chicken Mushrooms (pgs. 36–37) also provide flashes of bright orange in the woods, but they fruit **on trees or downed wood** rather than from the ground. They are thick, **fan-shaped caps** that typically grow in overlapping, shelf-like layers.

Green Mushroom Pimple
NOT RECOMMENDED

NOTES: Many experts believe that the main host of the Lobster fungus in our area is *R. brevipes*, which is edible but not considered choice. Although concerns have been raised about eating Lobsters when the identity and edibility of the host is unknown, they have been safely consumed for a long time and are sold commercially in some areas. The host species may affect the flavor of the Lobster. Some Lobsters taste like seafood, while others are bland; some may be peppery or curry-like. Lobster mushrooms should be fresh and firm; they should not be eaten if they are old and soft, or if they lack the bright orange, pimply surface. Some people may experience intestinal upset after eating Lobster Mushrooms.

False Morels: Gyromitras (several)

Gyromitra spp.

Gyromitras are often found in the spring woods by people seeking Morels (pgs. 26–30). The two can be confused from a distance, but closer inspection reveals some significant differences.

HABITAT: Gyromitras grow singly, scattered or in groups from the ground in forests; on rare occasions they fruit from well-decayed wood.

DESCRIPTION: The Gyromitras discussed here have caps that look lumpy and irregular. Stems are white to pale tan, sometimes with pinkish or violet tinges. Gyromitras have a somewhat brittle texture.

- Conifer False Morel (*G. esculenta*; found primarily near conifers) is up to 4 inches wide and may be nearly 6 inches tall, although it is usually shorter. Caps are covered with **rounded, brain-like wrinkles** and are typically **reddish-brown** but may be yellowish-brown or purplish-brown; they are attached to the stems in several places, sometimes overall. The stems may be smooth or creased; they are medium width and are often enlarged at the base. Stems and caps have **pale, chambered flesh inside**. This species is often referred to simply as the False Morel, a name used here to cover several *Gyromitra* species.
- Snow Mushroom (*G. montana*; also listed as *G. gigas*) is found at **elevation**, often near melting snowbanks. The yellowish-brown to medium-brown caps are up to **7 inches** wide; caps are **free from the stems** at the bottom, often flaring away slightly. Stems are 2 to 5 inches tall and very thick, almost as wide as the cap; they appear folded or ribbed.

Conifer False Morel

Snow Mushroom

green = key identification feature

California False Morel

Saddle-Shaped False Morel

- California False Morel (*G. californica*; also listed as *Pseudorhizina californica*) appears **puffy** and often **lobed**. Caps are typically 2 to 6 inches across; they are pale to dark brown and partially free from the stem, attached towards the top. Stems are short and fluted; several sharply creased **ribs continue onto the cap underside**, where they fan out towards the cap margin like the spokes of an umbrella. Unlike other Gyromitras, the stems have **pinkish tones**.
- Saddle-Shaped False Morel (*G. infula*; found near conifers and in mixed woodlands) occurs in **late summer and fall**, fruiting **on downed wood** or woody humus. Caps are brown and usually **saddle-shaped**. See pg. 194 for more information on several *Helvella* species with a similar appearance.

SPORE PRINT: Spore prints of Gyromitra are generally not taken.

SEASON: All but the Saddle-Shaped False Morel appear in spring.

OTHER NAMES: Lorchels.

COMPARE: Morels (pgs. 26–30) may appear similar at first glance, but their caps are **pitted and ridged** and the insides are **completely hollow**. • Elfin Saddles are related to the Saddle-Shaped False Morel, and appear similar; see pg. 194 for more information on these mushrooms.

NOTES: All Gyromitras should be considered inedible and possibly **toxic**. Although some people eat Conifer False Morels, sometimes even boiling them in several changes of water to remove toxins, some Gyromitras contain toxic compounds that can cause severe illness or death; they are especially **deadly** when raw, and the toxic effects may be cumulative.

Deadly Galerina

Galerina marginata

This pretty little mushroom prefers cool weather; it typically graces the woods in spring, then again in fall. Unfortunately, it is one of the most **toxic** mushrooms around. It contains amatoxins, the same deadly poisons found in some Amanitas; for more information on this toxin, see pg. 61.

HABITAT: Deadly Galerina are saprobes, getting their nutrients from dead wood. They grow in **clusters** on decaying coniferous and deciduous wood; they are often found on rotting logs that are mossy.

DESCRIPTION: Deadly Galerina are small to medium-size mushrooms, with caps that are generally 1½ inches wide or less; large specimens may be up to 3 inches across. The caps are **rust-colored, tawny or brownish** with a tacky but not slimy surface; they fade and become paler with age or upon drying. They are rounded or bell-shaped when young, opening up and becoming fairly flat with maturity. Stems are slender and generally 2 to 3 inches long; they often curve as they emerge from a rotting log or from a cluster. They are pale gray to brownish; the lower portion of the stem may be darker and somewhat shaggy. White mycelium (root-like fungal filaments) can sometimes be seen where the stem grows out of the wood. A **fragile, short skirt-like ring** is present on the

green = key identification feature

Buff-colored gills, skirt-like ring
TOXIC

Velvet Foot
EDIBLE

upper half of the stem of young specimens. The ring is **whitish** at first, turning brownish as it catches falling spores. It often disintegrates, leaving behind a **thin, collar-like ring zone**. Gills are **buff-colored or beige** at first, becoming **rust-colored**; they are attached to the stem and closely spaced.

SPORE PRINT: **Rust-colored**.

SEASON: Deadly Galerina are most common in spring and fall but may appear in summer during periods of cool weather.

OTHER NAMES: Autumn Galerina, *G. autumnalis*.

COMPARE: Several small to medium-size mushrooms are colored like Deadly Galerina for at least part of their development, and are found in similar habitat. Here are some differences to look for; spore prints are often key to identification.

- Velvet Foot (*Flammulina velutipes*) has **whitish to pale yellowish** gills. Caps are **slimy** when moist. Stems have **no ring**; with age the lower portions develop a **velvety, dark brown to blackish** coating. Spores are **white**.
- Honey Mushrooms (pg. 104) are **larger and beefier** than Deadly Galerina; they have a **sturdy ring** on the stem and a **white** spore print.
- Caps of Stuntz's Blue-Legs (*Psilocybe stuntzii*) are **deep brown to olive-brown** when young, fading to yellowish-brown. Gills are pale at first, becoming **violet-brown to blackish**. Stems are yellowish-brown. Young specimens **stain blue** when bruised or cut. Spores are **dark purplish-brown**.
- Caps of Spring Scalecap (*Kuehneromyces lignicola*; also listed as *Pholiota lignicola*) are **slimy** when moist. Stems are **very thin** and often have patches of brownish veil remnant below the ring zone. Its spore print is cinnamon-brown.

NOTES: Velvet Foot and Honey Mushroom are popular edibles. Great care must be taken when collecting them for the table, to avoid the **toxic** Deadly Galerina.

Amanitas (numerous)

Amanita spp.

It's probably safe to say that if you asked most people to name just one poisonous mushroom, they would mention the Amanita, although each person might have a different picture in their mind as to what this fungus looks like. Many people would think of the delicate, all-white Destroying Angel, with its skirt-like ring on the stem and its fragile cup at the base. Others might conjure up an image of the Fly Agaric, with its brightly colored cap dotted with numerous small but thick white patches.

The *Amanita* genus is a large, diverse group of mushrooms, encompassing hundreds of species in a wide palette of colors. The species discussed in this book have caps with gills underneath and stems that are centered under the caps; many other key characteristics are microscopic. Common traits shared by many—but not all—are the presence of a ring on the stem and a fragile, cup-like structure called a ***volva*** around the base of the stem. Many also have patches on the caps. All three of these characteristics are remnants of a ***veil***, a thin membrane that covers all or part of the developing mushroom.

All Amanitas start their lives encased in a ***universal veil***, a thin membrane that surrounds the developing mushroom entirely, making it resemble a small, rough-skinned egg; this is often referred to as the ***egg stage***. As the mushroom grows, it breaks through the universal veil. The volva is the part of the universal veil surrounding the base of the stem after the mushroom

Amanitas, from egg to button stage (different species shown)

green = key identification feature

has emerged from the egg-like sac; it is often necessary to dig around the base to uncover evidence of the volva, which may be covered by dirt and sometimes has disintegrated entirely. The patches on top of the cap, when present, are another remnant of the universal veil; patches may be thick, wart-like and persistent, or thin, insubstantial and easily washed away by rain.

Skirt-like veil remnant

Some Amanitas also have a ***partial veil***, a thin membrane attached to both the stem and the lower edge of the young, unopened cap. As the cap expands, the partial veil stretches to cover the gills, finally breaking away from the cap when it becomes too wide. The partial veil remnant often remains attached to the stem under the cap, hanging down and appearing skirt-like or ring-like; fragments may also hang like broken tissue from the edges of the cap.

Some Amanitas are notorious because they contain ***amatoxins***, extremely poisonous substances that cause liver and kidney failure and, often, death; the fatality rate for this type of poisoning, according to the North American Mycological Association, is as high as 50 percent unless prompt, sometimes radical treatment is effected. Other Amanitas have no amatoxins but contain other poisonous substances that cause failure of the nervous system, severe gastric problems or hallucinations. A few lack any toxins and are, surprisingly, edible; however, due to the possibility of confusion with toxic species, **no Amanita should be eaten** by any but the most experienced of foragers—and even then, it is risky business that is best avoided.

HABITAT: All Amanitas grow **from the ground**. Most are found near living trees; the mycelium (root-like fungal filaments) has a symbiotic relationship with tree roots (mycorrhizal). They grow singly, scattered or in loose groups.

DESCRIPTION: Although there are many differences in appearance between the numerous *Amanita* species, all share some common aspects. Young Amanitas at the button stage have rounded or egg-shaped caps that are generally 1 to 3 inches across. As the specimen matures, the cap opens up like an umbrella, becoming wider and flatter; mature specimens of the species discussed here are generally 3 to 6 inches wide. The surface texture of the cap varies depending on species. Stems are stocky on young specimens, becoming moderately sturdy to slender; all of the toxic species discussed here have a ring or skirt on the stem, although it may deteriorate or fall off with age. All Amanitas have some remnant of the universal veil at the base; it can be cup-like and quite obvious, but it is sometimes buried or broken up. Gills are closely spaced and generally free from the stem or just attached; they are typically white.

- The **Death Cap** (*A. phalloides*) contains amatoxins (pg. 61) and is one of the most **deadly** mushrooms known; ***ingestion of a single cap can kill an adult***. This graceful-looking mushroom is common in our area. It is not native to North America but has become naturalized in forests; it also appears in hazelnut and sweet chestnut orchards. It is becoming increasingly common in urban areas, where it is found in grassy areas near trees, particularly oak and beech. Caps are up to 6 inches wide and **yellowish-brown, bronze, greenish-yellow or olive**; edges are often paler. The surface is smooth and may appear shiny or metallic; one or two thin, large pale patches may be present. Stems are up to 7 inches tall and fairly slender at maturity; the base is often enlarged. A **delicate, skirt-like ring** is present near the top of the stem. The volva is thin and fragile, and is often buried, requiring you to dig around the base to see it. Both the ring and volva may disintegrate with age. The Death Cap fruits in summer and fall.
- The **Destroying Angel** (*A. ocreata*) grows near deciduous trees, particularly oak; it fruits in **spring**. It is about the same size as the Death Cap and equally **deadly**. The Destroying Angel is typically **white** overall but may have pinkish-beige tones; the center of the cap may be yellowish, pinkish or brownish. The cap has a **smooth, silky** texture; very rarely there may be a patch of veil remnant on the cap. Stems may be smooth or slightly shaggy. The ring and veil are similar to those of the Death Cap, and also may disintegrate with age. The Destroying Angel is uncommon in our area.

Death Cap

Destroying Angel

Smith's Amanita

Smith's Amanita

- Smith's Amanita (*A. smithiana*) is white overall and often presents a raggedy appearance. Young, fresh specimens have numerous small veil fragments that are **cottony or powdery** on the caps; stems are similarly decorated, and have a ragged ring. The fragments and ring often wash off with rain or fall off with age, leaving the cap and stem fairly smooth; at this point, specimens are sometimes mistaken for Matsutake, a prime edible (pgs. 46–47). Caps of mature Smith's Amanita are up to 6½ inches wide. Stems may be up to 7 inches tall and are fairly sturdy; the base is swollen and **bulbous**, with **ragged, irregular rings** that are remnants of the volva. A **long, tapering root-like extension** is often present, growing into the soil from the base of the stem; it may be nearly a foot long but is fragile and difficult to dig up. Smith's Amanita is found near conifers, often fruiting on badly decayed wood. It is most common in fall, but may be found in summer. It is **deadly**. The Western Woodland Amanita (*A. silvicola*; inedible and possibly toxic) looks like a **shorter, more stout** version of Smith's Amanita.

- Gemmed Amanita (*A. gemmata*) has **pale yellow, golden or buff-colored** caps with **numerous white warts**; caps are typically 2 to 4½ inches wide. Stems are up to 5 inches tall and fairly sturdy; they typically become wider towards the base. A thick ring is present on the upper stem, but it often disintegrates with age and may be missing entirely. The volva is **short** and may appear collar-like, or may flare outwards to form a rim. It is common in our area, and found near conifers in forests and urban areas from late spring into fall. It is **very toxic**, producing a variety of symptoms.

Gemmed Amanita

Fly Agaric (3 photos)
Above: *A. muscaria* var. *flavivolvata*

- **Fly Agaric** (*A. muscaria*) grows near deciduous and coniferous trees, fruiting from late spring into fall. Its caps, which may be up to **10 inches** wide when fully opened, are **heavily speckled** with whitish to buff-colored **wart-like patches** that often have a pyramid shape; cap edges may be faintly ribbed. A thin, skirt-like ring is generally present under the cap, although it may become ragged or fall off completely with age. Stems are whitish to pale buff and up to 11 inches tall; bases are swollen and **bulbous**, with **ragged, concentric rings** that are remnants of the volva. Our area has several varieties, each with different cap colors. The red-capped subspecies (var. *flavivolvata*) is most common in our area; caps are **scarlet to reddish-orange**, fading to orangish or yellowish-orange, and the ring under the cap is **yellowish**. Caps of other varieties are yellowish, orange or whitish. Fly Agaric should never be consumed. It is **toxic**; among other unpleasant symptoms, including sweating, nausea and delirium, it can cause a coma-like condition that may last for many hours.

- The **Panther Amanita** group (referred to as *A. 'pantherina'*; the true *A. pantherina* does not appear in North America) are known as springtime species, although they may also fruit in summer and fall. Cap colors range from dull yellowish to tan to **dark brown**; paler versions resemble Gemmed Amanita (pg. 63) but Panthers are often much larger, with caps up to **7 to 8 inches** wide. The whitish wart-like patches may be quite numerous, but they wash off or disintegrate with age. Caps are slimy when wet, and edges are usually finely ribbed. Stems are whitish to buff-colored and typically scaly; they may be up to 7½ inches tall but are often shorter. A white, skirt-like ring is present at the top of the stem, or sometimes towards the middle; it may become ragged with age. The stem base is bulbous; the cup-like volva at the base may flare outward at the top to form a rim. It is a **toxic** species that causes symptoms similar to those caused by Fly Agaric.

Panther Amanita

SPORE PRINT: White.

SEASON: Spring through fall; varies by species.

OTHER NAMES: Most Amanitas are called by more than one common name; refer to the scientific names when researching or discussing them.

COMPARE: Small **Puffballs** (pgs. 230, 232) resemble the egg stage of the Amanita; for this reason, all small puffballs collected for the table should be cut in half and inspected as described on pg. 49 to ensure that the specimen is not an Amanita egg. • **Common Volvariella** (*Volvopluteus gloiocephalus*; also listed as *Volvariella speciosa*) have a cup at the stem base, but stems have **no rings** and their spore print is **pinkish-tan to pinkish-brown**. Caps are dull white to grayish-brown or tan; they often appear silky or metallic. • **Shaggy Parasols** (pg. 86; edible) have **large, shaggy scales** on the caps; they have a ring on the stem but **no volva**. • **Smooth Parasol** (pg. 151) is whitish overall; young specimens have a **boxy or lumpy** cap. The thin ring on the stem is persistent and **movable**. Smooth Parasol is edible, but difficult to separate from toxic Amanitas without microscopic analysis; consumption is not advised.

Common Volvariella

NOTES: Sadly, it is not uncommon to hear of a family who has come to America from another country and picked mushrooms that resemble edible species of their homeland—only to discover, too late, that toxic *Amanita* species resemble familiar favorites from home. Beginners should always get assistance from knowledgeable foragers before eating any mushrooms they have gathered.

Satan's Bolete

Toxic Boletes (numerous)

Rubroboletus spp., *Boletus 'luridiformis'*

Like the edible King Bolete (pgs. 31–33), the mushrooms discussed here look like a typical cap-with-stem shape but reveal a **spongy pore surface** when turned over. These pores are the ends of tubes where the spores are produced. Some of the most brightly colored Boletes are **toxic** and cause severe gastrointestinal distress—particularly if eaten raw. The easiest way to identify some of the most toxic varieties is by the color of the pore surface and by the tendency of the flesh to **stain or bruise blue or bluish-green**. The Boletes described here are rare in our area.

HABITAT: Boletes grow **from the soil** and humus, singly or in loose groups, in mixed woods. Most have a symbiotic relationship with trees.

DESCRIPTION: The Boletes discussed here have reddish or orangish-red pore surfaces and are sometimes known, in general, as Red-Mouthed Boletes. Another common characteristic of this group is that some or all parts **stain blue** when cut or bruised. Satan's Bolete and Red-Pored Bolete are known to be **very toxic**; the others described here are generally listed as inedible and possibly toxic, although some people report no adverse reactions from eating well-cooked specimens.

green = key identification feature

- **Satan's Bolete** (*R. eastwoodiae*) has an **extremely bulbous, cushion-like** stem that is often as wide as the cap—sometimes wider. The top of the stem narrows down to a neck-like shape, which may be unnoticeable when viewed from above. The **umbrella-like** caps are up to 11 inches wide and fairly thick. They are pale gray to buff-colored when young, turning **pale to medium pink** with maturity; the surface may develop fine cracks, and old specimens fade to olive-gray. Pores are **very fine** and dark red on young specimens; the pore surface becomes paler as the pores expand, and may appear pinkish, orangish or yellowish, especially at cap edges. Stems are up to 5½ inches tall and **pale to rosy pink**, fading somewhat with age; the neck becomes orangish with age. Reddish reticulation (mesh-like texture) is present towards the top of the stem, sometimes further down. The flesh turns blue when exposed to the air; pores bruise blue or bluish-black. Satan's Bolete fruits under oaks, primarily in late fall.
- Caps of **Red-Pored Bolete** (*R. pulcherrimus*) are up to 8 inches wide and fairly flat when mature, sometimes with an irregular outline; they may be smooth or finely velvety. Caps of young specimens are deep rosy pink to reddish-brown with a pinkish edge, becoming grayish to olive-brown with age. The pores are **angular or irregularly shaped**; they are dark red on young specimens, turning orangish-red to reddish-brown with age. Stems are up to 6 inches tall and nearly as wide at the base, tapering to about half width near the cap. They are reddish to orangish-red, with **darker reddish reticulation** in the top two-thirds, sometimes overall. Cut flesh turns blue, then fades to bluish-yellow; pores quickly turn blue when bruised. Red-Pored Bolete is found in coniferous and mixed-wood forests; it fruits from summer to fall.

Satan's Bolete

Red-Pored Bolete

R. haematinus

Slender Red-Pored Bolete

- *R. haematinus* doesn't look much like a Red-Mouthed Bolete at first; the pore surface of young specimens is **yellow**. It soon changes to pale red, then turns dark red before becoming reddish-brown with age; the **pores near the cap edge remain yellow** throughout. Caps are light brown to yellowish-brown with reddish tints, particularly near the edge; mature specimens may be nearly 8 inches wide. Stems are typically 3 to 4 inches tall and half as wide; they are usually wider at the base but not bulbous. They are **yellowish**, and the top two-thirds is covered with pale reddish reticulation that may break up over time. The flesh and pores turn bluish when bruised or cut. *R. haematinus* is associated with true firs (*Abies* spp.) at **subalpine elevations** in the fall.
- Caps of young Slender Red-Pored Bolete (*Boletus 'luridiformis'*) are **dark brown** and often **velvety**; they become reddish-brown to olive-brown and are up to 4½ inches wide at maturity. The pore surface is orangish-red to brick-red. The robust stems are up to 4 inches tall, yellow, and covered with **reddish granules**; there is **no reticulation**. The flesh and pores turn bluish when bruised or cut. Slender Red-Pored Bolete is found in coniferous and mixed-wood forests, particularly on the coast; it fruits from late summer to fall.

SPORE PRINT: Brown to olive-brown.

SEASON: Summer through late fall.

OTHER NAMES: All species discussed above were previously placed in the *Boletus* genus (and some were in other genera before that). In 2014, many of the red-pored Boletes were moved to a newly created genus, *Rubroboletus*, whose members have red to orangish-red pore surfaces and reddish caps, and discolor blue when bruised or cut (in addition to various microscopic characteristics). Satan's Bolete—also known as Alice Eastwood's Bolete—was formerly listed as *Boletus satanas*, and *Suillellus eastwoodiae* prior to that; its current, accepted scientific name is *R. eastwoodiae*. However, the *eastwoodiae* species designation had been used in the past to refer to the Red-Pored Bolete, under the name

B. eastwoodiae; after microscopic study it was renamed *B. pulcherrimus* in 1976, and that name was later changed to *R. pulcherrimus*. The Slender Red-Pored Bolete was formerly listed as *B. erythropus*; it is also called Dotted Stem Bolete, and may be listed as *Neoboletus luridiformis* in some sources.

COMPARE: Young **Peppery Bolete** (pg. 192) have yellowish-brown to reddish-brown caps that fade with age; they are typically 2 to 3 inches wide and sticky when moist. Pores are angular and **cinnamon-brown**, darkening to reddish-brown. Stems are up to 3¾ inches tall and colored like the caps. Unlike the Red-Mouthed Boletes, **no part of Peppery Bolete turns blue** (although a very similar species, *Chalciporus piperatoides*, does turn blue); pores bruise brownish. It is generally regarded as inedible. • **Gastroid Bolete** (*Gastroboletus turbinatus* group) and other *Gastroboletus* species are related to other Boletes, but have **very short stems**, sometimes appearing to be almost stemless; they are often **partially buried** in the humus under conifers. They typically appear **distorted or underdeveloped**, often looking like a cut-off cap lying on the ground, or perhaps a flattened, distorted puffball. Caps are 2 to 3 inches wide and often **irregular** in shape; the surface is reddish-brown to yellowish-brown. Pores are orangish-red to yellowish. Pores and flesh **quickly turn blue** when cut. It is generally regarded as inedible.

Gastroid Bolete (2 photos)

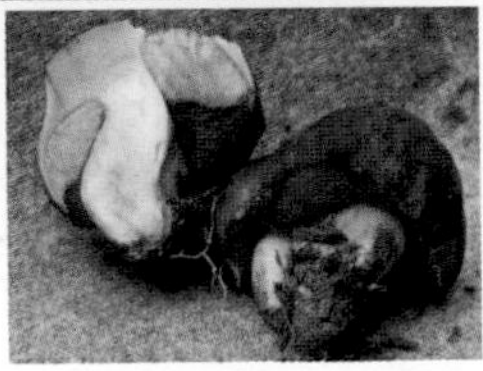

NOTES: Adding to the uncertainty when attempting to identify toxic Boletes, there is a good deal of variety among individual specimens depending on geography, age, and growing conditions. Though the names and descriptions discussed here get confusing, **the key point is simple**: *Boletes with red, orange or yellow pore surfaces that bruise blue should not be eaten*. That may cause you to skip a potentially edible variety, but you will also avoid getting sick. Red-Pored Boletes have been implicated in one death; the other Boletes discussed here are not known to be lethal but the gastrointestinal distress they cause can be quite severe, and affects some people more than others.

Brown Roll-Rim

Paxillus involutus

Although city dwellers may have seen this mushroom in urban parks, they probably didn't stop to investigate; other than its size and its habit of growing in large, scattered groups, it is plain-looking and unlikely to attract much attention.

HABITAT: Brown Roll-Rim is mycorrhizal, growing in association with both hardwoods and conifers; it favors birch, particularly those that have been planted in parks and landscaped areas. It may also be found in wooded areas and near bogs, but is less common in these natural habitats.

DESCRIPTION: This mushroom gets its common name from its **rolled-under cap edges**, which are particularly evident on young specimens. Caps are 2 to 6 inches wide, and are yellowish-brown, dull olive-brown or pale reddish-brown. Young specimens are finely hairy; older specimens have

green = key identification feature

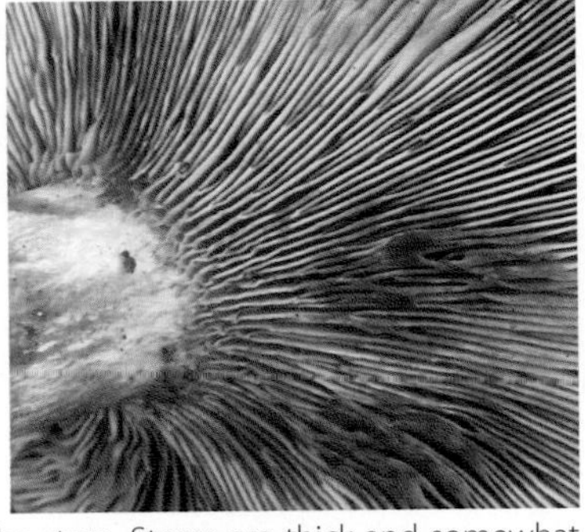

a smooth cap surface that may be sticky when moist. Brownish spots and other irregular markings are often present, and the caps may have subtle concentric rings. Gills are cream-colored when young, turning brownish with age or handling; they are **closely spaced to crowded** and run down the stem. Near the stem the gills are often forked or irregular, sometimes forming small, angular pockets. The gills can be **separated from the cap** in small sheets by teasing the edge next to the stem. Stems are thick and somewhat stubby, typically **shorter than the width of the cap** on mature specimens; they are colored like the cap or somewhat darker. There is no ring. All parts **bruise brown** when handled.

SPORE PRINT: Yellowish-brown to rust-brown.

SEASON: Summer through late fall.

OTHER NAMES: Poison Pax, Birch Pax.

COMPARE: Spring Paxillus (*P. vernalis*) appears very similar, but it is larger, with caps up to **7¼ inches** wide. Caps and stems are **paler**; stems are proportionally **thinner**. Its spore print is usually a **darker brown**. Microscopic examination is sometimes used to positively separate Spring Paxillus from Brown Roll Rim. • The Sweater (pg. 153; **toxic**) also has rolled-under cap edges and may sometimes appear to be a small specimen of Brown Roll-Rim, but it is typically **paler**, ranging from dingy white to grayish-white to buff-colored. Caps are less than 2 inches across and are often mottled with watery-looking spots. Stems are often flattened, and may be curved or twisted. Its spore print is **white**.

NOTES: Brown Roll-Rim was formerly considered edible, but it is now known that long-term consumption can cause Immune Hemolytic Anemia, an autoimmune disease that is life-threatening.

Deadly Parasol

Lepiota subincarnata

This pretty little mushroom is common in our area. Unfortunately it is **deadly**; it is responsible for one known fatality (in British Columbia) and has caused other poisonings, at least one of which required a liver transplant.

HABITAT: Deadly Parasol are saprobes that are fairly common in urban landscaped areas, where they fruit in lawns, on wood chips and in areas with disturbed ground. They also are found in deciduous and coniferous woods, where they act as decomposers of forest duff.

DESCRIPTION: Young specimens have rounded to bun-shaped caps that are pale pinkish-tan, with a felt-like texture. The caps expand and flatten out, often developing a central hump (called an umbo); at maturity they are typically less than 1½ inches wide and fairly flat to somewhat wavy or irregular. The center of the cap is covered with **pale reddish-brown to pinkish-brown fibrous scales**, which break up to form **concentric, broken rings** around the edge of the cap; the background between the scales is cream-colored to pale pinkish. The broad, closely spaced gills are white to pale cream on young specimens and barely free from the stem;

green = key identification feature

with age, the distance between the stem and the gills increases, and the gills become somewhat darker. Gills stain pinkish when damaged. A silky veil covers the gills of young specimens; it breaks up to form a fibrous ring that quickly vanishes, leaving an **indistinct ring zone** on the stem, at or above the midpoint. Stems are up to 2 inches tall and of medium thickness. Above the ring zone, the stem is white and silky; it is cream-colored below, with brownish to pinkish-brown scales arranged in broken bands. • Some sources list ***L. josserandii*** as a distinct species that is less pinkish overall, with a slightly larger cap; it is noted that if this is a separate species, it is difficult to separate from *L. subincarnata*. Other sources list *L. josserandii* as a synonym for *L. subincarnata*.

SPORE PRINT: White.

SEASON: Summer through fall.

OTHER NAMES: Fatal Dapperling, *L. helveola*.

COMPARE: Brown-Eyed Parasol (pg. 92) is **larger** overall, up to 2 inches wide and 3 inches tall; the scales on the cap are **darker reddish-brown**. Edibility of the Brown-Eyed Parasol is unknown; it is not eaten, due to its similarities to the Deadly Parasol.

NOTES: Deadly Parasol contains amatoxins, the same deadly poisons found in some Amanitas; for more information on this toxin, see pg. 61.

FROM THE SOIL NEAR LIVE TREES

LATE SUMMER THROUGH LATE FALL

Poison Pie

Hebeloma crustuliniforme group

The cap of this toxic mushroom resembles the well-browned crust of a pie; perhaps that's how it got its tasty-sounding name.

HABITAT: Poison Pie is mycorrhizal, associating with both conifers and hardwoods. It fruits in woods and in grassy areas near trees, appearing singly, scattered and in arcs or fairy rings.

DESCRIPTION: *H. crustuliniforme* is a European species that might not be the same species as the ones found in North America. The name is used to encompass a closely related group of *Hebeloma* species with very similar visual characteristics; this species complex is not well understood at this time. Caps of the most widely encountered form are typically 2 to 3 inches across and **cream-colored to pale tan**, usually with a darker center and paler edge. Gills are crowded and are barely attached to the stem, or may be notched. They are cream-colored when young, and are noted for developing **tiny droplets of moisture** on the edges in wet weather; the droplets dry out, leaving **brown spots** on the edges.

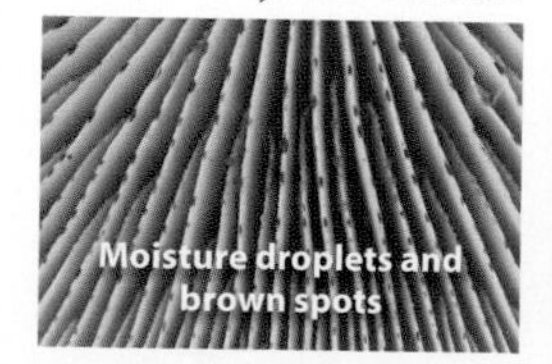

Moisture droplets and brown spots

green = key identification feature

Stems are 3 to 5 inches tall and moderately wide; the base may be somewhat enlarged or club-shaped. Young specimens have whitish stems that become tan with age; the top parts of the stem are granular or minutely scaly, while the lower parts are fibrous. There is no veil or ring. Poison Pie smells like **radishes**.

SPORE PRINT: Dull rust-brown.

SEASON: Late summer through late fall.

OTHER NAMES: Fairy Cake Mushroom.

COMPARE: *H. incarnatulum* is very similar in appearance to Poison Pie, but its stems have **bulbous** bases. Its gills **do not develop** the moisture droplets or brown spots. It is often found in mossy areas. Other differences are microscopic. • Veiled Hebeloma (*H. mesophaeum* group) is about half the size of Poison Pie. Caps have **dark reddish-brown to wine-brown** centers. A **cobwebby white veil** covers the gills of young specimens, leaving remnants on the cap margin and a **ring zone** on the stem. The radish-like odor may be faint. Found near conifers. • Scaly-Stalked Hebeloma (*H. sinapizans* group) is similar in size to Poison Pie. Its gills develop similar moisture droplets and brownish spots, but its caps have more **brownish hues** overall. Stems are covered with **scales or fibers** that may be brownish; stems discolor to brownish when handled. There is no veil or ring. Scaly-Stalked Hebeloma is uncommon in our area. • Brownish Cortinarius (pg. 130) are somewhat similar, but all have a **cobwebby veil** that leaves a **ring remnant** on the stems; gills do not develop moisture droplets.

NOTES: Poison Pie and the other Hebeloma species here are **toxic**, causing severe gastrointestinal problems including vomiting and diarrhea.

Veiled Hebeloma

Scaly-Stalked Hebeloma

Tiny Fragile Mushrooms (numerous)

Various species

HABITAT: Tiny fragile mushrooms of various types grow in an array of habitats, including woodlands and fields, on dead wood and on debris. They typically grow in scattered groups but may be found singly or in clusters.

DESCRIPTION: Tiny mushrooms are very common but are so small that they are often overlooked unless they are brightly colored and/or growing in a large cluster. The mushrooms included here have **long, thin stems**. Caps are **fragile** and rounded or conical; they are generally less than 1 inch wide at maturity, and many are less than ½ inch wide. Microscopic examination is required to identify many species; indeed, a hand lens is needed to properly examine them in the field. • ***Marasmioid*** species, comprised of species from multiple genera including *Marasmius, Marasmiellus, Mycetinis, Micromphale, Gymnopus* and others have **tough** stems that may be wiry. They are found during or after periods of **wet weather**, growing from decaying organic matter on the ground. *Marasmius* can withstand periods of dry weather, shriveling and going dormant for weeks. They are revived by rain, returning to fresh condition and resuming spore production; they are sometimes referred to as Resurrection Fungi. • Many ***Mycena*** species are also tiny and fragile, but their stems are **brittle** rather than tough or wiry. They may be brightly or subtly colored, or have brownish hues like those on pg. 162. • ***Hemimycena, Parasola, Atheniella, Roridomyces, Collybia*** and ***Strobilurus***, as well as some ***Coprinopsis*** and ***Conocybe***, also fall into the tiny, fragile category.

SPORE PRINT: If you want to try to place your tiny fragile mushrooms into a genus, the first step is making a spore print. Here are some generalizations to get you started. *Marasmioid* species, *Mycena, Atheniella, Hemimycena, Roridomyces, Collybia* and *Strobilurus* have white spores. *Conocybe* have brownish to rust-brown spores. *Coprinopsis* have dark brown to blackish spores. *Parasola* have blackish spores.

SEASON: Spring through fall, depending on species.

COMPARE: See also Little Brown Mushrooms (pg. 124), Orange to Red Waxy Caps (pg. 114) and Fuzzy Foot (pg. 120) for other small mushrooms; most of these have somewhat larger caps and shorter stems and are a bit less fragile.

NOTES: These tiny mushrooms are too small to eat, and it's unknown if they are edible.

Marasmius pallidocephalus

Mycena epipterygia

Conocybe spp.

Roridomyces roridus

Snowmelt Clitocybe

Clitocybe albirhiza

HABITAT: This saprobic mushroom is one of the species that is found at higher elevations in the period immediately following snowmelt. It grows scattered or in large clusters from the ground near spruce and other conifers, typically in the duff layer. It is fairly common.

DESCRIPTION: This small to medium-size mushroom stands 1¼ to 3¼ inches tall. Caps are up to **4 inches wide** and are warm beige or pinkish-beige, often with subtle **concentric rings**; young specimens have a whitish bloom, and the entire cap becomes darker when it is wet. The moderately thin stems are colored like the cap. Gills are closely spaced and **colored like the cap**, becoming slightly darker with age. They are attached to the stem and may run slightly down it. The most distinctive feature of this mushroom is the presence of a mass of **white rhizomorphs** (thick root-like strands) at the base of the stem.

SPORE PRINT: White.

SEASON: Early spring into early summer.

OTHER NAMES: None.

COMPARE: Several other mushrooms are common near conifers shortly after snowmelt. • ***C. glacialis*** (also known as *Lyophyllum montanum*) has a cap that is less than 2 inches wide and is **silvery gray** with a whitish bloom when young. Although *C. glacialis* lacks the rings of Snowmelt Clitocybe, the center of the cap is sometimes darker than the edges. A rounded knob (called an umbo) is often present at the center of the cap. Gills are closely spaced and attached to the stem; they are **putty-colored to grayish**. Instead of rhizomorphs, *C. glacialis* has a dense mat of **downy white mycelium** (root-like fungal filaments) at the base of the stem, which is up to 2¼ inches tall and colored like the cap. Mature *C. glacialis* lose the bloom on the cap and may turn **grayish-brown to yellowish-brown** overall, making the specimen appear completely different from younger ones. • ***Melanoleuca angelesiana*** is part of the *M. melaleuca* group, closely related species that are difficult to differentiate. It has a smooth, brownish cap up to 3½ inches wide. The stem is grayish to brownish and up to 2 inches tall; it is **streaked with fibers** which are white on young specimens, becoming darker with maturity. It somewhat resembles mature specimens of *C. glacialis*, but the white mycelium at the stem base is **sparse** rather than dense.

NOTES: The mushrooms discussed here are generally regarded as inedible.

Snowmelt Clitocybe
C. glacialis (young)
C. glacialis (mature)
Melanoleuca angelesiana

Subalpine Waxy Cap

Hygrophorus subalpinus

HABITAT: This is one of the "snowbank mushrooms," species that start fruiting as the snow begins to melt. Subalpine Waxy Cap likes cold weather. It first appears at low elevations in early spring, moving into higher elevations as the season progresses. It grows singly or in small groups from the ground near conifers, with which it has a mycorrhizal relationship. It is fairly common.

DESCRIPTION: This sturdy-looking mushroom is **bright white**, yellowing slightly with age. The cap is typically 2 to 5½ inches wide and slightly funnel-shaped at maturity; stems are 4 inches tall or shorter and typically one-half to one-third as wide. Gills feel **waxy** and are fairly closely spaced. They are attached to the stem and may run slightly down it. A **rounded bulb** may be present at the stem's base, but it is often buried. A veil remnant may be seen as a **thin ring** on the lower part of the stem; patchy veil remnants may cling to the cap edge.

SPORE PRINT: White.

SEASON: Early spring at lower elevations, continuing into fall at higher elevations.

OTHER NAMES: None.

COMPARE: The *Hygrophorus* genus includes several other snowbank mushrooms. • ***Hygrophorus vernalis*** has a **sticky, buff to pinkish-buff** cap less than 2 inches wide; its stem is up to 2¼ inches tall and **not stocky**. ***Hygrophorus goetzii*** is similar but its cap is **rosy-pink**, especially when young; gills are **pinkish** and more **widely spaced**. Both are found in the same habitat as Subalpine Waxy Cap but are far less common; they fruit from spring into summer. • Salmon Waxy Cap (*Cuphophyllus pratensis*, also listed as *Hygrocybe pratensis* and *Camarophyllus pratensis*) is **pale orangish** and up to 4 inches tall with a **dry** cap up to 3 inches wide. The cream-colored to orangish gills are fairly widely spaced and run down the pale stem. It fruits from **late fall into winter**. • Purple-Red Waxy Cap (*Hygrophorus purpurascens*) is similar in stature to Subalpine Waxy Cap, but its cap is **pinkish with reddish splotches or streaks**. A **faint, fibrous ring** may appear toward the **top of the stem**. It fruits from early spring into early summer, occasionally appearing into fall. • March Mushrooms (*Hygrophorus marzuolus*) appear from early spring into early summer. Caps of mature specimens are **dark gray** and up to 4 inches wide. Stems are stocky and up to 3½ inches tall; they are whitish to grayish. Gills are pale and **widely spaced**, and run down the stem slightly.

NOTES: The species listed here are edible but not considered choice.

Subalpine Waxy Cap
Hygrophorus vernalis
Salmon Waxy Cap
Purple-Red Waxy Cap
March Mushroom

Spring Agrocybe

Agrocybe praecox

HABITAT: Spring Agrocybe are saprobes, getting nutrients from **woody debris** and other decaying matter that may be underground. They appear in lawns and other grassy habitat, and are common in **mulched areas**, particularly those with wood chips. Often found in large groups, but may also be scattered.

DESCRIPTION: The caps of young specimens are up to 1¾ inches wide, with a white partial veil over the gills. As the cap expands, the veil is pulled apart, often leaving fragments that hang from the cap edge. Caps are cream to buff-colored when young, becoming yellowish-brown with age; the center is often slightly darker and may be raised. Fresh caps have a silky-smooth texture. Mature caps are up to **3½ inches** wide and often develop **shallow, pale cracks**, especially during dry weather. Gills are closely spaced and attached to the stem; they are **cream-colored** at first, turning pale brown, then darker brown as spores develop. Stems are colored like the cap or slightly lighter, becoming darker with age. They are up to **4 inches tall** and slightly grooved, particularly towards the top. There may be a **thin, pale, irregular ring** that becomes darkened by falling spores, but the ring may be incomplete or absent. **Whitish, slightly thick** mycelium (root-like fungal filaments) are often attached to the stem base.

SPORE PRINT: Dark brown.

SEASON: Spring through summer, sometimes into early fall.

OTHER NAMES: Spring Fieldcap, Spring Agaric, *Pholiota praecox*.

COMPARE: Several similar *Agrocybe* require a microscope for positive identification. ***A. molesta*** (also called *A. dura*) is one of these; it grows exclusively in grass. • Common Agrocybe (*A. pediades)* is colored similarly to Spring Agrocybe, but is **smaller**. Caps are no more than 2¼ inches wide, typically smaller; stems are up to 2½ inches tall and **quite thin** at maturity. No ring is present; the mycelium at the stem base is **fine** rather than thick. It fruits in grassy and disturbed areas. *A. semiorbicularis* is used as a synonym for *A. pediades*, although there may be microscopic differences between the two. • Mulch Mushroom (*A. putaminum*) is similar in size to Spring Agrocybe, but its caps are coated with a **fine, whitish dusting**; its stems are more **stocky** with a **bulbous base** and the mycelium is **fine** rather than thick. There is no ring. Gills are **grayish-brown**, becoming darker as the spores are released. It fruits in areas mulched with wood chips.

NOTES: The species discussed here are not collected for the table.

Spring Agrocybe

Common Agrocybe
Mulch Mushroom

Meadow Mushroom

Agaricus campestris

HABITAT: Growing singly, in groups or rings in **grassy areas such as meadows, fields and lawns.** They are saprobes, feeding on decaying organic matter.

DESCRIPTION: This common mushroom looks like its relative, the grocery-store Button Mushroom (*A. bisporus*). When young, the Meadow Mushroom has a **veil over the gills** and a smooth, rounded cap that is whitish to pale gray and may feel silky. With age, the cap expands and pulls the veil apart, leaving a **thin ring** on the stem; the cap is up to 4½ inches wide when fully opened, and the ring may disappear with age. Gills are closely spaced and **pink** at first, maturing to brownish-black; they are not attached to the stem. The stem is generally 1 to 2½ inches tall and moderately thick; it may taper slightly at the base.

SPORE PRINT: **Blackish-brown or dark purplish-brown**.

SEASON: Spring through fall, especially during cool, rainy periods.

OTHER NAMES: Field Mushroom, Pink Bottom, Champignon.

COMPARE: Wood Mushroom (*A. silvicola*) and Horse Mushroom (includes *A. arvensis* and *A. fissuratus*) have caps that **turn yellowish when rubbed**. Gills of young specimens are **whitish to pale gray**. Both have a **large, skirt-like ring** and a **sweet, anise or almond odor**; stems are typically 4 or 5 inches tall and have bulbous bases. Wood Mushroom is found in **forested areas**; its caps are up to 4½ inches wide. Horse Mushroom is found in grassy areas; its caps are up to **8 inches wide** and the veil (and, later, the underside of the ring) has patches that create a **cog-wheeled** appearance. • Spring Agaricus (*A. bitorquis*; also listed as *A. rodmanii* and sometimes called Pavement Mushroom) is firm-textured and **stubby**. Its **prominent, band-like ring** is flared or free at the top and may also be free at the bottom, appearing **double-edged**. It grows singly or in clusters in **hard-packed soil**, often near sidewalks and roads. It can fruit largely underground, and the cap is often seen **poking partially above the soil**. It may start fruiting in **early spring**, and can be found into fall.

NOTES: Spring Agaricus is a choice edible; Meadow Mushrooms are also collected for the table. Wood Mushrooms and Horse Mushrooms are edible, but may cause intestinal problems. Be cautious when collecting *Agaricus* species for the table; **toxic** Amanitas (pgs. 60–65) look similar but have **white spores**. Also watch out for Yellow-Foot Agaricus (*A. xanthodermus*), a mildly toxic look-alike whose **stem base turns bright yellow when cut or scratched**.

Meadow Mushroom

Wood Mushroom
Horse Mushroom
Spring Agaricus

Shaggy Parasols (several)

Chlorophyllum spp.

HABITAT: Three saprobic mushrooms which can be called Shaggy Parasols are found in our region; their habitat preferences are slightly different and can provide a clue to their identity. The most common is *C. brunneum*, which is typically found on compost heaps and in gardens. *C. olivieri* fruits in forested areas, favoring conifers; it may also appear in gardens and parklands. The least common, *C. rachodes*, is found in gardens, parks and along forest edges.

DESCRIPTION: Shaggy Parasols get their common name from **large, shaggy scales** on the caps. They are fairly large mushrooms. Opened caps are 4 to 5 inches wide or even larger; centers are smooth and darker in color. Gills are closely spaced and not attached to the stem; they are whitish on young specimens, becoming darker with age. Stems are smooth and whitish to cream-colored, turning darker with handling or age; they are up to 7 inches tall and somewhat slender. Stems have **prominent rings**, and the bases are covered with fuzzy white mycelium (root-like fungal filaments). The flesh **turns orangish, pinkish or reddish** when cut. • ***C. brunneum*** has **reddish-brown** scales on a pale, fibrous background. The cap underside may appear **bluish-green** in the area around the stem where the gills end. The stem has a **bulbous base with a flattened shoulder**. • ***C. olivieri*** also has a bulbous, shouldered base, but its dominant coloring is **olive-gray to tan**. Scales are fibrous and tend to curl up at the tip. There is **much less color contrast** between the scales and cap background than on *C. brunneum* or *C. rachodes*. • The stem base of ***C. rachodes*** is **club-shaped, widening gradually** with no abrupt shoulders. Scales on the cap resemble those of *C. brunneum*, although they may be slightly lighter in color. Other differences between *C. rachodes* and *C. brunneum* are microscopic.

SPORE PRINT: Whitish; spores of *C. olivieri* may appear yellowish.

SEASON: *C. brunneum* is found from **spring** through fall; *C. olivieri* and *C. rachodes* generally fruit later and are found from summer through fall.

OTHER NAMES: *C. brunneum* was formerly known as *Macrolepiota rachodes*.

COMPARE: The *Lepiota* species on pg. 92 have pale, scaly caps with dark centers, but Lepiota are **smaller and more delicate** than the *Chlorophyllum* species.

NOTES: Shaggy Parasols are edible and considered choice by some, but may cause stomach upset in others. Ensure that the spore print is white, to avoid the **toxic** *C. molybdites*, which has **green** spores and is very rare in our area.

C. brunneum

C. olivieri

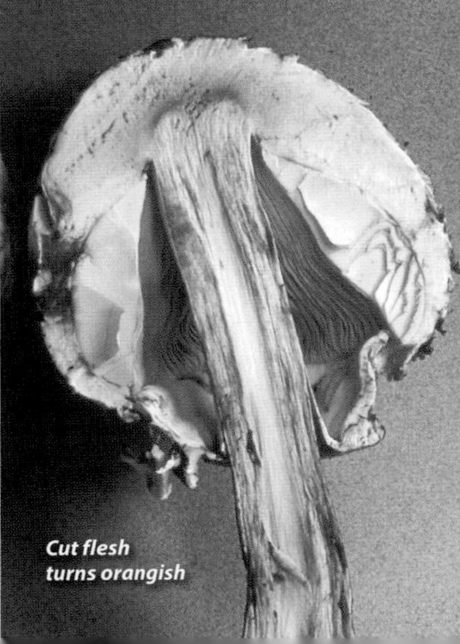
Cut flesh
turns orangish

FROM THE SOIL NEAR TREES

LATE SPRING THROUGH FALL

Funnel Caps (several)

Clitocybe spp., *Ampulloclitocybe clavipes*

HABITAT: Funnel Caps are saprobes that grow from the ground near trees in areas with moss, conifer needles or leaf litter, depending on the species. They fruit singly, scattered or in groups, and sometimes in rings or large arcs.

DESCRIPTION: As the name suggests, these mushrooms have **funnel-shaped caps** when mature. Caps are typically 2 to 3½ inches wide but may be smaller; edges are wavy or irregular and paler than the center. Gills run down the stem and are white, cream-colored or pale buff; spacing is close to moderately wide except as noted. Stems have no ring; copious fine white mycelium (root-like fungal filaments) is present at the base. • Caps of Small Scaly Clitocybe (*C. squamulosa* var. *montana*) are medium brown to cinnamon-brown; they are finely scaly in the center, becoming finely fibrous toward the edge. Stems are colored like the cap and under 2 inches tall; they may be attached to the cap slightly off-center. Bases may be slightly club-shaped. Found under conifers, less frequently in mixed woods. • Caps of Funnel Clitocybe (*C. gibba*) are **pale** pinkish-tan to reddish-tan. Gill spacing is close to **crowded**. Stems are up to 3 inches tall and somewhat **slender**; they are whitish to buff and may have a slightly swollen base. Found primarily under deciduous trees, especially oak; also in mixed-wood forests. • Caps of Club-Footed Clitocybe (*Ampulloclitocybe clavipes*) are dull brownish to grayish-brown. The stem is **stocky** and up to 2¼ inches tall; it is dirty whitish to buffy or pale brown, and may be attached to the cap slightly off-center. The base is usually **club-shaped** and may be up to 1¼ inches wide. Found primarily under conifers; also in mixed-wood forests.

SPORE PRINT: White.

SEASON: Small Scaly Clitocybe fruits from late spring through late summer, sometimes into fall. Funnel Clitocybe is found from summer through fall. Club-Footed Clitocybe fruits from late summer into late fall.

OTHER NAMES: *C. squamulosa* is also listed as *C. sinopicoides*. Also note that many members of the *Clitocybe* genus have been moved into the *Infundibulicybe* genus, and the situation is still in flux. Genetic studies are ongoing, but there is much work to be done and many species have not been properly identified.

COMPARE: The Sweater (pg. 153) is a **small** mushroom that fruits in **grassy areas**, such as pastures and open woods; it is dingy white, pale gray or buff overall.

NOTES: All Funnel Caps should be regarded as inedible; some are **toxic**.

Small Scaly Clitocybe

Funnel Clitocybe

Club-footed Clitocybe

FROM THE SOIL

EARLY SUMMER THROUGH FALL

Crowded White Clitocybe

Clitocybe dilatata

HABITAT: This saprobic mushroom often fruits in **large, dense clusters** along roads, trails and paths, primarily in disturbed areas with **sandy or gravelly soil**.

DESCRIPTION: The misshapen, often lumpy-looking caps with lobed or wavy edges may be nearly 6 inches wide, although they are usually smaller. They are light gray when young, soon turning **chalky white**, often with pale buffy or gray blotches. Gills are closely spaced and attached to the stem, often running slightly down it; they are white, buff or pale pinkish-buff. Stems are white and up to 4¾ inches tall, with a fibrous texture; they may be slightly curved and are often attached to the caps **slighty off-center**. The stem has no ring. Crowded White Clitocybe has a mild odor, or no odor; it is often listed as **toxic**.

SPORE PRINT: **White**.

SEASON: Early summer through fall.

OTHER NAMES: Also listed as *Lyophyllum connatum* and *Clitocybe connata*.

COMPARE: Several mushrooms have wavy-edged caps that may be off-center on the stem. • Caps of Cloudy Clitocybe (*Clitocybe nebularis*) may be **9 inches wide**; stems may be nearly 6 inches tall. Caps are grayish to pale grayish-brown with a **fine whitish bloom** and darker centers. It has a **disagreeable odor** that may be skunk-like or rancid. The spore print is **pale yellowish**. It is not usually collected for the table. • Caps of Sweetbread Mushroom (*Clitopilus prunulus*) are 2 to 4 inches wide; stems are up to 3¼ inches tall. Gills turn **pale pink** with age; the spore print is **pinkish-buff to salmon-colored**. Also called The Miller because it smells like **grain or bread dough**. It fruits in **open woods and grassy areas**. Edible but not advised for amateurs due to similarities with toxic species. • Fried Chicken Mushroom (*L. decastes*) fruits in large clusters in disturbed areas, but caps are **grayish-brown to yellowish-brown** with **silky streaks** and a **soapy texture**; they are less than 5 inches wide. It has a mild odor and is edible, but may cause digestive upset. • The **toxic** Sweater (pg. 153) is **much smaller** than the others here, standing 1½ inches tall or less; caps are less than 2 inches wide and are dingy-looking, often mottled with wet-looking splotches. It fruits in **rings or small groups** in **grassy areas**.

NOTES: This group of similar-looking mushrooms offers a cautionary lesson in the importance of good identification practices when foraging for the table.

Crowded White Clitocybe

Cloudy Clitocybe

Sweetbread Mushroom

Fried Chicken Mushroom

FROM THE SOIL AND GROUND DEBRIS

SUMMER THROUGH FALL

Brown-Eyed Parasol

Lepiota cristata

HABITAT: This saprobe is locally common in urban areas, fruiting along paths, in parks and areas mulched with wood chips, on rotten logs and in grassy areas; it also grows occasionally in forested areas. It may appear singly or in groups, sometimes clustering together so closely that the caps become deformed.

DESCRIPTION: Although small, this mushroom stands out due to its white cap decorated with a rounded, **reddish-brown center ringed by small scales** of the same color. The cap is rounded or softly conical when young, opening up to become slightly rounded or nearly flat; it is typically **1 to 2 inches wide** at maturity. Edges are sometimes wavy or split. The center may be slightly raised, providing a bell-shaped profile, or more abruptly raised, appearing nipple-like. Gills are not attached to the stem; they are white to cream-colored and closely spaced. A veil covers the gills of young specimens. As the cap expands, the veil breaks, forming a fragile ring on the stem or hanging in fragments from the edge of the cap. The slender stems range from **1¼ to just over 3 inches tall** and may be slightly curvy; they are whitish at the top, becoming tan to pinkish towards the base. Whitish mycelium (root-like fungal filaments) are present at the base. Most specimens have an unpleasant odor that has been compared to rubber or coal gas; some observers, however, report a mildly fruity fragrance.

SPORE PRINT: White.

SEASON: Summer through fall.

OTHER NAMES: Stinking Parasol.

COMPARE: The cap of ***L. magnispora*** also has a brown center, but the scales surrounding it are **much smaller** and the overall color is more buffy. The edge of the cap is **very raggedy**, and the stem is **shaggy**. *L. clypeolaria* is very similar to *L. magnispora*, but the eye on the cap is paler and the stem is less shaggy. • The center and surrounding scales on ***L. felina*** are **brownish-black**. The **edge of the stem ring has dark spots**, as does the **base of the stem**. • Caps of ***L. aspera*** (also listed as *L. acutesquamosa* and *Echinoderma asperum*) are up to **3 inches** wide, and generously dotted with **pointed, pyramid-shaped** brown scales. The veil over the gills is **cobweb-like**, and forms a **large, skirt-like hanging ring** on the stem, which is fairly **stocky**. • Shaggy Parasols (pg. 86) have dark circles at the center of the cap, but are **much larger** overall.

NOTES: The species discussed here are considered inedible and possibly **toxic**.

Brown-Eyed Parasol

L. magnispora

L. felina

L. aspera

FROM THE SOIL NEAR TREES

LATE SUMMER THROUGH FALL

Pale Milk Caps (several)

Lactarius spp.

HABITAT: Lactarius are mycorrhizal, growing from the soil in association with trees.

DESCRIPTION: Milk Caps produce milky **latex** when cut. Gills of the species listed here are closely spaced, and attached to the stem or running slightly down it. Stems are fairly thick and are generally about as tall as the mature caps are wide. Lactarius have no rings. • Two of the species here have cap edges that are **bearded** (hairy); young caps of both are sticky when moist. Pitted Milk Cap (*L. scrobiculatus*) have caps up to **6 inches wide** that are cream-colored, pale yellowish or yellowish-orange; mature caps have fine scales. Gills are whitish to pale yellow, developing brownish stains. Latex is scant and white, **quickly turning yellow**. Stems are pale, with **darker pockmarks**. Found near **conifers**. Bearded Milk Cap (*L. pubescens* var. *betulae*) has cream-colored to pale pinkish-buff caps up to 3¼ inches wide. Caps are smooth at the center, becoming fibrous towards the edges. Gills are cream-colored to pale pinkish. Latex is scant and white, **changing slowly to yellow**. Stems are pale and have no pockmarks. Found near **birch trees**. • Caps of *L. pallescens* are 1½ to 4 inches wide; they are **smooth**, and sticky when moist. Young caps are whitish, turning pale gray, often with yellowish or faintly purplish areas. Gills are whitish, turning cream-colored and developing brownish or orangish stains. The white latex is **copious** and stains the gills **lilac-purple**. Stems are smooth and whitish, becoming dingier with age; they are sticky in damp weather. Found near conifers. • Coconut Milk Cap (*L. glyciosmus*) has a **coconut-like odor**. Caps are 1 to 2¾ inches wide, and pinkish-gray, pinkish-buff or beige; they are dry and feel velvety to slightly rough. Gills are pinkish-buff to pale beige, becoming lilac-gray with age. Latex is scant and **remains white**. Stems are colored like the cap or paler. Found near birch trees.

SPORE PRINT: Whitish to cream-colored, sometimes pale yellow.

SEASON: Late summer through fall.

OTHER NAMES: *L. torminosus* is also called Bearded Milk Cap, and is distinguished from *L. pubescens* primarily by microscopic examination.

COMPARE: Also see Orangish Milk Caps (pg. 116) and Dark Milk Caps (pg. 136).

NOTES: Coconut Milk Cap is generally regarded as edible. The other Lactarius discussed here are inedible, and are often listed as possibly **toxic**.

Pitted Milk Cap
Pitted Milk Cap
stem detail
Bearded Milk Cap
L. pallescens
Coconut Milk Cap

White Leucopax

Leucopaxillus albissimus

HABITAT: White Leucopax are saprobes that break down leaf litter and other ground debris. They grow scattered or in groups, frequently in rings. Found in forested areas under trees; they prefer conifers but also fruit in mixed woods. They are **resistant to decay**; specimens may persist for weeks or even months.

DESCRIPTION: Medium to large mushrooms, with caps that are typically 4 to 8 inches wide, sometimes larger. Caps of young specimens are rounded and **whitish to cream-colored**, with a smooth, dry surface that may be velvety; edges are turned under. Older specimens are flattened and yellowish to tan; the surface may develop cracks with age or in dry weather. Cap edges are wavy and often **finely ribbed**. Gills are white to cream-colored, turning yellowish or buffy with age. They are closely spaced and run down the stem slightly; the gills can be **separated from the cap in sheet-like sections**. Stems are white and smooth when young, becoming beige and rougher with age; there is no ring. Medium-size specimens are 3 to 4 inches tall; larger specimens may be up to **11 inches** tall. Stems are often thicker in the lower half, tapering slightly at the bottom. The base is surrounded with a **dense mat of white mycelium** (root-like fungal filaments) that is tangled with pine needles and other duff.

SPORE PRINT: White.

SEASON: Fall.

OTHER NAMES: Also called Large White Leucopax.

COMPARE: Bitter Brown Leucopax (*L. gentianeus*; also listed as *L. amarus*) has many similar features, but its caps are **medium brown to reddish-brown**. It is slightly smaller; caps are generally 3 to 5 inches wide and stems are 2 to 4 inches tall. It fruits from late summer through fall, in the same type of habitat as White Leucopax. See additional photo on pg. 133. • Giant Clitocybe (*Aspropaxillus giganteus*; also listed as *L. giganteus* and *Clitocybe gigantea*) are often even larger than White Leucopax; caps are commonly **6 to 11 inches wide**, although size varies. Mature specimens have wide, **funnel-shaped** caps that are buff to tan; they are **brittle and break easily**. Stems are 4 inches tall or less, even on large specimens; bases **lack the white mycelium** found on the Leucopax species.

NOTES: The Leucopax discussed here are tough and inedible, with a strong odor and an unpleasant or bitter taste. Giant Clitocybe is also inedible.

White Leucopax
Bitter Brown Leucopax
Giant Clitocybe

FROM THE SOIL OR DOWNED WOOD

SPRING THROUGH FALL

Common Collybia

Gymnopus dryophilus

HABITAT: These saprobes are found in deciduous, coniferous or mixed-wood forests. They grow singly, scattered, in small groups or in clusters, usually from the soil but also from well-rotted wood or wood chips. Common in our area.

DESCRIPTION: Caps are smooth and up to 2¼ inches wide; they are **orangish-brown to brownish-yellow**, turning paler with age or in dry weather. Young caps are rounded, becoming flat or developing a wavy top. Edges may also be wavy. Caps have a **greasy** feeling and are **hygrophanous** (pg. 11), becoming darker when moist; they become paler when dry, starting at the edges. Gills are **white to pinkish-buff** and closely spaced; they are attached to the stem, but may be deeply notched just before meeting the stem. Stems are 1½ to 3 inches tall and whitish, tan or buff-colored near the cap, darker toward the base; they are smooth and brittle, and may grow in a curved fashion. **White mycelium** (root-like fungal filaments) is often visible at the base. Stems have no ring.

SPORE PRINT: **Whitish to pale yellow**.

SEASON: Spring through fall.

OTHER NAMES: Oak Collybia, *Collybia dryophila*.

COMPARE: Two *Gymnopus* species have similar caps that are a bit **smaller** than Common Collybia, and **long, thin** stems. Caps and stems are **reddish-brown** on young specimens, fading with age. Both grow in **clusters**. Clustered Collybia (*G. acervatus*; also listed as *C. acervata*) fruits **on wood chips or rotting wood**. Stems have **fine white hairs** at the bases or over the lower half. Tufted Collybia (*G. confluens*, also listed as *C. confluens*) fruits **from the ground**. Stems are covered with **downy hairs**. • All parts of *G. peronatus* are **yellowish to brownish-yellow**. Stems are **densely hairy** on the lower part; mycelium may be **yellowish** or white. • *G. fuscopurpureus* (also listed as *C. fuscopurpurea*) is **dark brown to reddish-brown overall**. Stem bases have **reddish-brown hairs**; mycelium is **not present**. • Buttery Collybia (*Rhodocollybia butyracea*; also listed as *C. butyracea*) are a bit **larger** than Common Collybia. Caps have a **greasy feeling** and are dark reddish-brown at first, turning tan to brownish-yellow; gills are white to pale pinkish with **jagged edges**. Stem bases are often **swollen to club-like**. Spores are **buff to pinkish-buff**.

NOTES: Buttery Collybia is edible. The *Gymnopus* above are generally tough and sometimes bitter; some are known to be **toxic**. None should be eaten.

Common Collybia
Clustered Collybia
G. peronatus
G. fuscopurpureus
Buttery
Collybia

Conifer Powdercap

Cystoderma fallax

HABITAT: These saprobes fruit singly, scattered or in small groups in areas with needle duff or moss, primarily under conifers; also found on rotting wood.

DESCRIPTION: This small mushroom is common in our area. Caps and stems of fresh specimens are covered with **mealy granules or small scales**; most wear off the cap, which may feel powdery on mature specimens. Caps are **pale cinnamon-brown to brownish-yellow** and less than 2 inches wide. Edges of mature caps may be wavy or puckered. Gills are white to pale pinkish-buff; they are closely spaced and attached to the stems or slightly notched. Stems are up to 2¾ inches tall and ¼ inch thick. A **substantial ring** that looks like the **top edge of a sheath** is present in the upper third of the stem; the ring is **whitish on the inside** and often flares upward. Above the ring, stems are smooth and pale; below the ring they are granular or scaly and colored like the cap or darker.

SPORE PRINT: White.

SEASON: Spring through late fall.

OTHER NAMES: Sheathed Powdercap, *Cystoderma carcharias* var. *fallax*.

COMPARE: Golden False Pholiota (*Phaeolepiota aurea*; also listed as *Pholiota aurea*) has granular caps and stems, but its spores are **yellowish-brown to orangish-buff**. Caps are up to **7 inches wide** and are orangish-tan to golden brown. Stems are up to **8 inches tall** and colored like the cap, with a large, flaring or skirt-like ring. • Three related mushrooms with granular caps and stems are roughly the same size as Conifer Powdercap, but their stem rings are **fragile or lacking**. Instead, numerous small veil remnants often hang off the cap edge, looking like fine white teeth. Caps of *Cystoderma amianthinum* are **light orangish to brownish-yellow**; the centers may be darker and often have a slight hump (umbo). Thin wrinkles may run from the center to the edges, but these are not always present. Caps of *Cystodermella cinnabarina* are **brick-red to reddish-brown** and may be up to 3 inches wide. Stems are a bit longer than the other two species listed here, and proportionally thicker. *Cystodermella granulosa* (also listed as *Cystoderma granulosum*) is very similar to *Cystoderma amianthinum*, but its caps are **reddish-brown, orangish-brown** to tawny and generally unwrinkled. Other differences between these three species are microscopic.

NOTES: The species listed here should be considered inedible.

Conifer Powdercap

Golden False Pholiota

Cystoderma amianthinum

Cystodermella cinnabarina

Cystodermella granulosa

Golden Pholiota (several)

Pholiota limonella/aurivella group

HABITAT: The Pholiota discussed on this spread are saprobes that feed on wood. They grow in groups or clusters on living, dying or dead trees and fallen logs, both coniferous and deciduous.

DESCRIPTION: Golden Pholiota refers to several *Pholiota* species that can't be positively separated from one another without a microscope. The two most commonly noted in our area are *P. aurivella* and *P. limonella*. The **yellow** to yellowish-orange caps are **very slimy** and sprinkled with **flattened, reddish-brown to purplish scales** that may eventually fall off. Young caps are conical to rounded, with a webby veil over the gills that leaves a thin, band-like remnant near the top of the stem. With age, caps becomes flattened, often with a raised hump (called an umbo) in the center; mature caps are up to 6 inches wide but usually much smaller. Gills are whitish to pale yellow, darkening to reddish-brown; they are attached to the stem and closely spaced. Stems are typically 2 to 5 inches tall; they are silky and whitish near the top, becoming scaly and often darker below the veil remnant.

SPORE PRINT: Rusty brown.

SEASON: Late spring through fall.

OTHER NAMES: *P. limonella* is sometimes called Lemon-Yellow Pholiota.

COMPARE: **All parts** of Yellow Pholiota (*P. flammans*) are **bright yellow to orangish-yellow** when young; caps darken as they mature. Stems and young caps have **tufted scales**. • Caps and stems of Scaly Pholiota (*P. squarrosa*) are **pale tan to buff**, and covered with **curved, dark** scales. The cap surface is **dry**, and young gills are **pale yellowish**, developing a **greenish tinge** as they age. Bristly Pholiota (*P. squarrosoides*) appears very similar to Scaly Pholiota; however, its cap surface is **slimy** between the scales and its gills are **whitish, never developing the greenish tinge**. • Poplar Pholiota (*Hemipholiota populnea*; also listed as *P. populnea* and *P. destruens*) has **yellowish-brown to tan** caps that may be up to **7½ inches wide** when mature; cottony whitish scales are often present, particularly on the edge of the cap, but may be absent. Stems may be nearly 6 inches tall; they are **whitish** and covered with small scales, and the base is often **enlarged**. Gills are whitish on young specimens.

NOTES: Scaly Pholiota is **toxic**. Most other *Pholiota* species are poor table fare; they are best admired for their beauty and unique form.

P. aurivella

Poplar Pholiota
Yellow Pholiota
Scaly Pholiota

Honey Mushrooms (several)

Armillaria spp.

HABITAT: Honey Mushrooms digest wood. Some are parasites that attack living trees, wreaking havoc in forested areas. Others are saprobes that decompose fallen logs or dead trees. Species listed here are both parasites and saprobes.

DESCRIPTION: The Honey Mushroom group includes numerous, closely related species. Three are fairly common in our area. All have a veil over the gills; cap edges are finely ribbed on mature specimens, and stems are fibrous. Gills are closely spaced and attached to the stem or running slightly down it; they are white to cream-colored when young. **Dark rhizomorphs** (thick root-like strands) may be seen at the stem base. • ***A. solidipes*** is the biggest, with caps up to 5 inches wide and 7-inch stems. Caps are yellowish-brown, pinkish-beige or reddish-brown; **numerous dark scales** are concentrated in the center, becoming sparser toward the edges. Gills turn pale orangish with age. The **stout** stems are whitish, becoming brown toward the bases, which may be thickened or club-like. Stems have many fluffy patches. A **thick, fluffy, whitish ring** with brown markings underneath is present near the top. Usually found in **dense clusters** on conifer wood, including hidden roots; it also attacks hardwoods. • ***A. sinapina*** is similar to *A. solidipes* but smaller. The ring may be yellow, and there are **small yellowish tufts** from the universal veil on the stem, particularly at the base. Fruits **singly or in small groups**, primarily on conifers. • Caps of ***A. nabsnona*** are up to 2¾ inches wide and orangish-brown; they may have fine dark hairs but **no scales**. Gills turn pinkish-tan with age. Stems are 3 to 4 inches tall and **narrow**; in age they are **blackish-brown** near the base, paler toward the caps. Fruits in groups on **hardwoods**, often in **swampy areas**.

SPORE PRINT: White.

SEASON: Summer through fall; *A. nabsnona* may occasionally fruit in **spring**.

OTHER NAMES: *A. solidipes* is also listed as *A. ostoyae*.

COMPARE: Several other cool-weather mushrooms that fruit on dead logs may be confused with Honey Mushrooms, but their gills are **yellowish**, becoming **brownish** or grayish; spores are **brownish**. These include Deadly Galerina (pgs. 58–59; **toxic**), Jumbo Gym (pg. 112) and Smoky-Gilled Woodlover (pg. 108). Please read the pages noted for more information.

NOTES: Honey Mushroom caps are generally regarded as edible; they may cause gastric upset. Stems are tough but can be used to make broth.

A. solidipes
A. solidipes,
scales on cap
A. nabsnona
A. sinapina

FROM THE SOIL NEAR LIVE TREES

LATE SUMMER THROUGH FALL

Man on Horseback

Tricholoma equestre

HABITAT: Mycorrhizal, growing from the ground near conifers. Common in our area.

DESCRIPTION: This sturdy, medium-size mushroom has yellowish caps up to 5 inches wide, with slightly darker centers; they become dull brownish-yellow with age . Caps are **sticky** when moist. Edges may be wavy, and the center may have a slight hump (umbo). Stems are whitish to pale yellow; they are 1¼ to 4 inches tall and often about one-third as wide. There is no ring on the stems. Gills are closely spaced and **medium yellow**; they are attached to the stem, sometimes appearing slightly notched. Its odor is **coconut-like** or grain-like.

SPORE PRINT: White.

SEASON: Late summer through fall.

OTHER NAMES: Yellow Knight, Canary Trich, *T. flavovirens.*

COMPARE: Several Tricholoma that appear similar to Man on Horseback are found in our area. None are reported with a coconut-like odor; most have a grain-like odor. All but *T. subsejunctum* are uncommon in our area. • ***T. intermedium*** has **white** gills. Its caps may be somewhat darker, and its stems are thinner. • Caps of ***T. davisiae*** are pale **yellowish-green to whitish**, usually with a **dry** surface; the umbo is **sharply pointed** and often much darker than the rest of the cap. Stems are moderately thin. Gills are pale **yellowish-green** on young specimens. • ***T. subsejunctum*** has a greenish-yellow cap that is **streaked with black to dark brownish fibers** radiating out from the center. Caps are tacky or slightly sticky when moist. Gills are whitish or cream-colored at first; they become yellow toward the cap edge or may turn completely yellow. Stems are up to 4¼ inches tall; they may have a bulbous base. Found under both conifers and hardwoods. It is listed by some sources as *T. sejunctum*, but that is a European species that grows strictly with hardwoods. • ***T. sulphureum*** (sometimes called Sulfur Knight) has caps that are usually less than 3 inches wide; stems are somewhat thin. Caps are **dry** and yellowish, or with reddish-brown centers. Gills are yellow and **somewhat widely spaced**. As its name suggests, this species has a **strong, unpleasant, chemical odor** that has been compared to coal tar. Found under both conifers and hardwoods.

NOTES: Man on Horseback is often considered a choice edible, but reports of poisonings traced to this species in Europe have created doubt. The other species listed here are considered inedible.

Man on Horseback

T. intermedium

T. davisiae

T. subsejunctum

T. sulphureum

Smoky-Gilled Woodlover

Hypholoma capnoides

HABITAT: These saprobes fruit in clusters on decaying conifers such as downed logs and stumps. They are common in our area and may be abundant.

DESCRIPTION: Caps of young specimens are softly conical to bell-shaped, becoming fairly flat as they age; mature caps are up to 2 inches wide. The surface is pale yellowish-orange to tan; the center may be darker and sometimes has a slight hump (called an umbo). In wet weather, the cap surface may be **sticky** or merely moist. Gills are closely spaced and attached to the stem; they are whitish at first, becoming **pale gray** and maturing to grayish-brown. A cobwebby veil covers the gills of young specimens; this soon breaks apart, often leaving patches on the cap edge. The stem has **no ring** but there may be a subtle fibrous ring zone toward the top. Stems are fairly slender and up to 4 inches long; they are pale at the top, becoming darker towards the base.

SPORE PRINT: Purplish-brown to grayish-brown.

SEASON: Late summer through late fall.

OTHER NAMES: Conifer Tuft. The *Hypholoma* species listed here were originally in the *Naematoloma* genus; older texts refer to them with that genus name.

COMPARE: Sulfur Tuft (*H. fasciculare*) is similar in stature, but more **brightly colored** overall. Gills of young specimens are **greenish-yellow**. It is common in our area, and fruits in large clusters on downed logs of conifers and **hardwoods**, as well as from **buried roots**. • ***H. dispersum*** is more **delicate**, with caps that are 1½ inches wide or less and **very thin** stems that are pale when young, becoming **dark reddish-brown** below the ring zone with age. Caps are **brownish-orange** with paler edges; they are **slippery** when moist. Stems have pale, silky hairs in an arrangement that is often described as a **snakeskin pattern**; it is evident on the dark, mature stems. Found near conifers. *H. marginatum* is often listed as a synonym; some sources list them as similar but separate species. • The ***Pholiota malicola*** group includes *P. malicola, P. alnicola,* and *P. flavida*. All are medium-size mushrooms. Caps are yellowish, tawny or rust-colored; gills of young specimens are **yellowish**. They grow in clusters on decaying wood and have **rust-brown** spores. Many have a **sweet odor** similar to green corn.

NOTES: Smoky-Gilled Woodlover has a **mild taste**, and is edible but not favored; if it is collected for the table, care must be taken to avoid Sulfur Tuft, which is **bitter** and **toxic**. The others listed here should be considered inedible.

Smoky-Gilled Woodlover
Sulfur Tuft
Smoky-Gilled Woodlover, sticky caps
H. dispersum
P. alnicola

Questionable Stropharia

Stropharia ambigua

HABITAT: This saprobe is common in our area, often fruiting in massive "troops" on wood chips in landscaped areas. Also found in natural areas, growing singly or scattered on decaying material under conifers and hardwoods, notably alder.

DESCRIPTION: These striking mushrooms range in size from 1¼ to nearly 6 inches wide, and 2 to 7 inches tall. Fresh caps are pale yellow, straw-colored, yellowish-orange or yellowish-brown, fading to pale tan. The surface is smooth and **slimy or glossy** when moist. Gills are close to crowded and attached to the stem or barely free from it. They are pale gray at first and covered with a **cottony white veil** that splits, leaving **shaggy remnants on the cap edge**; mature gills are purplish-brown. Stems are sturdy and whitish; there may be an irregular ring, but this disappears quickly. Below the ring zone the stem is covered with **dry, soft white scales** that give it a **shaggy** appearance. White rhizomorphs (thick root-like strands) are found in the substrate at the base of the stem.

SPORE PRINT: Purplish-brown to purplish-black.

SEASON: Most common in fall through early winter, but also found in winter and spring.

OTHER NAMES: Ambiguous Stropharia.

COMPARE: *Leratiomyces riparius* (also listed as *S. riparia*) has a buff-colored cap that is usually 1 to 2 inches wide. Its stem is generally **thin** and often **curved or bent**, and is less shaggy. Some sources say that *L. percevalii* is the same as *L. riparius*, or that differences are largely microscopic. • Caps of Conifer Roundhead (*S. hornemannii*) are **reddish-brown** when young, fading to brownish-buff; they are 1½ to 5½ inches wide. Stems are stocky and 2 to 4 inches tall, with **prominent skirt-like white rings**; stems are shaggy below the ring. • Wine Caps (*S. rugosoannulata*) have **wine-red** caps up to 6 inches wide that fade to buff; the stocky stems are white when fresh, turning buffy with age. The veil over the gills has an irregular edge that resembles a **gear or cogwheel**. The stem ring is **thick and persistent**, retaining the cogwheel-shaped edge. • Older, faded specimens of Blue-Green Stropharia (pg. 144) appear similar to Questionable Stropharia, but Blue-Green Stropharia is **much smaller**; caps are typically 1 to 2 inches wide and stems are 3 inches tall or less.

NOTES: Most sources list Questionable Stropharia as edible but not very good. Wine Caps are edible and choice; the others here are not collected for the table.

Questionable Stropharia

L. riparius

Conifer Roundhead

Wine Cap, fresh

Wine Cap, faded

Jumbo Gym (several)

Gymnopilus ventricosus, G. 'junonius'

HABITAT: Jumbo Gyms are saprobes that feed on the rotting wood of conifers and, less commonly, hardwoods. They usually grow in clusters that can be dense or loose, and are found at the bases of dead or dying trees, on stumps, and on buried wood; they may also fruit higher up on the trunks of dead trees.

DESCRIPTION: Several **very large** *Gymnopilus* species with **yellowish-brown to yellowish-orange** coloration are found in our area. It is not uncommon to find mature specimens with caps that are 7 to 10 inches wide—sometimes larger. Caps are rounded at first; they are dry and covered with very fine scales, although the center may be smooth. With age, the caps turn up, exposing the gills; mature caps are flattened and may be wavy. Gills are closely spaced and attached to the stem, often slightly notched; gills of young specimens are pale tan to yellowish, covered with a pale, webby veil. As the cap expands the veil breaks, leaving patches hanging off the cap edge. A **pale, upturned ring** remains on the stem; it is soon darkened by the spores, eventually deteriorating into a **dark ring zone**. In our area, ***G. ventricosus*** is the most common of these large Gyms. Stems are **sturdy and thick**, becoming **wider at or below the center**. Stems are yellowish to pale brown, often with darker streaks on the lower half. ***G. 'junonius'*** is less common in our area. It is slightly smaller, with a **proportionally thinner stem**; other differences are microscopic.

SPORE PRINT: Rusty orange.

SEASON: Spring through fall.

OTHER NAMES: *G. 'junonius'* is also listed as *G. spectabilis*.

COMPARE: ***G. sapineus*** is one of a group of **small** Gyms whose caps are **orangish to reddish-brown**, usually with paler edges and yellow gills; most differences are microscopic. Caps of *G. sapineus* are 1 to 2 inches wide, with **many fine scales**; stems are less than 3 inches tall. Its veil is yellowish. • ***G. punctifolius*** is **medium-size** and uncommon in our area. Caps are **mixed hues** of blue, yellowish, blue-green and tan. Gills are **olive-colored**; there is **no veil** or stem ring. • **Golden-Gilled Gym** (*G. luteofolius*) is also medium-size and uncommon in our area. Caps are covered with **purplish-red to maroon scales**, becoming mostly orangish with age. Gills are yellow, becoming bright rust-orange.

NOTES: The species above are inedible. *G. 'junonius'* is hallucinogenic, although some report that this effect is absent in specimens from the West coast.

G. ventricosus

G. 'junonius'

G. sapineus

Golden-Gilled Gym

G. punctifolius

Orange to Red Waxy Caps (several)

Hygrocybe and *Hygrophorus* spp.

HABITAT: Waxy Caps fruit from the soil and humus in wooded areas that are generally a bit damp; some are found in bogs. They appear singly or in groups.

DESCRIPTION: Numerous Waxy Caps with orangish to reddish attributes are found in our area; exact identification is often difficult. All are small to medium in size. Caps of young, fresh specimens are brightly colored, fading with age. Caps feel **waxy or slimy** when wet, although the degree of sliminess varies. Except where noted, gills are closely or fairly closely spaced, and attached to the stems or barely free. Species here have no stem rings. • Caps of young *Hygrocybe singeri* are **orange to reddish** and often **sharply conical**. Gills are whitish to yellowish. Stems are **dry to slightly sticky**. Stems are yellowish to orangish and **twisted at the base**. All parts **turn blackish** when handled. • Young *Hygrocybe miniata* have rounded **bright red** caps that flatten and fade to orange with age. Gills are yellow to orangish and **widely spaced**; they may **run slightly down the stems**, which are reddish to orangish. • Caps of *Hygrocybe coccinea* are **deep red** and broadly conical or rounded. Gills are pinkish to reddish and may be somewhat widely spaced. Stems are red to reddish-orange. • Young *Hygrocybe flavescens* have rounded, bright **yellow to yellowish-orange** caps. Gills are yellow. Stems are colored like the caps.

SPORE PRINT: White.

SEASON: Spring through late fall.

OTHER NAMES: *Hygrocybe* species are often listed in the *Hygrophorus* genus. *Hygrocybe singeri* has been referred to as *Hygrocybe conica*, a similar species that is found in eastern North America and Europe but not in our area.

COMPARE: Larch Waxy Cap (*Hygrophorus speciosus)* have caps that are bright orangish-red when young; they fade to orange or yellow, but the center may remain darker. Caps are rounded, sometimes with a gentle hump (umbo) in the center. Gills are white to pale yellow and **fairly widely spaced**. Stems are white to pale yellowish and often have a club-like base; they are **sheathed in gluten**, which stains the stem orangish as it dries. A slimy **ring zone** may be present above the gluten sheath. Larch Waxy Caps are mycorrhizal, fruiting in woods and bogs under conifers, particularly larch (*Larix* spp.)

NOTES: *Hygrocybe singeri* is inedible. *Hygrocybe coccinea* resembles some inedible species and should be avoided. The others above are edible but not choice.

Hygrocybe singeri

Hygrocybe miniata

Hygrocybe coccinea

Hygrocybe flavescens

Larch Waxy Cap

Orangish Milk Caps (several)

Lactarius spp.

HABITAT: Mycorrhizal, growing from the soil in association with conifers.

DESCRIPTION: Milk Caps produce milky **latex** when cut. Gills of the species listed here are closely spaced, and attached to the stem or running slightly down it. Young caps are rounded, becoming vase-shaped to flattened; the species here are typically 3 to 5 inches wide at maturity. Stems are sturdy and generally about as tall as mature caps are wide; they have a whitish bloom at first. Lactarius have no rings. • ***L. 'deliciosus'*** is a group of Lactarius whose caps are mottled or zoned (having concentric rings) with colors ranging from dull to deep orangish, to orangish-brown or tan, to greenish. Mature caps develop **greenish blotches**. Gills are **dull to bright orange**. Stems are orangish and may have darker pits. Latex is **orange** and sparse. Cut or bruised surfaces turn **turquoise-green**. • ***L. rubrilacteus*** has pale orange to orangish-brown caps with subtle to distinct concentric zones. Gills are **dull reddish to grayish-buff**. Latex is **dark red** and sparse. Stems are pinkish-orange to brownish-orange. All parts stain grayish to greenish when bruised. Usually associated with pines and Douglas fir. • Caps of ***L. olympianus*** have concentric zones of orange to reddish-orange. Gills are **whitish to dingy yellow**, discoloring to orangish-brown when bruised. Latex is **white**; it does not change color but stains the gills darker as it dries. Stems are whitish, becoming yellowish-brown with age. • ***L. aestivus*** is **orange overall**, with a zoned cap that may be darker in the center. Latex is **bright orange** and sparse. The stem may have a spotted or pitted appearance.

SPORE PRINT: Most species here produce whitish to pale yellowish spores; those of *L. olympianus* are cinnamon-buff.

SEASON: Late spring through fall.

OTHER NAMES: *L. rubrilacteus* is also called Bleeding Milk Cap.

COMPARE: Candy Caps (*L. rubidus*) are slightly smaller, with thinner stems. Caps and stems are light brown to orangish-brown; caps are **not zoned** but may have darker centers. Gills are light orange; latex is **whitish and watery**. Fresh Candy Caps have a mild taste and little odor, but develop a **maple-like** odor and taste when dried; they are highly prized. Several inedible lookalikes have a **peppery or acrid taste** when fresh; their milk is white and **not watery**.

NOTES: *L. aestivus* is edible with a good texture. The *L. 'deliciosus'* group and *L. rubrilacteus* are edible but grainy in texture. *L. olympianus* is considered inedible.

L. 'deliciosus' group (all 3 above)

L. rubrilacteus

L. olympianus

Candy Caps

FROM THE SOIL NEAR TREES

SUMMER THROUGH LATE FALL

Common Laccaria

Laccaria laccata

HABITAT: Common Laccaria are mycorrhizal, growing from the soil in association with hardwoods and conifers. They may be scattered or in groups, and are found in leaf litter or conifer debris, in both sandy and boggy areas.

DESCRIPTION: These small, common mushrooms have **dull orange, orangish-brown to pinkish-brown** caps that are smooth to finely scaly. Caps are **hygrophanous** (pg. 11); they are darker when moist, becoming paler when dry. Mature specimens have rounded to fairly flattened caps up to 2 inches wide; they may have wavy or frilly edges that are often split, appearing somewhat irregular in shape. Cap centers are often depressed; edges may have subtle ribbing. Gills are **pinkish to tan, thick and widely spaced**. They are attached to the stem; additional short gills are attached around the edge of the cap. Stems are up to 4 inches long and moderately slender, often appearing somewhat twisted or curved. They are dry and fibrous, with fine hairs or scales on the surface, and are typically a **darker shade of the cap color**. The stem has no ring. **White** mycelium (root-like fungal filaments) is often visible at the base.

SPORE PRINT: White.

SEASON: Summer through late fall.

OTHER NAMES: Deceiver, *L. laccata* var. *pallidifolia*.

COMPARE: Western Amethyst Laccaria (*L. amethysteo-occidentalis*) has a **purple to brownish-purple** cap that fades to buff; it may be over **3 inches** wide. Gills are **bright purple**, fading to lavender with age. Stems are up to **5 inches tall** and vary quite a bit in color, ranging from purplish-brown to various shades of brown or purple; they have a **shaggy or grooved** texture and are often twisted. Mycelium is **purple and unchanging**. • Two Laccaria in our area have **purplish mycelium that fades to white**. *L. nobilis* is up to 3 inches wide and over 4 inches tall. Compared to Common Laccaria, its caps and stems are **more scaly**, and gills **more closely spaced**. This is typically found at higher elevations. Two-Colored Laccaria (*L. bicolor*) has **purplish** gills under an orangish-tan to pinkish-tan cap; gills become buff with age. • *L. montana* looks like a **smaller** version of Common Laccaria; caps are less than 1½ inches wide and stems are less than 2 inches tall. Found only at **middle to high elevations**.

NOTES: Common, Western Amethyst and Two-Colored Laccaria are edible but not sought after. Edibility of *L. nobilis* and *L. montana* is uncertain.

Common Laccaria
Western Amethyst Laccaria
L. nobilis
Two-Colored
Laccaria

ON DECAYING WOOD AND WOODY DEBRIS

LATE SUMMER THROUGH LATE FALL

Fuzzy Foot

Xeromphalina campanella, X. enigmatica

HABITAT: These saprobes feed on decaying logs and stumps, usually growing in clusters or "troops" which can be dense or loose. *X. campanella* is very common in our area and fruits on coniferous wood. *X. enigmatica*, a recently described species also found in our area, may also fruit on birch or other hardwoods; mating studies and microscopic examination are used to separate the two species.

DESCRIPTION: Although small, Fuzzy Foot are easy to spot. Caps are orange, orangish-brown or yellowish-brown and ¼ to 1 inch wide; they are broadly convex to nearly flat. The surface is smooth and may appear shiny. Cap centers are **darker and sunken**; edges have subtle **ribbing** and are thin enough to be somewhat **translucent**, especially when moist. Gills are pale yellow to orangish and widely spaced; they **run down the stem** a fair amount. There are numerous **cross-veins** between the gills (visible with a hand lens). Stems are slender and up to 2 inches long; they are yellowish at the top, turning **reddish-brown** and **velvety** below, and often grow in a curved fashion. **Orange tufts** of stiff hairs grow around the base. Stems have no ring.

SPORE PRINT: White to light buff.

SEASON: Late summer through late fall.

OTHER NAMES: Cross-Veined Troop Mushroom.

COMPARE: Caps of *X. brunneola* are usually ½ inch wide or less; they are **darker orangish-brown to reddish-brown** and their edges are **opaque**. This species is less common in our area, and has not yet been reported in Oregon. • Caps of *X. cornui* are **pale yellow to amber**, and may be a bit larger than ½ inch wide. Stems are very thin and up to 2¼ inches tall; they are **dark golden-brown to brick-colored**, sometimes appearing almost blackish. The gills run down the stem and may appear arc-like. It fruits on coniferous debris and in **sphagnum bogs**. • Caps of *X. fulvipes* (sometimes listed as *Heimiomyces fulvipes*) are rich yellowish to tawny in the center, with a paler edge. Stems are up to **3¼ inches tall** and **blackish-brown**, slightly paler at the top. Its gills are attached to the stem but **do not run down it**. It typically fruits on coniferous debris. • Also see Tiny Fragile Mushrooms (pg. 76) for other mushrooms that are similarly sized.

NOTES: *X. campanella* and *X. cornui* have a mild odor and taste; the others listed here are bitter, and may have a disagreeable odor. Due to their small size, none are collected for the table.

X. campanella

FROM THE SOIL NEAR TREES

LATE SUMMER TO EARLY WINTER

Wooly Pine Spike

Chroogomphus tomentosus

HABITAT: Wooly Pine Spikes grow from the ground, widely scattered or in groups. They are mycorrhizal, associating with conifers. They also parasitize certain *Suillus* species, interfering with the mycorrhizal relationship between the *Suillus* and the surrounding trees. Very common in our area.

DESCRIPTION: These distinctive mushrooms are orangish-tan to buffy overall. Young specimens have **wooly caps that are rounded and cushion-like, sitting atop a stem that is nearly as wide as the cap**; they resemble a peg or spike. As caps expand they become broadly convex; at maturity they are up to 3½ inches wide and fairly flat, with a **dry, finely fibrous or scaly** surface. The widely spaced gills run down the stems; a dry, webby veil covers gills of young specimens, quickly deteriorating but sometimes leaving hairy remnants on the stem, below the gills. Stems may be nearly 6 inches tall and are fairly thick, sometimes flattened and wide; the stem base tapers abruptly to a point. Flesh inside the caps and stems is orangish.

SPORE PRINT: **Blackish** to dark gray.

SEASON: Late summer to early winter.

OTHER NAMES: Also listed as *Gomphidius tomentosus*.

COMPARE: Two Chroogomphus are called Pine Spike; both are slightly smaller than Wooly Pine Spike. Caps may have a pointed center (umbo) and are **slimy** when moist. Gills are yellowish-brown, becoming brownish-gray. Stems are orangish-tan to yellowish-brown. Caps of *C. vinicolor* are more conical, especially when young; they are often **reddish-brown**, although color varies quite a bit. Caps of *C. ochraceus* are **purplish-brown, grayish-brown to olive-tan**, often mottled with a combination of colors; caps become shiny and metallic-looking when dry. • Giant Pine Spike (*C. pseudovinicolor*; uncommon in our area) has dark **reddish-orange to burgundy-colored** caps up to **6 inches wide**; they are flattened and often wavy but have **no hump** in the center. The **stubby** stems are orangish-tan and loosely covered with patches of **reddish fibers**. Spores are **greenish to olive-gray**. • Young Wooly Pine Spike may be mistaken for Chanterelles (pgs. 42–44), but Chanterelles have **gill-like folds** under the caps rather than true gills, and their spores are **pale yellow to white**.

NOTES: The Chroogomphus discussed here are edible but not choice. Mushroom expert David Arora states that they are better when dried before cooking.

Wooly Pine Spike

C. vinicolor

C. ochraceus

Giant Pine Spike

LBMs: Little Brown Mushrooms

Various species

HABITAT: Little Brown Mushrooms (LBMs for short) grow in all habitat types and may be found in woodlands and fields, on dead wood, or on debris. Some are mycorrhizal, living in a symbiotic relationship with live trees; others are saprobes that help decompose dying and dead material.

DESCRIPTION: This catch-all term is used even by professional mycologists to refer to any of a number of common, **small to medium-size brownish mushrooms** that are difficult to identify precisely—and are usually considered not worth the bother. *Naucoria, Deconica, Entoloma, Kuehneromyces, Leptonia, Panaeolus, Psathyrella, Psilocybe, Tephrocybe* and *Tubaria* are a few of the genera included in this group. Some *Agaricus, Agrocybe, Cortinarius, Galerina, Inocybe, Pholiota* and *Pluteus* also fall into this category, although some species in these genera can be more readily identified and appear elsewhere in this book. Some LBMs are **toxic**; none should be eaten due to the difficulty in identification.

SPORE PRINT: If you want to try to place LBMs into a genus, the first step is making a spore print. Here are some generalizations to get you started. *Tephrocybe* have white spores. *Agrocybe, Cortinarius, Galerina, Inocybe, Kuehneromyces, Pholiota* and *Tubaria* have brownish to reddish-brown spores. *Naucoria* have olive-brown to brownish spores. *Agaricus* and *Psathyrella* have dark brown to blackish spores. *Deconica* and *Psilocybe* have purplish-brown spores. *Entoloma, Leptonia* (considered by some authorities as an *Entoloma*) and *Pluteus* have pinkish-brown spores. *Panaeolus* have blackish spores.

SEASON: Early spring through late fall, depending on species.

OTHER NAMES: Little Boring Mushrooms.

COMPARE: Some of the tiny fragile species discussed on pg. 76 are brownish. Also see Common Agrocybe in the "Compare" section on page 82, and "Fairy Ring" Mushroom on pg. 157.

NOTES: It's frustrating to find a large crop of mushrooms that you can't identify—but it's also very common, since field guides can't cover everything you're likely to find. You may enjoy studying them to hone your observation skills and to see how far you get in attempting to identify them. Since you should never eat any mushroom that you can't identify with ***absolute certainty***, you should never eat unidentified or poorly identified LBMs.

Deconica montana

Psathyrella spadicea

Kuehneromyces lignicola

Leptonia spp.

Cortinarius spp.

Inocybe lacera

Deer Mushroom

Pluteus exilis group

HABITAT: Deer Mushrooms are saprobes that fruit on rotten logs, sawdust piles, wood chips, decaying roots and stumps. They are found in both hardwood and coniferous forests, growing singly, scattered or in groups.

DESCRIPTION: The *Pluteus exilis* group is a complex of several species that are very similar in appearance, and can be separated only with microscopic examination. *P. exilis* is reportedly the most common in our area. Caps are brownish, ranging from medium brown to blackish-brown and becoming paler in dry weather. **Subtle streaks** often radiate from the center of the cap, which often has a distinct hump. The surface is smooth, sometimes glossy; it is tacky in damp weather. Bell-shaped when young, the caps expand to become broadly convex or flat; mature caps may be 5 inches wide. Stems, which are often slightly curved, are typically 3 to 5 inches tall and up to ¾ inch thick; they are white to cream-colored and may be streaked with dark fibers. There is no ring on the stem, and **no cup at the base**. Gills are closely spaced and **free from the stem**; they are white at first, turning pale salmon-pink as spores develop.

SPORE PRINT: Salmon-pink.

SEASON: Spring through fall.

OTHER NAMES: *P. exilis* was originally called *P. cervinus*, the name of a European species that looks very similar and which is also called Deer Mushroom. DNA studies showed that most of the Deer Mushrooms in our area were not *P. cervinus*; however, *P. cervinus* has been positively identified in California, and may also be found in our area. Differences between the two are microscopic.

COMPARE: Black-Edged Pluteus (*P. atromarginatus*) is darker and duller; caps and stems are both **streaked with dark fibers**. Gills have **blackish-brown edges**. Stems are proportionally thinner than those of *P. exilis*. It fruits on conifer wood and debris. • Caps of ***P. petasatus*** may be **6 to 7 inches** wide. They are whitish to light gray with a somewhat darker center; the surface often appears **metallic or shiny**. It is uncommon in our area; it prefers hardwoods, and often appears in urban areas. • Willow Shield (*P. salicinus*) is **small**, less than 2 inches wide and 3 inches tall. Caps are brownish to grayish, turning bluish-gray or greenish in the center; the white stems turn **bluish** with age.

NOTES: Willow Shield is mildly hallucinogenic and is not collected for the table. The other Pluteus are edible and considered good but not choice.

P. exilis

P. petasatus

Willow Shield

Black-Edged Pluteus

FROM THE SOIL NEAR LIVE TREES

SPRING THROUGH FALL

Bright Gill Cortinarius

Cortinarius spp.

HABITAT: These mycorrhizal mushrooms grow under trees. All species listed here associate with conifers; Cinnamon Cort is also found in hardwood forests, and often appears at elevation or in boreal forests.

DESCRIPTION: Cortinarius have a **cobwebby veil** (called a *cortina*) covering the gills of young specimens. The veil disintegrates with age, leaving a ring or ring remnant on the stem. Young caps are conical, becoming wider and fairly flat, often with a central hump (umbo). Our area has several Corts with **dry** caps and gills that are **brightly colored** on young specimens (becoming darker with age); these belong to the *Dermocybe* subgroup of Corts. Those listed in this paragraph are small, typically 1 to 2 inches wide and 1 to 2¾ inches tall. • Caps of Cinnamon Cort (*C. cinnamomeus*) range from cinnamon-yellow to olive-brown to dark reddish-brown. Gills are **bright orange** when young. Stems are yellowish-brown to olive-yellow. • Young Red-Gilled Cortinarius (*C. ominosus*; sometimes listed as *C. semisanguineus*, a name that more properly refers to a similar red-gilled species) has **deep red to reddish-purple** gills under a yellowish-brown to reddish cap. Stems are dull yellow to yellowish-brown. It sometimes fruits on rotten conifer wood. • Caps of *C. malicorius* (uncommon in our area) are yellowish-olive with a darker, reddish-brown center. Gills are **medium-orange to cinnamon** when young. Stems are pale yellow with darker bases. Cap edges and stems are **coated with orangish fibers**. • Caps of the *C. croceus* group are olive-yellow, pale to dark yellowish-brown or reddish-brown. Stems are yellowish at the top, becoming yellowish-brown to yellowish-gray below. Gills are **mustard-yellow to yellowish-green** when young.

SPORE PRINT: Brownish, ranging from rust-brown to reddish-brown.

SEASON: Spring through fall.

OTHER NAMES: Some sources refer to Cortinarius as Webcaps.

COMPARE: *C. californicus* is uncommon. It is **hygrophanous** (pg. 11), becoming darker when wet. Caps may be nearly **4 inches** wide; stems are up to **6 inches** tall. Gills are **deep red to reddish-orange**. Caps are dark reddish-brown when moist, fading to dull orangish-brown when dry. Stems are orangish.

NOTES: The Cortinarius discussed here are considered inedible and possibly **toxic**. The *Dermocybe* subgroup of Corts has pigments that bind to fabric, so they are often used for dyeing fibers.

Cinnamon Cort
Cortina
Red-Gilled Cortinarius
C. malicorius
C. croceus group
C. californicus

Brownish Cortinarius

Cortinarius spp.

HABITAT: These mycorrhizal mushrooms grow under trees. All species listed here associate with both conifers and hardwoods except *C. clandestinus*, which fruits in mossy areas with conifers, particularly Douglas fir and hemlocks, and may be found at both low and high altitudes.

DESCRIPTION: Cortinarius have a **cobwebby veil** (called a *cortina*; see photo on pg. 13) covering the gills of young specimens. The veil disintegrates with age, leaving a ring or ring remnant on the stem. Young caps are conical, becoming wider and fairly flat, often with a central hump (umbo). Our area has several Corts with **brownish** caps. Those listed in this paragraph are medium-size, typically 2 to 3 inches wide and 1½ to 3¾ inches tall. Gills are close to crowded and attached to the stem. • *C. clandestinus* is the most common in our area. Its **dry** caps are **yellowish olive-brown** with a heavy layer of **dark brown to blackish scales** that are concentrated in the center. Gills are pale yellowish, developing olive-brown tones and finally becoming orangish-brown. The veil leaves a faint yellowish-brown ring zone, and the lower stem may have a **fibrous, greenish-yellow sheath**. • Caps of Bulbous Cortinarius (*C. glaucopus*) are **sticky to slimy**, and range from reddish-brown to yellowish-olive to grayish-brown. Gills are **lilac to purplish**, becoming grayish-brown to cinnamon-brown. Stems are **bluish to violet** on young specimens, becoming yellowish-brown; the stem base is **bulbous**. The ring zone is faint. • Stems of Early Cortinarius (*C. trivialis*) are **slimy** and have a **prominent cobwebby ring** that is white at first, but turns brownish as spores develop. Below the ring, stems have **scaly rings** of dried slime. Caps are also **slimy**, and are yellowish-brown to pale olive-brown; colors may be mottled. Gills are bluish-gray, becoming brownish.

SPORE PRINT: Brownish to rusty brown.

SEASON: Spring through fall.

OTHER NAMES: Some sources refer to Cortinarius as Webcaps.

COMPARE: Caps of Gypsy Mushroom (pg. 160) are pale yellowish-brown with whitish fibers in the center that make it appear **frosted**. Stems have a **persistent white ring**. • Bright Gill Cortinarius (pg. 128) have many similar features, but their gills are **very brightly colored**.

NOTES: Early Cortinarius is said to be edible, but is usually avoided because some Cortinarius are **toxic**. The others listed here are inedible.

C. clandestinus
Bulbous Cortinarius
Early Cortinarius

FROM THE SOIL NEAR TREES

SUMMER THROUGH FALL

Reddish-Brown Tricholomas

Tricholoma spp.

HABITAT: Tricholomas are mycorrhizal, fruiting near trees, typically in groups.

DESCRIPTION: Trichs are generally fairly large, with thick caps and sturdy stems. Caps of the Tricholoma discussed here are darker in the center; the edges are paler and often wavy, sometimes splitting with age. Gills are closely spaced and attached to the stem; they are usually notched just before meeting the stem. With the exception of *T. vaccinum*, the Trichs listed here have no veil. Stems are firm, pale and dry, and often swollen at the base. • Several reddish-brown Trichs in our area have caps that are **dry**, becoming scaly with age. Shingled Trich (*T. imbricatum*) is a fairly large mushroom, often up to **6 inches wide** and nearly **5 inches tall**. Caps are dull reddish-brown to cinnamon-brown; edges may be faintly ribbed, and the cap surface around the edges may appear **broken** on older specimens. Gills are pale buff, becoming spotted with age. *T. vaccinum* has many of the same attributes as Shingled Trich but is smaller; caps are usually less than 3 inches wide. A **wooly, light brown veil** covers the gills on young specimens, leaving **hairs on the cap margin** but no stem ring. Both of these species fruit near conifers. • Several reddish-brown Trichs in our area have caps that are **sticky** when moist; debris may be stuck to the caps even when they are dry. Caps of Red-Brown Trich (*T. 'pessundatum'* group) are **medium to dark reddish-brown** and streaked with fine fibers. Gills are whitish, becoming darker and spotted. Red-Brown Trich associates with both conifers and hardwoods. Caps of Poplar Trich (*T. populinum*) are paler reddish-brown, sometimes fairly pale overall. They fruit near **aspen and cottonwoods**.

SPORE PRINT: White.

SEASON: Summer through fall.

OTHER NAMES: *T. pessundatum* is a European species; the name is used here to cover a group of several related conifer-loving *Tricholoma* species that have slightly different attributes but are difficult to separate from one another.

COMPARE: Bitter Brown Leucopax (pg. 96) is a medium-large mushroom with dull brown to reddish-brown caps. Gills are white and do not develop spots; they can be **separated from the cap in sheet-like sections**. It has a **very bitter taste** and usually associates with conifers. See additional photo on pg. 97.

NOTES: Poplar Trich is edible, but care must be taken to ensure proper identification. The other species here are considered inedible and some may be **toxic**.

Shingled Trich
T. vaccinum
Red-Brown Trich
Poplar Trich
Bitter Brown Leucopax

FROM THE SOIL NEAR TREES

SUMMER THROUGH FALL

Blackening Russulas

Russula spp.

HABITAT: Russulas are mycorrhizal species that grow from the ground, typically scattered or in small groups, in forested areas.

DESCRIPTION: Russulas are sturdy mushrooms, with thick stems and fleshy caps. Stems will **snap like chalk when bent** due to the brittle texture of the flesh. Caps often appear somewhat mottled, and usually have a depression in the center; edges may be wavy. Gills are firm and somewhat **brittle**; when pressed, they tend to break rather than to bend. Stems have no ring. The *Russula* species discussed here are generally 1 to 3 inches tall; all **bruise blackish** when handled or cut. • ***R. nigricans*** has whitish caps that turn dark brownish-gray to black with age; they are up to 6 inches wide. Gills are fairly **widely spaced** and thick; they are cream-colored to pale yellow when young. *R. nigricans* **bruises red at first**, slowly turning black. It is found in coniferous or mixed-wood forests. • Caps of ***R. 'densifolia'*** are **sticky** when moist, becoming **shiny** when dry; they are cream-colored at first, soon turning brownish, and are generally no more than 4 inches wide. Gills are **crowded** and cream-colored. The staining is the same as *R. nigricans*. *R. 'densifolia'* is found under hardwoods, conifers or in mixed-wood forests. • Members of the ***R. 'adusta'*** **group** closely resemble *R. 'densifolia,'* but differ in that they may—or may not—show a more subtle pinkish stage before they blacken. They are found only with conifers, and have a mild taste as opposed to the usually acrid taste of *R. 'densifolia.'* It is very difficult to positively separate these two without the use of a microscope. • ***R. albonigra*** **quickly turns blackish when bruised, without any reddish or pinkish phase**. Caps may be up to 7 inches wide, and may be slightly sticky when moist. Gills are closely spaced and whitish when young.

SPORE PRINT: White.

SEASON: Most common from summer through fall; some may appear in spring.

OTHER NAMES: Russulas are sometimes called Brittle-Gills. *R. atrata* is listed in some references; it may be the same as *R. albonigra*, or may be a slightly different species. Research to identify and separate members of this group of Russulas is ongoing and the scientific names are in flux.

COMPARE: Other Russulas do not blacken when bruised; see pgs. 152, 163 and 164 for some examples.

NOTES: Blackening Russulas should be considered inedible; some are very **toxic**.

R. nigricans

R. 'densifolia'

Dark Milk Caps

Lactarius spp.

HABITAT: Lactarius are mycorrhizal, growing from the soil in association with trees; all the species here except *L. necator* associate with conifers. The species here are fairly common in our area.

DESCRIPTION: Milk Caps produce milky **latex** when cut. Gills of the species listed here are closely spaced and attached to the stem or running slightly down it. Stems have no rings. • Velvety Milk Cap (*L. fallax*) has dark brown to blackish caps less than 3 inches wide, with a **suede-like** feel. Gills are white, turning orangish-buff; gill edges may be dark brown (on subspecies *L. fallax* var. *fallax*). Latex is abundant and white, slowly staining gills dull reddish to orangish. Stems are 3 inches or taller; they are brownish and **slender**, with a **velvety** texture. Sometimes found on rotting wood. • Caps of Slimy Milk Cap (*L. pseudomucidus*) are nearly 4 inches wide and covered with a **thick layer of slime** when moist, becoming shiny when dry. They are dark brownish-gray, grayish or brownish. Gills are bright white when fresh, becoming yellowish-gray. Latex is thin and white, and may be abundant or scant; it dries to yellow but stains the gills brownish. The **slimy** stems are grayish and up to 4 inches tall; bases are paler. • Red Hot Milk Cap (*L. rufus*) gets its name from its **extremely peppery** taste, as well as its **reddish-brown** caps which may be 4 inches wide or more. Caps are dry to somewhat moist; they may become wrinkled in age. Gills are whitish, becoming pale orange. Latex is white and usually abundant; it does not stain the gills. Stems are up to 4 inches tall and about one-third as wide; they are dry and brownish-orange to pinkish-brown. • Two Milk Caps appear very similar, separated mainly by their habitat. ***L. necator*** fruits under **birch trees**; ***L. olivaceo-umbrinus*** associates with conifers. Caps and stems of both are **drab olive-green to olive-brown**, often with orangish undertones. Caps are typically 3 to 4 inches wide. Stems are thick and up to 3 inches tall; they are often pitted. Gills are pale, becoming **dingy olive-gray**. Latex is plentiful and white, staining the gills olive.

SPORE PRINT: Whitish to cream-colored or pale yellowish.

SEASON: Late summer through fall.

OTHER NAMES: *L. necator* is also listed as *L. turpis* and *L. plumbeus*.

COMPARE: See also Pale Milk Caps (pg. 94) and Orangish Milk Caps (pg. 116).

NOTES: The Milk Caps listed here are considered inedible; some may be **toxic**.

Velvety Milk Cap

Slimy Milk Cap

Red Hot Milk Cap

L. necator (as *L. turpis*)

L. olivaceo-umbrinus

FROM THE SOIL NEAR LIVE TREES

LATE SPRING THROUGH FALL

Rosy Gomphidius

Gomphidius subroseus

HABITAT: Rosy Gomphidius grow from the ground, widely scattered or in groups. They are mycorrhizal, associating with conifers, particularly Douglas fir and spruce. They also parasitize certain *Suillus* species, interfering with the mycorrhizal relationship between the *Suillus* and the surrounding trees.

DESCRIPTION: Caps of young Rosy Gomphidius are rounded and cushion-like, with rolled-under edges. As they expand they become broadly convex; at maturity they are nearly 3 inches wide and flat or vase-like. They are dull to **deep pinkish or rosy-red** and are **very slimy or sticky** when moist; the surface can be **peeled off** as a colorless, sticky film. Gills are white and have a waxy feel; they are widely spaced and run down the stem. A **translucent, slimy veil** covers the young gills; it breaks apart to become a **slimy, fibrous ring** at the top of the stem, which soon becomes blackish from spores that also turn the gills smoky-gray. Stems are **slimy** below the ring zone and may appear somewhat **textured** due to the unevenness of the slime; they are 2 to 3 inches long and up to one-quarter as wide. When young they are white at the top with a **yellow base**; they may become dingy yellowish overall with age.

SPORE PRINT: Grayish-black to blackish.

SEASON: Late spring through fall.

OTHER NAMES: Rosy Slime Spike; very young specimens often have a spike-like or peg-like appearance, with a sturdy stem topped by a very small, domed cap.

COMPARE: Several other Gomphidius are found in our area; like Rosy Gomphidius, all have slimy caps, white gills that run down the stem, white stems and blackish spores. Clustered Slime Spike (*G. oregonensis*) is larger, up to **6 inches wide and tall**. Cap colors are **variable**; they may be dingy beige, pinkish-beige, dull reddish-tan or purplish-gray. It often grows in **clusters** that may be fused; with age it develops **numerous black splotches** overall, sometimes turning entirely black. Purple Slime Spike (*G. glutinosus)* is similar to Clustered Slime Spike, but its caps are more **purplish** and typically 2 to 4 inches wide. It tends to grow singly rather than in clusters. Other differences are microscopic. ***G. maculatus*** is uncommon; its caps are less slimy and it has **no veil**. Stems are often streaked and dark. Its gill turn **reddish** when bruised. Found near **larch** trees.

NOTES: The Gomphidius listed here are edible but reportedly bland; the cap skin is usually peeled off before cooking.

Rosy Gomphidius

Clustered Slime Spike

Gills and ring darkened by spores (*G. glutinosus* shown)

Purple Slime Spike

Purplish Cortinarius

Cortinarius spp.

HABITAT: Cortinarius are mycorrhizal. All species discussed here associate with conifers; Violet Cort may also be found near hardwoods.

DESCRIPTION: Cortinarius have a **cobwebby veil** (called a *cortina*; see photo on pg. 13) covering the gills of young specimens. The veil disintegrates with age, sometimes leaving a ring remnant on the stem. Spores are brownish; they typically darken the mature gills and ring remnant. Caps are conical at first, becoming wider and fairly flat, often with a central hump (umbo). Gills are attached to the stem, sometimes running down it slightly. Our area has several Corts with purplish attributes. • Many Corts have **dry** caps. The two discussed here are fairly large, with caps up to **5 inches** wide. Violet Cort (*C. violaceus*) is **deep violet to violet-black overall**, with **purplish** flesh; older specimens fade to brownish. Caps are hairy or scaly, with a **rough** texture. Gills are fairly widely spaced. Stems are up to **7 inches** tall, with a swollen or club-shaped base. It has a **mildly sweet odor** that some compare to cedar wood. Lilac Cort (*C. traganus*) has pale lilac caps and stems; gills are **brownish-yellow** and closely spaced. Stems are less than 4 inches tall and roughened with irregular pale patches. Flesh is **brownish**. Lilac Cort has a **pear-like odor**. • Other Corts have caps that are **slimy or sticky** when wet. The two discussed here are medium-size, with caps that are typically 2 to 3 inches wide; stems are 2 to 3 inches tall and moderately slender. Gills of both are closely spaced. *C. occidentalis* are violet-blue overall when young, fading to grayish-purple or tan. Flesh is bluish to bluish-gray; it **stains purplish** when cut or bruised. This species has little odor. *C. subfoetidus* (uncommon in our area) is noted for its **highly sweet, unpleasant** odor. Caps are bluish-lavender to pale pinkish lilac; the centers fade to pinkish-tan but the edges remain lavender. This species has a universal veil that leaves a **lilac-colored sheath** on the lower part of the stem.

SPORE PRINT: **Rust-brown to cinnamon-brown**.

SEASON: Summer through fall.

OTHER NAMES: *C. occidentalis* is also listed as *C. mutabilis*.

COMPARE: Young Blewits (pg. 142) are purplish overall, but they have **no veil** and **no ring zone** on the stem; spores are **pale pink to pinkish-buff**.

NOTES: Violet Cort is edible but not choice. The others listed here should be considered inedible; some may be **toxic**.

Violet Cort
Lilac Cort
C. occidentalis
C. subfoetidus

Blewit

Lepista nuda

HABITAT: These common saprobes get nutrients from decaying matter, including leaf litter, compost, grass clippings and wood mulch. Found on lawns, under brambles and hedgerows, and in parks and forests, both deciduous and coniferous. They fruit singly or in small groups and may grow in a ring.

DESCRIPTION: Young Blewits are **lavender, violet-blue or purplish** overall. Mature specimens are **tan to brownish**, often with slight mottling; gills may retain some purplish coloration. Caps are 1½ to 6 inches wide with a smooth surface that may feel waxy when moist. Young Blewits have softly rounded caps with slightly rolled-under edges, but as the mushrooms age the caps flare out and may develop wavy edges and irregular tops; some have a rounded point in the center. Gills are closely spaced and attached to the stem; they may be slightly notched at the stem, appearing to curve upwards. Stems are 1 to 3 inches tall and **stocky** with a rough texture; there is no ring. The base is often swollen or bulbous and may have a network of **fine purplish or bluish mycelium** (root-like fungal filaments). Blewits have a sweet, floral fragrance.

SPORE PRINT: **Pale pink to pinkish-buff**.

SEASON: Late summer through fall.

OTHER NAMES: All of the *Lepista* species listed here are also listed in the *Clitocybe* genus, with the same species names (*Clitocybe nuda*, for example).

COMPARE: Grass Blewit (*L. tarda*) is smaller overall, with a **slender, fibrous** stem. They are found more frequently in grassy, landscaped or cultivated areas rather than in woods and other natural areas. Coloration is more brownish overall but they have lilac tinges, particularly in the gills. Caps are often very wavy and may appear lobed. • ***L. glaucocana*** are similar to Blewits but more brownish to pale pinkish or lilac overall; they never have the darker violet tones of young Blewits. They are uncommon in our area. • Caps of Field Blewit (*L. saeva*) are buff-colored to yellowish-brown, lacking any purple tones. Stems are whitish to grayish with **purple tinges**. Found in deciduous woods. • Purplish Cortinarius (pg. 140) may resemble Blewits, but they have a **cobwebby veil** and **brownish** spores.

NOTES: Blewits are edible but opinions vary as to desirability. Always look for any trace of a cobwebby veil (present on inedible *Cortinarius* species but not found on Blewits) and make a spore print of your mushrooms before eating.

Blewit
Colorful young Blewit
with basal mycelium
Grass Blewit
L. glaucocana

Blue-Green Anise Clitocybe

Clitocybe odora

HABITAT: These colorful Clitocybes are saprobes; in our area, they are found on conifer needles and other debris. They grow scattered or in small groups.

DESCRIPTION: Two varieties of this mushroom are found in our area; both smell like **anise**. Caps are smooth and **dry**. They are **bluish-green, pale bluish or greenish**, often with a **slight whitish bloom**; they fade to pale bluish-gray or grayish-brown, and may be whitish in dry weather. Edges are rolled under at first and there may be a raised hump (called an umbo) in the center. As they mature, caps flatten out and edges become wavy; mature caps are up to 3 inches wide. The closely spaced gills are attached to the stem or run slightly down it. Gills of *C. odora* var. *odora* are **whitish, buff-colored or pinkish-buff**; those of *C. odora* var. *pacifica* are **bluish-green to greenish**. Stems are up to 2¼ inches tall and about **one-third as wide**; they are **white** in var. *odora*, and **pale greenish or greenish-blue** in var. *pacifica*. There is **no ring** on the stems.

SPORE PRINT: **Dingy whitish to pale pinkish-buff**.

SEASON: Summer through late fall.

OTHER NAMES: Anise-Scented Clitocybe, Aniseed Funnel.

COMPARE: Anise Clitocybe (*C. fragrans*) also has a sweet, anise-like odor. Caps are smaller than Blue-Green Anise Clitocybe. They are **pale yellowish-beige**; when dry they are **whitish**, and may be mistaken for a pale Blue-Green Anise Clitocybe. However, stems of Anise Clitocybe are **thinner** and often **longer**; caps have **ribbed, somewhat translucent** edges and a slightly **greasy** feel, and spores are **white**. *C. deceptiva* is similar to *C. fragrans*, but more **yellowish** overall and darker when moist, with **pinkish-buff** spores. • Blue-Green Stropharia (*Stropharia aeruginosa*) are similar in size to Blue-Green Anise Clitocybe, but caps are **sticky or slippery** when moist. Caps fade to yellowish. Gills are pale at first, turning **chocolate-brown**; spores are **purplish-brown**. Stems have a **thin ring**, and are **scaly** below the ring. *S. caerulea* is very similar to *S. aeruginosa* but slightly smaller; microscopic examination is used to positively separate the two.

NOTES: Blue-Green Anise Clitocybe is edible but very strongly flavored. Anise Clitocybe is best avoided; Blue-Green Stropharia is inedible and possibly **toxic**.

C. odora var. *odora*

C. odora var. *pacifica*

Anise Clitocybe

Blue-Green Stropharia

Grayish Tricholomas (several)

Tricholoma spp.

HABITAT: Tricholoma are mycorrhizal, fruiting singly, scattered or in loose groups under trees. They prefer cooler weather and are often found at elevation.

DESCRIPTION: Cap edges of the Tricholoma discussed here are paler than the centers; they may be slightly wavy, and often split with age. Stems are dry, thick and whitish, sometimes discoloring from handling or with age. Gills are closely spaced and attached to the stem; they are usually notched just before meeting the stem. With the exception of Cucumber Trich, there is no veil or stem ring. • Caps of Leopard Trich (*T. pardinum*) may be **6 inches wide** or larger. They are whitish to pale gray and **generously spotted with dark scales**. Stems are 2 to 6 inches tall and often enlarged at the base. Gills are whitish, sometimes flushed with pink. Found under conifers and hardwoods, fall to early winter. • Fibril Trich (*T. virgatum*) has caps up to 3½ inches wide; they are grayish to silvery, sometimes with a purplish cast. Caps are **conical with a pointed knob** in the center; **dark fibers radiate outward** from the knob. Stems are up to 5 inches tall, and smooth to slightly hairy. Gills are whitish to grayish. Found in mixed woods and under conifers, late summer through fall. • Cucumber Trich (*T. vernaticum*) has a **cucumber-like odor**. Caps are up to 5½ inches wide, and are whitish to pale grayish-brown; they are smooth and somewhat **moist but not sticky**. Stems are up to 5½ inches tall and have a **slight ring** that may be inconspicuous or absent. Below the ring, the stem is **sheathed with filmy veil remnants** that may be slightly darker than the stem. Gills are whitish to pale grayish, turning dingy buff with age. Found under conifers in **spring**. • Streaked Trich (*T. portentosum*) has **slimy to sticky** caps that are brownish-gray to purplish-gray; they are typically 2 to 3 inches wide but may be larger. Caps are somewhat conical with a **darker, raised knob** in the center; **dark fibers radiate out** from the knob. Gills are white. Stems are 2 to 4 inches tall and may appear twisted; the base may be somewhat bulbous. Both gills and stem may turn **yellowish**. Found under conifers and hardwoods, late summer to late fall.

SPORE PRINT: White.

SEASON: Spring through fall.

OTHER NAMES: Cucumber Trich was formerly called *Armillaria olida*.

COMPARE: Soapy Tricholoma (pg. 168) smells like soap; cut stems stain pinkish.

NOTES: Streaked Trich is edible. The others are inedible; Leopard Trich is **toxic**.

Leopard Trich
Cucumber Trich
Fibril Trich
Streaked Trich

FROM THE SOIL NEAR LIVE TREES

SPRING THROUGH FALL

Grisettes

Amanita spp.

HABITAT: Grisettes are mycorrhizal, growing in association with trees. Species discussed here grow singly or scattered, near both conifers and hardwoods.

DESCRIPTION: Grisettes are a section (subgroup) of the *Amanita* genus. All have the universal veil (pg. 9) and free gills that are common to other Amanitas; however, Grisettes **lack a partial veil** over the gills, so the stems have **no ring**. Other characteristics common to Grisettes include **distinct, fine ribbing** along the cap edge, and a long stem that is wider at the base but **not bulbous**. Caps of young specimens are conical and often have white patches from the universal veil. At maturity caps are nearly flat, typically with a hump in the center (umbo). • The largest in our area is the Western Grisette (*A. pachycolea*), which may be **7 inches wide and 10 inches tall**—or taller. Caps are brownish-gray, dark gray or dark brown, sometimes with a pale, halo-like ring between the center and the edge; patchy veil remnants are typically **absent** from caps of this species. Stems are pale and have fine scales that may form a chevron-like pattern. The volva (a sac-like cup at the base of the stem) is **large, thick and felt-like**; it is white and often has rust-colored stains. • *A. vaginata* var. *vaginata* is a name used for a medium-size Grisette that is fairly uncommon in our area. It has grayish to grayish-brown caps up to 4 inches across. Stems are white to grayish and up to 6 inches tall; the volva is **thin** and whitish. White Grisette (*A. vaginata* var. *alba*) is very similar but **whitish** overall. • Constricted Grisette (*A. constricta*) is medium-size, with grayish to brownish-gray caps and whitish, scaly stems that may be grayish at the base. The volva is white outside, often with rust-colored stains. It is **firmly attached to the stem** for much of its length, becoming free and **flaring out** at the top to reveal the gray interior.

SPORE PRINT: White.

SEASON: Spring through fall.

OTHER NAMES: *A. vaginata* is a European species. This name is applied in a general sense to many species in the U.S. The species listed here (as well as others that are similar) are collectively referred to as *Amanita* sect. *Vaginatae* sensu.

COMPARE: Most other Amanitas (pgs. 60–65) have rings on the stems. Rings may be large and easy to spot, or small and fragile; they may disappear with age.

NOTES: Grisettes are edible but disintegrate quickly once picked; however, even many experts do not eat them, due to possible confusion with **toxic** Amanitas.

Western Grisette

Volva of Western Grisette

A. vaginata var. *vaginata*

Constricted Grisette

Train Wrecker

Large Lentinus

Train Wrecker

Neolentinus lepideus (also known as *Lentinus lepideus*)

This saprobe grows singly or in small groups on downed trees, logs and stumps, primarily conifers but also hardwoods; it also fruits on buried wood as well as fenceposts and other lumber. It is called Train Wrecker because it has been blamed for breaking up railroad ties, causing derailments. Mature caps are up to 5 inches wide and are whitish to buff-colored with **numerous small, brownish scales**; caps are convex to flat, often with surface cracks. Gills are closely spaced and whitish, bruising brownish; they generally run down the stem. Gill edges become **jagged or serrated** with age. A **membrane-like veil** covers the gills of young specimens, breaking apart to leave a thin stem ring which may disintegrate. Stems are up to 4 inches tall and 1 inch thick; they may be slightly off-center. They are colored like the cap and have numerous curved whitish to brownish scales. The spore print is white. It fruits from spring through fall; specimens decay slowly ᐧnd may be found even in dry weather. Its odor has been compared to anise.

ᐧMPARE: Large Lentinus (*N. ponderosus*; also listed as *L. ponderosus*) has caps ᐧo **20 inches** wide; stems are stubby, generally less than 7 inches tall and ᐧhird as wide. There is **no veil or stem ring**. The cap surface breaks up **ᐧrge, light brown scales**. Stems are smooth or lightly ridged, with **fine ᐧ-brown scales** over the lower part. Most common at higher elevations.

ᐧoung caps of both species are edible but likely to be tough; if the mush- ᐧrowing on treated wood, they should not be eaten.

ᐧy identification feature

Smooth Parasol

Leucoagaricus leucothites (also listed as *Lepiota naucina, Leucoagaricus naucinus*)

This attractive, common saprobe resembles several other mushrooms—and that is a problem, because while Smooth Parasol is edible, some of the others are inedible, even **deadly**. Smooth Parasol is **whitish overall**, although caps and stems may discolor with age or from handling. Caps of young specimens are somewhat **marshmallow-shaped**, soon becoming widely bell-shaped to convex; they are up to 4 inches wide at maturity, with a smooth, somewhat glossy surface. Gills are closely spaced and free from the stem; they are whitish when young, becoming pinkish or buffy before turning brown in age. The white partial veil breaks open to leave a **persistent, movable ring** on the stem, which is typically about 4 inches tall and often has a bulbous base. Its spore print is **white or pale pinkish**. Smooth Parasols grow singly or scattered in lawns, parks, gardens and other landscaped areas; it may also fruit along roads and paths, occasionally in wooded areas. Most common in fall, they also appear in spring and summer.

COMPARE: Gray Parasol (*Leucoagaricus barssii*) is similar in many aspects, but its caps are **grayish to brownish** and **coarsely scaly**, particularly in the center. It is found in similar habitats, but also appears in agricultural fields and near manure piles. • Several *Agaricus* spp. (pg. 84) appear similar, but their gills are **pink**, becoming brownish with maturity; spores are **dark brown**.

NOTES: Some **toxic** Amanitas (pgs. 60–65) are very similar in appearance and also have white spores, making it extremely unwise to consume Smooth Parasol.

Short-Stemmed Russula

Russula brevipes

These large, common mushrooms often seem to burst through the soil when nearly fully formed, their dry caps covered in dirt, duff and pine needles. They are **whitish overall**, becoming **dingy and stained** with age. Caps are up to **7 inches** wide, sometimes larger; the **stout** stems are 2 to 3 inches tall and about half as wide. Caps often become **vase-like** with age and develop yellowish to yellowish-brown spots and stains. Gills are closely spaced and attached to the stem, sometimes running down it slightly; they are brittle and become yellowish with age, developing brownish stains. Stems have no rings. Short-Stemmed Russulas are mycorrhizal and are usually found in forests, where they appear singly, scattered or in groups. Spores are white to cream-colored. This species has variations that are not well-studied. Many associate with conifers, while others are found in hardwood or mixed-wood forests; other differences are microscopic. They fruit from summer through fall.

COMPARE: Cascade Russula (*R. cascadensis*) is similar in appearance but much **smaller**, less than 4 inches wide and 2 inches tall. Caps stain **orangish-buff**, and its taste is very **peppery or acrid**. Other differences are microscopic.

NOTES: Opinions vary as to the edibility of this species; some sources consider it inedible, while others list it as edible but not tasty. This is one of the species that is attacked by the parasitic mold *Hypomyces lactifluorum*, which turns the Russula into a Lobster Mushroom (pgs. 54–55), a much better edible than the original species.

The Sweater

Clitocybe rivulosa (also known as Ivory Funnel Cap and *C. dealbata*)

This small, **toxic** mushroom appears in pastures, urban grassy areas and open woods; it often grows in a ring. It is dingy white, pale grayish-white or buff-colored overall; the cap may appear pinkish when it is moist and often becomes **mottled with darker, wet-looking splotches**. Mature caps are generally ½ to 1⅝ inches wide; the edge is turned under. The cap surface is irregular but smooth, becoming dry with maturity. Gills are **closely spaced** and run down the stem for a short distance on older specimens; they are creamy white at first, turning pale buff to tan with age. Stems are 1 to 1½ inches tall and often slightly **flattened**; they may be **slightly curved or twisted**. The cap is often attached to the stem slightly off-center. The stem has no ring. Several specimens may grow together from a common base. Its spore print is white; it is found from summer into fall.

COMPARE: Crowded White Clitocybe (pg. 90) is much **larger**, with lobed to wavy-edged caps up to **6 inches** wide; it grows in **large, tight clusters** in areas with sandy or gravelly soil. • Funnel Caps (pg. 88) are up to 3½ inches wide and **brownish to pinkish-tan** with a **deep funnel shape**. They grow near trees in areas of moss, conifer needles or leaf litter. • "Fairy Ring" Mushroom (pg. 157) grows in similar habitat as the Sweater and is about the same size, but its caps are **buff to tan**, its stems are **slender** and its gills are more **widely spaced**.

NOTES: Very toxic. The Sweater contains muscarine, which causes intense sweating, salivation, tear formation and intestinal distress.

Golden-Fringed Waxy Cap

Hygrophorus chrysodon

This fairly common mushroom is easy to identify when it's bearing its hallmark: tiny **golden-yellow flakes** on the cap (particularly on the edge) and at the top of the stem. Other than the yellow accents, it is white to cream-colored overall, with a **waxy** feeling; caps and stems are **slimy** when moist. Caps are smooth and rounded to slightly humped, and are usually 2 to 3 inches wide. Gills are fairly widely spaced and run down the stem. A fleeting veil covers the gills of young specimens; it disappears rapidly, leaving a bit of slime on the stem but no ring. Stems are 2 to 3 inches tall and of moderate width; they may taper slightly at the base. Spores are white. They are mycorrhizal, growing from the ground near conifers, sometimes in mossy areas. They fruit from summer into winter. The golden flakes wash off over time, making indentification difficult.

COMPARE: Ivory Waxy Cap (*H. eburneus*; also called Cowboy's Handkerchief) is similar, but it is pure white overall, **lacking the yellow flakes**; stems are a bit taller and noticeably **thicker**. Its caps are covered with **thick slime** which may drip off the edges. • Glutinous Waxy Cap (*H. gliocyclus*) is cream-colored overall. Caps have a **yellowish to buff-colored center** and paler edges; they are **very slimy**. Stems are shorter and wider, appearing **stubby**; they are covered in a **sticky sheath**, and a **sticky, band-like ring** is present near the top on young specimens.

NOTES: The species listed above are edible but bland; Ivory Waxy Cap and Glutinous Waxy Cap are unpleasantly slimy.

Almond Waxy Cap

Olive-Brown Waxy Cap

Almond Waxy Cap

Hygrophorus bakerensis (also known as Mt. Baker Waxy Cap)

This attractive mushroom has a **noticeable scent of almond extract**, especially when young. Caps are distinctly **bicolored**, with a white to ivory edge and dark centers that are yellowish-brown to reddish-brown. Caps are slimy when moist and typically **2 to 5 inches** wide; edges of mature caps are wavy, and there is often a distinct hump (umbo) in the center. Beads of moisture may be present on the caps, gills or stems, particularly in warm weather. Gills feel **waxy** and are whitish when young, developing pinkish or yellowish tones with maturity. They are moderately closely spaced and attached to the stem or running slightly down it. Stems may be up to 6 inches tall but are usually shorter; they are white, often darker near the base. There is **no veil** or ring; spores are white. This mycorrhizal species grows scattered or in groups near conifers, from fall into winter.

COMPARE: *H. discoideus* is similar in coloration to Almond Waxy Cap but is much **smaller**, typically less than 2 inches wide and 3 inches tall. It **lacks the almond odor**. It has a gelatinous **universal veil** that leaves the lower part of the stem **slimy**. • Gray Almond Waxy Cap (*H. agathosmus*) is similar in size and odor to Almond Waxy Cap, but its caps are **gray to brownish-gray overall**. • Olive-Brown Waxy Cap (*H. hypothejus*) has caps that are **brownish overall**; colors range from olive-brown to yellowish-brown to orangish-brown, with darker centers. Caps are typically 3 inches wide or less. It has a **mild, non-almond odor**.

NOTES: The waxy caps listed here are regarded as edible but bland.

The Prince

Agaricus augustus

This common mushroom starts out with a small, **marshmallow-shaped** cap that expands and flattens to become **10 inches wide**—or more. Caps are whitish to pale buff, covered with **numerous brownish scales**; with age the cap background becomes yellowish to yellowish-brown, giving the cap a golden appearance. Caps **bruise yellowish** when rubbed or damaged. Gills are closely spaced and pale tan to warm gray on young specimens, becoming grayish-brown before maturing to chocolate-black; they are free from the stem on mature specimens. A white veil that often has **cottony patches on the underside** covers the gills of young specimens. The veil breaks as the cap expands, forming a **large-skirt-like ring**. Stems are up to **10 inches tall** and sturdy; they are white to cream-colored, with whitish to brown-edged scales below the ring that give a **shaggy** appearance. The Prince is a saprobe that fruits scattered or in groups, typically in lawns, disturbed areas, along paths and on ground debris near conifers and hardwoods. Spores are chocolate brown; it fruits from spring through fall.

COMPARE: Buck's Agaricus (*A. buckmacadooi*; previously listed as *A. moelleri* and *A. praeclaresquamosus*) has caps less than 8 inches wide with small, flat, dark brown scales and appearing darkest over the center. Gills are **pinkish** at first, becoming dark brown. Stems are **smooth**. It has a **tar-like** smell and is **toxic**.

NOTES: The Prince has a strong, sweet odor that is usually compared to almonds or anise; this is most noticeable when the cap is bruised. It is a choice edible.

"Fairy Ring" Mushroom

Marasmius oreades (also known as Scotch Bonnet)

Although this mushroom is referred to as the Fairy Ring, that name is also used for other species so it is best to use the scientific name, *Marasmius oreades*. This saprobe is found in lawns and grassy areas and is common in urban settings, often growing in dense arcs or rings. The cap is **buff to tan** and often slightly darker in the center. Caps are rounded to bell-shaped at first but flatten out quickly; they are typically somewhat **wavy with a central hump** (umbo). Mature specimens are up to 2 inches wide. The tough stems are up to 3 inches tall and fairly slender; they are generally colored like the cap, with slightly darker bases. There is no ring. Gills are cream-colored to tan and **fairly widely spaced**. They are typically attached to the stem but **never run down it**; sometimes the gills appear slightly notched where they are attached to the stem. The spore print is white. These mushrooms are present from spring through fall.

COMPARE: Numerous small to medium-size mushrooms can be confused with *M. oreades*. The **toxic** Sweater (pg. 153) grows in similar habitat and is about the same size and overall shape. Its gills are **closely spaced** and **run down the stem slightly**, and its cap lacks the central hump. • Also see Spring Agrocybe (pg. 82), Common Laccaria (pg. 118) and Little Brown Mushrooms (pg. 124) for other mushrooms that may appear somewhat similar to *M. oreades*.

NOTES: *M. oreades* is edible; the stems are tough and should be discarded. Beginners must seek expert help to avoid **toxic** lookalikes.

Phaeocollybia kauffmanii group

Dark-Rooting Collybia Group

Phaeocollybia spp.

Although they are uncommon, a number of *Phaeocollybia* species are found in our area; they are related to *Cortinarius* species. They are an iconic Northwest species that is usually found in coastal areas. All have **tough, root-like stems that extend far below the soil**, sometimes up to three times as deep as the aboveground height. *P. kauffmanii*, pictured above, is typical. Caps are **slimy**, and can be up to 6 inches wide. Like many Phaeocollybia, they are conical when young, becoming bell-shaped to convex; they are generally some shade of orangish-brown and are usually paler at the edges. Gills are crowded to closely spaced and generally free of the stem, although they may be attached to the stem with a small tooth. They are pale buff when young, becoming darker with age. The aboveground portion of the stems is slender and usually 2 to 4 inches tall; stems are colored like the cap but paler at the top, becoming darker towards the ground. No stem ring is typically present. Spores are **cinnamon-brown**. This group is mycorrhizal, found in coniferous or mixed forests from spring through late fall.

COMPARE: Some members of the *Rhodocollybia* genus can appear similar, but they **lack the long, root-like stems**. Caps often feel greasy (see Buttery Collybia on pg. 98), and spores are **pinkish-buff, buff or yellowish**.

NOTES: It is fairly easy to recognize a member of the *Phaeocollybia* genus, but often challenging to determine exact species. Although the stems are tough, it can be very difficult to dig up the entire buried portion.

Shaggy-Stalked Flocccularia

Floccularia albolanaripes (also listed as *Armillaria albolanaripes*)

Young specimens of this mushroom are very attractive; their rounded, **bright yellowish to golden** caps are adorned with **pressed-down brown fibers**. Caps expand and flatten out with age, and may be over 4½ inches wide; the centers are **dark brown** and may have a slight hump. Stems are typically 2 to 3 inches tall and fairly thick, with a slightly enlarged base. Gills are closely spaced and **whitish to pale yellowish**; they are fairly wide, narrowing down to a notch just before attaching to the stem. A cottony white veil covers the gills of young specimens; it breaks apart as the cap expands, often leaving **ragged patches** hanging from the cap edge. The veil also leaves **shaggy remnants on the lower part of the stem**; with age, the shaggy remnants develop yellow or brownish edges. Caps become dull brown with age, retaining the dark brown fibers. Spores are white. Scattered populations of this species are found throughout our region, in both coastal and montane areas; they grow singly, in pairs or in small groups from the duff in conifer and hardwood forests, particularly near alder. Shaggy-Stalked Floccularia is found primarily in fall, but also fruits in spring.

COMPARE: Scaly Yellow Armillaria (*F. luteovirens*) is similar, but its caps are paler and are decorated with **raised yellow scales**. Edibility is uncertain. • Man on Horseback (pg. 106) has yellowish caps with **fairly subtle brownish scales** in the center. Its stems are **smooth** and its gills are **medium yellow**.

NOTES: Fresh, young specimens of Shaggy-Stalked Floccularia are a choice edible.

Gypsy Mushroom

Cortinarius caperatus (also listed as *Rozites caperata*)

The Gypsy is mycorrhizal, growing from the soil in a symbiotic relationship with conifers. It can be found in small or large groups and often fruits near blueberry or huckleberry bushes. The cap is often 3 to 5 inches wide and **yellowish to light brown**; it is covered with **fine white fibers**, mainly in the center, making it appear slightly **frosted**. Caps are conical when young, becoming convex and slightly knobbed; the cap surface is often wrinkled (*caperata* means "wrinkled" in Latin). The **attached** gills are closely spaced and putty-colored when young, darkening to rusty brown; they are often wavy or irregular-looking. They are initially covered by a partial veil that breaks to form a **persistent, thick white ring** on the stem, near the midpoint. Stems are up to 5 inches tall and white to light tan; they may be swollen at the base and the lower part of the stem is often streaked with pale orangish-tan stains. Spores are **rusty brown**. It fruits from summer to early fall.

COMPARE: Other *Cortinarius* species (pgs. 128, 130, 140) may look similar in some regards, but buttons typically have a **cobwebby cortina** (partial veil) and mature specimens lack the thick stem ring. • *Agaricus* species (pg. 84) may be tan with a prominent ring, but the gills are **free** from the stem and spores are **dark brown**. • Poison Pie (pg. 74) and other *Hebeloma* species appear somewhat similar, but they have **no rings** on the stems and their caps are **slimy or sticky**; they are **toxic**.

NOTES: The Gypsy is being studied for antiviral properties. It is a good edible when properly identified; some cooks discard the stems, which may be tough.

Plums and Custard

Tricholomopsis rutilans

This attractive, common mushroom, also known as Variegated Mop, grows scattered or in small clusters from **decaying conifer stumps and logs** that may be underground; also found on wood chips. Both cap and stem are yellowish and have a coating of **reddish to purplish-red fibers and scales** that are sometimes so dense on the cap that it may appear entirely red. Caps of mature specimens are up to 4¾ inches wide, often with a wavy or scalloped edge. Stems are stocky and up to 4 inches tall; the base may be somewhat flattened. The stem has no ring. Gills are deep yellow and closely spaced; they are attached to the stem or slightly notched. The flesh is yellow. The spores are **white**. It grows from late spring through fall, particularly during cool periods.

COMPARE: Golden-Gilled Gym (pg. 112) appears similar, but its stems are **pinkish-red to yellowish-orange** with a whitish bloom; they are often somewhat streaky. Gills are covered with a **partial veil** that leaves a faint, fibrous ring at the top of the stem; the ring may disappear with age. Spores are **bright orangish-brown**. • Decorated Mop (*T. decora*) is smaller, with a cap that is less than 3 inches across and a stem that is less than 3 inches tall. It is typically **golden yellow overall** and **lacks the reddish fibers**; it has **tiny brownish to blackish scales** that are concentrated on the center of the cap.

NOTES: Plums and Custard is considered a poor edible. Golden-Gilled Gym and Decorated Mop are considered inedible.

Faded specimens with "bleeding stem"

Bleeding Mycena

Mycena haematopus

Unlike many other members of the *Mycena* genus, this common species is easy to identify. It is a saprobe that fruits on **rotting wood**, usually in clusters; the stem bases **bleed a dark red juice** when crushed. Caps of young specimens are pinkish-brown, reddish-brown to purplish-brown at the center, becoming lighter towards the edges, which are finely ribbed, especially when moist; margins are typically scalloped or ragged. Young caps are conical or bell-shaped, becoming convex or flattened, sometimes with upturned edges; they are ¾ to 1¼ inches wide at maturity. Older caps fade to pale pinkish-brown. Gills are fairly closely spaced and attached to the stem; they are pale pink to pinkish and often develop dark spots or reddish-brown bruises. Stems are up to 4 inches tall and slender; they are reddish to reddish-brown, fading to grayish-brown. Spores are white. They can be found from spring through fall.

COMPARE: Terrestrial Bleeding Mycena (*M. sanguinolenta*) is quite a bit smaller, less than 1 inch wide and 3 inches tall. Like Bleeding Mycena, its stems bleed dark red juice when crushed. Caps are **reddish-brown to orangish-brown** and remain bell-shaped at maturity. Gills are pale pinkish-tan with **reddish edges**. It grows **from the ground** rather than on rotting wood and is usually found in conifer needle beds, mossy areas or in forest duff.

NOTES: These species are too small to be of interest in the kitchen, but they make nice subjects to hone your photographic skills.

green = key identification feature

Shrimp Russula

Russula xerampelina

Like many Russulas, this species can vary quite a bit in appearance, with cap colors ranging from reddish-purple to bright red, maroon, brownish-olive and so on. The main identifying factor is a **shrimp-like or fishy odor**, which may be musty and unpleasant, and becomes more pronounced when it is older or dried. Caps of mature specimens may be up to 6 inches across; they generally have a depressed center. Gills are firm and somewhat **brittle**; they are moderately close and attached to the stem, sometimes notched. They are creamy white, becoming **yellowish then brownish** when bruised or scratched. The spores are pale yellow. Stems are typically 2 to 3 inches tall and one-third as wide; they are whitish and often have a pinkish tone, particularly at the base. Shrimp Russula are common in our area and are found scattered or in groups in coniferous to mixed-wood forests, fruiting from summer through fall.

COMPARE: Several other Russulas in our area have caps with varied appearances, but have been identified as distinct species through microscopic differences. These include Rainbow Russula (*R. 'olivacea'*), which has a **fruity** odor and caps that are generally olive-brown when young; and Western Russula (*R. occidentalis*) whose flesh turns **red, then gray or black**, when bruised.

NOTES: The Russulas above are edible. Some people have digestive problems with them, so only a small amount should be eaten at first.

Rosy Russula

Russula rhodocephala (also listed as *R. sanguinea, R. sanguinaria, R. rosacea*)

This gorgeous, common mushroom is fairly easy to identify, if not to name (see "Notes" below). Caps are **bright scarlet or crimson**, sometimes reddish-orange to reddish-brown; they are somewhat **shiny**, even when dry. At maturity they are up to **4¾ inches** wide and shallowly funnel-shaped or irregularly wavy. Gills are moderately spaced and attached to the stem or running slightly down it; they are cream-colored, yellowing with age. Stems are **very stout** and shorter than the width of the mature cap; they are whitish flushed with pink, often **rosy pink to pale pink** overall. Flesh is whitish and unchanging, although the lower stems may bruise yellowish. There is no ring. Spores are **yellowish**. Rosy Russula are mycorrhizal, found near **pines**; they fruit singly or in groups from summer to fall.

COMPARE: American Russula (*R. americana*) is **smaller and less robust**, with bright red caps less than 2½ inches wide and moderate-width stems up to 2½ inches tall. Its spores are **buff-colored**, and it associates with **hemlock and fir**. • Caps of The Sickener (*R. emetica*) are scarlet pink to pale yellow or both; they are up to 3 inches wide. Stems are up to **4 inches** tall and whitish. They are found in **mossy areas** such as bogs (particularly sphagnum).

NOTES: The species described here as *R. rhodocephala* has been listed as *R. sanguinea*, a European species. Microscopic studies have found differences between *R. sanguinea* and the West Coast specimens, so the mushrooms found in our area have been designated as a separate species. All species listed here are inedible.

Chip Cherries

Leratiomyces ceres (previously listed as *Stropharia aurantiaca*)

These saprobes are common in gardens and areas that have been landscaped with wood chips, where they often fruit in very large groups; also found in other woody debris including sawdust. Caps are **deep orangish-red**; they are slimy when young and moist, becoming duller and dry with age. They are typically 2 to 3 inches wide and often have a distinct bump (umbo) in the center. Gills are closely spaced and attached to the stem, sometimes slightly notched; they are pale gray when young, becoming olive-brown and finally purplish-black from the spores. A whitish partial veil covers the gills of young specimens; fragments often cling to the cap edges and a thin ring may be present on the upper stem for a while before disintegrating. Stems are 1 to 3 inches tall and slender; they are sometimes twisted and may be slightly enlarged at the base. Young specimens have **whitish** stems; they become **orange-streaked** with age and handling. A mat of fine white to pale yellow mycelium (root-like fungal filaments) may be found at the base. Spores are dark purplish-brown. Chip Cherries fruit from early fall to winter.

COMPARE: Mulch Maids (*L. percevalii*) may also be found in the same areas as Chip Cherries, but their caps are yellowish-brown to beige; stems are pale tan and up to **4¾ inches** tall.

NOTES: Chip Cherries may have hitched a ride to the Pacific Northwest on wood, wood chips or sawdust coming from Australia. Edibility is unknown.

Lilac Bonnet

Mycena pura

This attractive saprobe is found in wooded areas, including hardwood, conifer and mixed-wood forests. It fruits in leaf litter and other forest duff and may grow singly, scattered or in clusters. Caps are small and conical at first; at maturity they are less than 2 inches wide and somewhat flattened except for a slight central hump (called an umbo). They are **hygrophanous** (pg. 11), becoming darker when moist; they appear shiny and somewhat translucent in wet weather, turning dull and opaque in dry weather. Cap color is **purplish** but variable, ranging from lilac to pale grayish-purple to pinkish-gray; they fade to pale gray or tan with age. Edges are **finely ribbed**. The closely spaced gills are attached or slightly notched just before meeting the stem; they are pale purple, whitish or light lilac. The thin, hollow stems are typically 2 to 3 inches tall and whitish to pale pinkish or lilac; they are often slightly flattened and may be somewhat wider towards the base. There is **no veil** over the gills, and no ring on the stem. This species has a mild **radish-like odor**. Spores are **white**. Lilac Bonnet fruits from spring into early summer, and then again in fall; it is common in our area.

COMPARE: Lilac Fiberhead (pg. 167; **toxic**) is similar in size and coloration, but it has a **cobwebby veil** over the gills of young specimens; the veil leaves **fine hairs** on the cap edges and the stem. It has a **bleach-like odor** and **brown** spores.

NOTES: Some sources say that this species may contain the **toxic** compound muscarine; it should be regarded as inedible.

Lilac Fiberhead

Inocybe lilacina (also listed as *I. geophylla* var. *lilacina*)

Young specimens of this small, common mushroom are **lilac to lavender-colored overall**, fading to pale lilac or grayish-brown, often with a brownish center. Caps are oval to conical when young, becoming bell-shaped or fairly flat with a central hump (umbo); mature caps are less than 2 inches wide. They are dry and finely fibrous, sometimes silky. Gills are closely spaced and attached to the stem, sometimes slightly notched; a **cobwebby veil** covers the gills of young specimens, disintegrating and leaving fine hairs on the cap edge and stem; there is no distinct ring. Stems are up to 2½ inches tall and moderately thin; the surface is silky to smooth and stem bases may be somewhat enlarged. Lilac Fiberheads have an unpleasant odor that has been described as bleach-like, pungent or spermatic. Spores are **dull brown**. This mycorrhizal species fruits near conifers, in areas with moss or forest duff; it is found from late summer through fall.

COMPARE: White Fibercap (*I. geophylla*) is very similar but it is white overall. Some consider Lilac Fiberhead to be a variant of this main species • **Lilac Leg Fibercap** (*I. griseolilacina*) are smaller, usually 1½ inches wide or less and 1½ inches tall. Caps are somewhat **scaly** and **grayish-brown**, becoming paler at the edges. Stems are pale lilac to pale brown and covered with fine, pale hairs. • Several *Cortinarius* species are purplish (pg. 140), but they are quite a bit **larger**; their spores are **rust-brown to cinnamon-brown**.

NOTES: Lilac Fiberhead and White Fiberhead are **toxic**; the others may be as well.

green = key identification feature

Soapy Tricholoma

Tricholoma saponaceum

These large mushrooms are mycorrhizal, associating with both hardwoods and conifers. Caps may be up to 7 inches wide; **color varies** quite a bit. They are often various shades of gray or yellow, but may also be olive or brownish; they often have slightly **greenish** tints. The surface is dry to moist, with a **greasy feeling**. Cap margins are rolled under on young specimens, becoming uplifted and often wavy with age; the center may have a broad hump (umbo). Gills are thick and moderately closely spaced; they are whitish to yellowish and attached to the stem, sometimes slightly notched. Stems are typically 2 to 4 inches tall and one-quarter as wide; they are often **slightly wider** at the midpoint, with a **tapered base** that may narrow quite a bit at the end, becoming root-like. The stems are whitish, usually with pinkish or pale orangish tints at the base; flesh inside the stem is **pinkish** at the base. There is no ring on the stem; spores are white. Soapy Tricholoma usually have an odor that is both sharp and sweet; it is often described as **soap-like**. They are very common in our area, fruiting from spring to fall.

COMPARE: Numerous Grayish Tricholomas (pg. 146) are found in our area. Caps of many are spotted or streaky; some are sticky, while others are fibrous. None have the soapy smell, or pinkish flesh inside the base of the stem.

NOTES: Many sources report that Soapy Tricholoma have an unpleasant, soap-like taste; others say that the taste is mild. They are generally regarded as inedible or possibly **toxic**.

Platterful Mushroom

Megacollybia fallax (also listed as *M. platyphylla, Tricholomopsis platyphylla*)

From late spring through summer, this saprobe can be found scattered or in small groups, growing near or on decaying conifer logs, stumps and buried woody debris. Caps are up to 3½ inches wide and grayish-brown, streaked with **fine, dark fibers** running from the center to the edges. On mature specimens, the top of the cap may be uneven; edges are often **wavy and/or cracked**. The whitish to cream-colored gills are very broad and **moderately widely spaced**. They are **attached to the stem**, sometimes slightly notched; gill edges near the cap may appear ragged on mature specimens. Stems are up to 4½ inches tall and fairly stout; they are white and streaked with fine vertical fibers. There is no ring on the stem. A few white rhizomorphs (thick root-like strands) are often visible at the base. Its spore print is **white**. It is fairly common in our area.

COMPARE: Deer Mushrooms (pg. 126) have streaked brownish caps and are found on rotting wood, but their gills are **free** from the stem and **closely spaced**; their spores are **salmon-pink**. • Some Grayish Tricholomas (pg. 146) have grayish-brown, gray or brownish caps, but they are mycorrhizal, growing from the soil near trees rather than from rotting wood. Their gills are **closely spaced**.

NOTES: Platterful Mushrooms are generally regarded as edible when young some people may experience gastrointestinal problems, so try only a small po tion at first. Some people refer to this species as Broadgill. It is generally fo east of the Cascades.

Scaber Stalks (several)

Leccinum spp.

HABITAT: These common mycorrhizal species grow under or near birch, aspen and conifers. Common Scaber Stalk is often found in urban areas.

DESCRIPTION: The hallmark of *Leccinum* species are **scabers**, minute raised scales covering the stems. The scabers of the species discussed here are darker than the stems, particularly on mature specimens. Caps are dull and smooth when dry but slippery when wet; stems are **whitish** with no rings, and typically wider at the base. The pore surface is whitish to buff-colored on young specimens, becoming brownish with age; pores **bruise brown**. • Caps of Common Scaber Stalk (*L. scabrum*) are **brownish** and less than 4 inches across. Stems may be bluish-green at the base and are usually **slender**; they are typically 3 to 5 inches tall. The flesh **remains white or turns pale pinkish** when cut. It is found near birch trees, and is also called Birch Bolete. • Caps of ***L. fibrillosum*** are **medium to dark reddish-brown** and up to **9 inches** wide; caps of young specimens are covered with **fine fibers**, becoming scaly with age. Stems are **chunky** and up to 4 inches tall. The white flesh turns **pinkish or purplish** when cut. It associates with spruce and pine. • ***L. insigne*** and ***L. 'aurantiacum'*** are both referred to as Aspen Boletes due to their association with aspen; *L. 'aurantiacum'* is also found with pines. Both are also called Orange-Capped Bolete because of their cap color, which varies from apricot to orange to brown. They are up to 6 inches wide and tall, with sturdy stems. Typically, *L. 'aurantiacum'* has a more intense orange cap, though it may fade with age. When cut, the flesh of both slowly **bruises purplish-gray to blackish**; flesh of *L. 'aurantiacum'* turns **pinkish to reddish** before turning purplish-gray. • Manzanita Bolete (*L. manzanitae*) is found near **manzanita and madrone**, particularly in coastal areas. Caps are **dark red to reddish-brown** and may be 8 inches wide or more; they are **slimy** when moist. Flesh slowly bruises smoky gray to purplish-gray.

SPORE PRINT: Olive-brown to brownish.

SEASON: Spring through fall.

OTHER NAMES: See text above.

COMPARE: Some sources question the presence of *L. aurantiacum* in our area; the species present here may be closer to *L. vulpinum*. Both names are European.

NOTES: Most *Leccinum* species listed here are considered edible, but the orange-capped species may cause gastrointestinal problems and should be avoided.

Common Scaber Stalk

L. fibrillosum

L. insigne

Slippery Jack, Slippery Jill

Suillus luteus, S. acidus

HABITAT: These common mycorrhizal mushrooms grow in a symbiotic relationship with living trees. They are found in scattered clusters primarily under **conifers**, particularly pines. Slippery Jack prefers red pine and other two-needle varieties; Slippery Jill prefers white pine and other five-needle species.

DESCRIPTION: *Suillus* species are called Slippery Boletes due to their frequently **slimy** cap surface. What makes Slippery Jack and Slippery Jill distinctive is the partial veil that breaks to form a **prominent ring** on the stem; like the caps, the rings are **slimy** in humid weather. The other notable feature is the **fine dots on the stem** above the ring. Pores **do not change color** when bruised. • Slippery Jack (*S. luteus*) has a **brown** cap with a pale yellow pore surface that darkens with age. Caps are up to 5 inches across and may become tan or yellowish with age. The ring on the stem is white on the underside; the side towards the cap becomes **dark purplish brown**. Stems are up to 3 inches tall and one-third as wide; they are white below the ring and typically yellowish above it. • Caps of Slippery Jill (*S. acidus*) are **olive-brown to tan** and typically less than 4 inches wide. The pore surface of young specimens is yellowish to olive-buff; it may be dotted with **beads of moisture** in damp weather. The ring on the stem is band-like and often thickened on the bottom; the underside is **colored like the cap** and the side towards the cap is **white** rather than purplish.

SPORE PRINT: Cinnamon-brown.

SEASON: Spring through fall.

OTHER NAMES: Slippery Jill is also called Olive-Capped Suillus and *S. subolivaceus*.

COMPARE: Caps of Tamarack Jack (pg. 178) are **reddish-brown with a yellow edge**. Pores are cream-colored at first, becoming yellowish; they **bruise brown**. Stems are **yellowish**, with **brownish to reddish-brown streaks** on the lower part. The stem ring is **cottony and white**; there are no fine dots above it. Flesh is **orangish-yellow** and **bruises brown** or pinkish-brown. It is found near larch trees. • The Short-Stemmed Bolete (*S. brevipes*) is very similar to Slippery Jack, but stems have **no ring** and lack the fine dots at the top. It is found under pines, preferring the two-needle and three-needle varieties.

OTES: The species above are edible. Caps remain slimy after cooking and the lime may cause digestive problems, so some cooks peel caps before cooking; wever, some people get a skin rash from handling the sticky, uncooked caps.

en = key identification feature

Slippery Jack
Slippery Jill

Zeller's Bolete

Xerocomellus zelleri, X. 'atropurpureus'

HABITAT: Although Zeller's Bolete is mycorrhizal and fruits from the ground near living trees (primarily conifers but also hardwoods), it may also be found growing on rotten, moss-covered logs and stumps. *X. 'atropurpureus'* is more common in our area except perhaps east of the Cascades.

DESCRIPTION: Two *Xerocomellus* species with very similar appearances are referred to here as Zeller's Bolete. Both have flattened caps that are **very dark**; those of *X. zelleri* are **brownish-black to purplish-black** and up to 3½ inches wide, while those of *X. 'atropurpureus'* may be **reddish-purple to wine-purple** and 4 inches or more wide. Caps of *X. zelleri* often have a **paler margin** and are **velvety** when young, becoming rough or wrinkly with age; those of *X. 'atropurpureus'* usually lack the pale edge and are not velvety. Both have **yellowish** pore surfaces that **do not bruise blue** except on waterlogged specimens. The flesh is yellowish and typically unchanging when cut, but may slowly turn bluish on older specimens. Stems are 1 to 3 inches tall and yellowish, but are so heavily covered with tiny red spots that they appear **reddish**, ranging from rosy red to dark red.

SPORE PRINT: Olive-brown.

SEASON: Spring through fall.

OTHER NAMES: *X. zelleri, X. truncatus* and *X. chrysenteron* were formerly listed in the *Boletus* genus.

COMPARE: Several similar Boletes in our area may be called Cracked-Cap Bolete; they were all thought to be *X. chrysenteron*, a European species not found in our area. The most common of this group is *X. 'diffractus.'* Cracked-Cap Boletes have **olive-brown to bright tan** caps up to 4 inches wide. They are dry and velvety when young, developing **numerous surface cracks** as they mature. The cap surface between the cracks is yellowish, becoming pinkish or reddish (the pinkish or reddish cap surface more reliable in *X. truncatus*, another of the Cracked-Cap Boletes). Pores are pale yellow to greenish-yellow, **bruising blue slowly**. • Caps of Smith's Bolete (*Boletus smithii*) are **olive-yellow to buff with reddish overtones**, sometimes reddish overall; they are up to 6 inches wide. Pores are yellowish, **immediately changing to blue** when bruised.

NOTES: Zeller's Boletes are edible and considered good. The others here are edible but not favored; they may be bland and mushy.

green = key identification feature

Zeller's Bolete

X. 'diffractus'

Black Foot Mushrooms

Polyporus badius, Polyporus leptocephalus

HABITAT: These common mushrooms are saprobes that get their nutrients from decaying wood. They grow singly or in groups from fallen trees, branches and sticks, primarily from deciduous trees but occasionally from conifers.

DESCRIPTION: These polypores have smooth, tough, funnel-shaped caps that grow flatter as they expand, often developing a wavy edge. Under the cap they have a fine white to pale buff pore surface that runs partway down the stem; pores are circular to honeycombed. Stems may be whitish, tan or brown at the top but are always **black at the base**; there is no ring. The stem location varies from centered to completely off to one side and everywhere in between. Stems may be so short that the mushroom may look like a shelf fungus at first glance. • Caps of Big Black Foot (*Polyporus badius*) are up to **6 inches** wide. They are typically **reddish-brown to orangish-brown**; edges may be paler and the center is often darker, at times nearly black. Stems are black at the base on young specimens, becoming almost **entirely black** on mature specimens. • Little Black Foot (*Polyporus leptocephalus*) is **smaller**, seldom larger than 2 inches wide. They have **uniformly colored** caps that are pale yellowish-brown, tan or cream-colored. Stems are black on the lower half, sometimes only on the base.

SPORE PRINT: White.

SEASON: Late spring through fall.

OTHER NAMES: Some recent references list *Polyporus badius* as *Picipes badius*. *Polyporus leptocephalus* may be listed as *Cerioporus leptocephalus*, *Polyporus varius* or *Polyporus elegans*.

COMPARE: Caps of Fringed Polypore (*Polyporus arcularius*; also called Spring Polypore) are tan to dark-brown and less than 1½ inches wide, with a smooth to wrinkled surface; edges are **fringed with fine hairs**. Pores are **honeycombed** and whitish to cream-colored; stems are colored like the caps, and **do not have a black base**. It fruits primarily on dead hardwoods. • *Polyporus melanopus* is similar to Big Black Foot but a bit smaller; its stems are velvety near the top. It fruits **from the ground** (possibly from buried wood) rather than from exposed wood.

NOTES: The mushrooms above cause white rot of dead trees; old specimens can be found year-round. They are not edible due to their tough texture.

Big Black Foot
Little Black Foot
Fringed Polypore

Larch Suillus (several)

Suillus spp.

HABITAT: Suillus have a mycorrhizal relationship with conifers, growing from the soil near live trees. All discussed here associate exclusively with **western larch**.

DESCRIPTION: Larch Suillus have a **partial veil** covering the gills of young specimens; a ring on the stem is usually present. Pores are angular or irregular in shape, often elongated; they may be arranged in rows that radiate from the stem.

• Two Larch Suillus have **dry, suede-like** caps that are **covered with hairs**. Caps of Hollow-Stalked Larch Suillus (*S. ampliporus*; also listed as *S. cavipes*) are up to 4 inches wide; the overall color is **tan, dark brown or orangish-brown**. Flesh and pore surfaces are pale yellow; **neither changes color** when bruised or cut. A slight, fibrous ring is often present; the stem is **brownish** below the ring, and the lower half is **hollow or pocketed** inside. Caps of Rosy Bolete (*S. ochraceoroseus*) are **pinkish, rosy red or dull red** overall and up to **7 inches** wide. The pore layer is yellowish to dull tan. Flesh is yellowish, and may turn **slightly blue** when cut. Stems are pale gray to yellowish, becoming brownish at the base. Large portions of the veil often remain attached to the cap edge; a thin ring may be present on the stem, but it deteriorates quickly.

• Two Larch Suillus have caps that are **sticky or slimy** in damp weather. The Grayish Larch Bolete (*S. elbensis*; also listed as *S. viscidus*) has grayish to yellowish-brown caps up to 4½ inches wide. The pore layer is whitish to grayish. Flesh is whitish; pores and flesh **slowly stain pale bluish-green** when bruised or cut. Caps of Tamarack Jack (*S. clintonianus*; also listed as *S. grevillei*) are up to 5½ inches wide and **reddish-brown with a yellow edge**. Pores are cream-colored to yellowish, **bruising brown**. The ring is **cottony and white**. Stems are **yellow**, with **brownish to reddish-brown streaks** below the ring. Flesh is pale yellow and **bruises brown** or pinkish-brown.

SPORE PRINT: Brownish to reddish-brown.

SEASON: Summer through fall.

THER NAMES: The alternate names listed for the *Suillus* species above apply to -uropean species that are not found in North America.

PARE: Slippery Jack and Slippery Jill (pg. 172) have **fine, glandular dots** on stems above **prominent** rings.

The species listed here are edible but not of particularly high quality.

key identification feature

Hollow-Stalked
Larch Suillus
Grayish Larch Bolete
Rosy Bolete
Tamarack Jack

Admirable Bolete

'Boletus' mirabilis

HABITAT: Unlike most other Boletes that grow from the soil in association with trees, the Admirable Bolete typically fruits **on well-decayed logs and stumps**, primarily of hemlock; it occasionally fruits from the ground near rotted wood.

DESCRIPTION: This handsome Bolete has **dark reddish-brown, dark brown to maroon-brown** caps that are covered with short hairs, providing a **plush or velvety** texture that may feel slightly rough. Caps are typically 2 to 7 inches wide; cap margins may be paler. Pore surfaces are pale yellow to olive-yellow, with small to moderately large pores that are rounded to irregular; they appear sunken around the top of the stem and **do not change color** when bruised. There is no veil or stem ring. The club-shaped stems are up to 8 inches tall and often have **bulbous bases** that may be 2 inches or more thick. Stems are **dark brown to reddish-brown**, sometimes with **yellowish or brownish streaks**. The tops of the stems typically have shaggy reticulation (mesh-like texture); the remainder may have long, bark-like ridges but may also be fairly smooth.

SPORE PRINT: Olive-brown.

SEASON: Summer through fall.

OTHER NAMES: Admirable Bolete is also called The Admiral, and may be listed as *Aureoboletus mirabilis, Boletellus mirabilis* and *Xerocomus mirabilis.*

COMPARE: Two Boletes with similar appearance are found in our area; they fruit **from the soil** rather than on wood and are found in mixed-wood forests. Both are slightly smaller than the Admirable Bolete; their caps have **fine, felt-like** surfaces. Suede Bolete (*Boletus subtomentosus*; also listed as *X. subtomentosus*) has **medium-brown to yellowish-brown** caps. Pores are yellow to buff-colored, becoming bright yellow with age; they **bruise blue**. Stems are **pale yellow to whitish** with **widely spaced reticulation** on the upper half. Flesh is whitish and may develop weak bluish stains when cut. • *Boletus fibrillosus* (pgs. 32–33) has dark brown to cinnamon-brown caps; stems are brownish and **lack the bulbous base**. Flesh and pores **do not change color** when cut or bruised.

TES: The Admirable Bolete is common in our area. It is edible and considered good find, with a taste that has been described as buttery and lemony; caps / become soft with age and exposure to rain, but stems remain firm and 'e. *Boletus fibrillosus* is generally considered a good edible; Suede Bolete are but generally not sought out for the table.

= key identification feature

Admirable Bolete

Admirable Bolete

Suede Bolete

Kurotake

Boletopsis leucomelaena, B. grisea

HABITAT: The Boletopsis discussed here are mycorrhizal, and fruit from the ground near trees. They may be found singly, scattered or in small groups in mixed woods. *B. leucomelaena* typically associates with spruce; *B. grisea* is more likely to be found near pine species. Both are common in our area.

DESCRIPTION: The name Kurotake is used to refer to several closely related *Boletopsis* species that are difficult to separate visually; they are sometimes referred to as the *Boletopsis leucomelaena* group, which also includes *B. grisea* and perhaps others that are as yet unnamed. These cap-and-stem mushrooms have pores, much like Boletes, but the flesh and pore surface are **tough**—somewhat like polypores (shelf mushrooms with pores; see pgs. 198–219). *B. leucomelaena* is sometimes described as being taller and thinner than *B. grisea*, with caps that are consistently darker. In general, caps of Kurotake are dingy white or gray when young, developing dark streaks or blotches over time; caps of mature specimens may be **dark gray or blackish** overall (particularly in *B. leucomelaena*) and are up to 8 inches wide. Edges are often wavy or irregular. The pore surface is **bright white**, darkening slightly with age; it extends down slightly onto the top of the stem. The pores are finely textured and angular to rounded in shape. Stems are 1½ to 4 inches tall and one-third to one-half as thick; they are dull white to pale gray, developing **darker streaks** with age. The stems may be attached to the caps somewhat off-center; stem bases are tapered. There is no ring.

SPORE PRINT: White to pale brown.

SEASON: Summer through fall.

OTHER NAMES: *B. subsquamosa* is used in some references to refer to the two *Boletopsis* species discussed here.

COMPARE: *Albatrellus* species have similar growth forms, but their coloration is usually quite different; they are found near conifers. **Flett's Polypore** (pg. 184) is one of the closest in color. Its caps are **grayish-blue**, and it develops orangish -racks or patches with age. ***A. avellaneus*** looks somewhat like a young, pale- -pped Boletopsis; its caps are **whitish to pinkish-tan, with orangish areas**. -s are less than 4 inches across.

· Kurotake are typically very bitter, but soaking in brine or drying tempers -terness; some consider it a choice edible when it is properly prepared.

key identification feature

B. leucomelaena

A. avellane

FROM THE SOIL NEAR LIVE TREES

SUMMER THROUGH FALL

Flett's Polypore

Albatrellopsis flettii

HABITAT: Flett's Polypore is mycorrhizal, fruiting from the ground near trees; it associates primarily with conifers but also appears in mixed woods. It may be found scattered or in groups and is common in our area.

DESCRIPTION: This fairly large mushroom is easy to recognize, with its **bluish** caps up to 8 inches wide. The blue tones range from pale blue, bright blue or royal blue on young specimens, to pale grayish-blue, smoky bluish-gray or greenish-blue on older specimens; colors may be mottled, and caps often develop orangish areas. The cap surface is dry and smooth, sometimes with a velvety feel; older specimens may develop extensive **surface cracks**. The flesh inside the caps and stems is **white**, with a tough texture. The pore surface is **bright white**, darkening with age and sometimes developing orangish stains; it extends down onto the top of the stem, sometimes for a fair distance. Pores are finely textured and angular to rounded in shape. Stems are 2 to 6 inches tall and about one-quarter as thick; they are dull white, developing orangish stains and becoming dingy gray with age. Flett's Polypore often grows in clumps containing several specimens **fused together** at the bases.

SPORE PRINT: White.

SEASON: Summer through fall.

OTHER NAMES: Blue-Capped Polypore, *Albatrellus fletti, Polyporus fletti.*

COMPARE: ***Albatrellopsis confluens*** (also listed as *Albatrellus confluens*) is closely related and very similar, but its caps are **buff-colored, pale orange, tan or pinkish-buff**. • The ***Albatrellus ovinus*** **group** includes *Albatrellus ovinus, Albatrellus avellaneus* (pg. 182) and *Albatrellus subrubescens*. Caps are **white or ivory-colored** when young, becoming **tan or pinkish-tan**. Flesh is **pale yellow**, and shows through the cracks that develop with age; pores turn **yellowish** when bruised or with age. • **Little Blue Polypore** (*Neoalbatrellus subcaeruleoporus*) is much **smaller**, less than 2 inches wide and 2½ inches tall; caps and pores are **bright blue to grayish-blue**. • Caps of **Greening Goat's Foot** (pg. 193) may be over 10 inches wide. They are yellowish-brown, bright yellow or greenish, often a mix of these colors; they are **hairy or plush** when young, becoming **scaly**. The white flesh and pores **bruise or stain greenish**. Stems are chunky and up to 4 inches tall.

S: All species discussed here are edible but not considered choice.

n = key identification feature

Flett's Polypore
Albatrellus ovinus

Chicken Fat Suillus

Suillus americanus (also listed as *S. sibiricus*)

This common mushroom is also called White Pine Bolete because it grows singly, scattered or prolifically from the soil near **white pine** (exclusively). It is fairly small, typically less than 4 inches wide and tall. It has **dull to bright yellow** caps that are **slimy** or slippery in damp weather; both the color and greasy feel account for its common name. Caps are fairly flat when mature, with a **slight peak** in the center; they may have reddish-brown patches around the edges, and are often marked with reddish streaks. There may be veil remnants hanging on the cap edge; the stem may have a faint ring but it is usually absent. The stem is **slender** and often bent; it has small, raised **brown dots** and **stains brown** when handled. The flesh is yellow and **stains pinkish-brown** when cut or bruised. Pores are fairly large and angular; like the cap, the pore surface is yellow. Chicken Fat Suillus has cinnamon-brown spore print and is found from late summer through early fall.

MPARE: Caps of less-common Slim Jack (*S. flavidus*; also listed as *S. umbonatus*, may be the same or a different species) are yellowish-buff to olive-buff and have a **distinct, raised hump** called an umbo; they often have reddish to streaks. Stems are whitish and have a **ragged ring** that is pressed tightly the ring is translucent at first, becoming brown from falling spores.

pecies here are edible but not prized; Chicken Fat is sometimes col- ble. Caps remain slimy when cooked and are often peeled before ople get a skin rash from handling the sticky, uncooked caps.

ation feature

Dotted-Stalk Suillus

Suillus 'granulatus' (also listed as *S. weaverae*)

Dotted-Stalk Suillus is mycorrhizal, growing from the soil near pines. Caps are **pinkish-buff, brown or tan**, often spotted or streaked with cinnamon-brown. They are typically 2 to 4 inches wide and shiny when dry but sticky when damp. The pore surface is cream-colored, becoming yellowish and coarser with age; it bruises dull cinnamon, and may be **dotted with beads of moisture** in damp weather. Stems are up to 3 inches tall and **white** with **minute tan dots** that are **more concentrated at the top**; stems become yellow with age, particularly at the top. There is **no ring**. Flesh is white to yellow and **does not change color** when cut. Spores are cinnamon-brown. Found from spring through fall; common.

COMPARE: Wooly Pine Bolete (*S. tomentosus*) has dingy buff to orangish-yellow caps that are **covered with fine, pale hairs** when young, developing **olive-gray to reddish-brown scales** as it ages. Stems are **yellowish** with brownish dots. Pores are brownish and flesh in the stems is yellowish; both pores and flesh slowly **stain blue** when bruised or cut. • Caps of Short-Stemmed Bolete (*S. brevipes*) are **dark brown** and **slimy**. Stems are less than 2 inches tall; they are whitish, turning yellowish, and have **no dots**. Pores are yellowish and do not stain. • *S. punctatipes* has dark brown caps that are very **slimy** and often streaked. Stems are white to yellowish, with **brown dots and smears** in the top half. Pores are **large** an whitish, turning yellow; they are arranged in **rows that radiate from the stem**

NOTES: Species here are edible; caps should be peeled to prevent stomach up

Tiger's Eye

Coltricia perennis

This attractive mushroom grows singly or in small groups **from the soil**, often in areas of disturbed ground such as paths and roadsides; it is usually found near conifers. Caps are funnel-shaped when young, opening up and becoming round to slightly irregular and up to 4 inches wide; they are **thin** and wavy, featuring **concentric rings in various shades of brown**. The surface is **velvety**, and the **texture often varies** from ring to ring. Young specimens are leathery, becoming brittle with age. The pores under the cap are elongated, eventually becoming angular; they run down the stem somewhat. They are whitish to buff-colored on young specimens, becoming darker with age; they bruise brown. Stems are fairly short, seldom longer than 1½ inches; they are orangish-brown and velvety, often wider at the base. Two or more individuals may fuse together at the base. Spores are yellowish-brown. Its growing season is from summer through fall. Common.

COMPARE: Shiny Cinnamon Polypore (*C. cinnamomea*) is less than 2 inches wide; young specimens are **shiny**, becoming velvety with age. Caps are more **reddish-brown**, with fainter ring zones. Found in hardwood forests; uncommon. • Caps of *C. montagnei* are up to **5 inches** wide and up to ¾ inch thick. The pores are arranged in **concentric gill-like plates**. It is rare. • Stems of Black Foot Mushrooms (pg. 176) are **black at the base**, sometimes nearly overall, and the pores are finer. They fruit **on decaying wood**.

NOTES: These mushrooms dry well and are used in decorative arrangements.

Green = key identification feature

Conifer Bolete

Caloboletus conifericola (also listed as Dark Bitter Bolete and *Boletus coniferarum*)

One of the keys to identification of this mycorrhizal mushroom is that all parts quickly **turn blue** when cut or bruised. Caps are typically 3 to 10 inches wide and **brownish-gray to olive-gray**, with a suede-like texture; the surface may develop cracks with age. The pores are very fine and pale yellow, darkening slightly with age; after bruising blue they become **brownish**. Stems are up to 5 inches tall and very sturdy; bases are often **club-shaped**. They are yellow at first, gradually becoming colored like the cap from the base upwards. **Fine reticulation** (net-like pattern) covers the stem at the top and often overall; it is pale and may be hard to see. Stems have no ring. The spores are olive-brown. This common Bolete fruits singly, scattered or in groups near conifers from summer through fall.

COMPARE: Two additional Boletes in our area have similarly colored caps, and turn blue when cut or bruised. Both are referred to as Bitter Bolete or Red-Stemmed Bitter Bolete, and are found in montane conifer forests. *C. 'calopus'* (also listed as *B. calopus*; common) is often slightly smaller. Stems are **deep red to scarlet** except at the top, which is yellowish. The reticulation is **paler** than the stem color, making it easy to see. Bitter Bolete may be found in mixed woods, under hardwoods as well as conifers. The less-common *C. rubripes* has reddish stems like *C. 'calopus,'* but there is **no reticulation**; the lower portion of the stem may be streaked.

NOTES: The species listed here are very bitter-tasting; they may surprise a forager who has mis-identified them as a King Bolete and then cooked them.

Bitter Iodine Polypore

Jahnoporus hirtus (also listed as *Polyporus hirtus, Albatrellus hirtus*)

This common saprobe typically fruits from the ground near conifer stumps and trees, decomposing buried roots and other wood; it may also grow directly on rotting stumps or logs. Caps are up to 7 inches wide and **brownish, tan or dark brown**, with a velvety surface. They are **irregularly shaped**, with **scalloped or wavy edges**; stems are often off-center, making the caps appear kidney-shaped. Pores are angular and whitish, becoming darker with age; they **run down the stem**, often covering a good portion of it. Stems are 1 to 4 inches tall and generally distinct, although they may flow from the cap in funnel-like fashion. They are whitish on young specimens, becoming brownish; the base is often deeply buried in the soil. Flesh is whitish, firm and tough, and thick where the caps merge with the stems. Spores are white. Bitter Iodine Polypores are found in the fall.

COMPARE: *Bondarzewia occidentalis* typically fruits in **rosette fashion**, with multiple caps coming from a common base. The grouping of caps may be over a foot wide. Caps are velvety and brownish to brownish-yellow overall; centers are dark, becoming paler towards the edges; they may appear faintly zoned. Pores are whitish and irregularly shaped, often becoming **tooth-like** with age; they may **weep milky fluid** when cut. Stems are indistinct and funnel-like. It is edible but somewhat tough and often bitter. *B. mesenterica* and *B. montana* are quite similar, and are sometimes considered part of a species group. Both are common.

NOTES: Bitter Iodine Polypore is bitter and inedible, with an iodine-like smell.

Western Painted Suillus

Suillus lakei

Young, fresh specimens of this common mushroom are distinctive and quite attractive, with yellowish to orangish-tan caps that are decorated with a **dense layer of scales and fibers** that are reddish-brown, brick-colored or dark brown. Caps are dry to slightly slimy and up to 6 inches wide, often with whitish veil remnants hanging from the edge. The scales may disintegrate with age, leaving the caps smooth and yellowish-brown to buff-colored. The angular pores are yellowish, bruising **brownish**; they may be arranged in rows that radiate from the stem. A thin whitish to yellowish ring is present towards the tops of the stems, but it soon disappears. Stems are typically about 3 inches tall on mature specimens; they are yellowish above the ring and **streaked with brownish or reddish fibers** below. Flesh is yellow, remaining unchanged or turning slightly pinkish when cut except at the stem base, which turns **slightly blue or bluish-green**, particularly on young specimens. Spores are cinnamon-brown. Western Painted Suillus are mycorrhizal, associating exclusively with **Douglas fir**, often the company of Rosy Gomphidius (pg. 138); they fruit from spring through fa

COMPARE: Blue-Staining Suillus (*S. caerulescens*) has **slimy** yellowish-bro reddish-brown caps streaked with scattered reddish fibers. Pores are turning **dull brick-red** when bruised. When cut, the yellow flesh st **blue** at the base of the stem.

NOTES: Both species are edible but not favored.

Peppery Bolete

Chalciporus piperatus (also listed as *Boletus piperatus*)

The caps of young Peppery Bolete are **yellowish-brown to reddish-brown**, fading with maturity; they are typically 2 to 3 inches wide and are sticky when moist. The pores are **cinnamon-brown**, darkening to reddish-brown; they are fine near the cap edge, becoming larger and angular near the stem. They may run slightly down the stem on young specimens; on older specimens, the pore surface becomes sunken around the stem. Pores stain brownish when bruised. Stems are up to 3¾ inches tall and **colored like the caps** except at the base, which is **yellowish** from abundant clinging myceliuym (threadlike fungal roots). There is no ring. Flesh is buff-colored except at the base, which is yellowish; the flesh picks up some pale purplish-brown staining when cut or bruised. No part of this mushroom stains blue. Spores are cinnamon-brown. Peppery Boletes are found singly or scattered under conifers, and sometimes under aspen and other ›ardwoods; they fruit from summer through fall and are common in our area.

›MPARE: *C. piperatoides* (also listed as *B. piperatoides*) is similar in size and overall ›arance to Peppery Bolete; however, the **pores stain bluish to bluish-black** ›bruised, and the flesh—particularly in the cap—may also turn bluish when ›es are olive-colored. Other differences are microscopic. Rare in our area.

the name suggests, Peppery Bolete has a distinctly peppery, hot taste. ›as inedible, although some sources say that cooking diminishes the *C. piperatoides* is also peppery and regarded as inedible.

›tification feature

Greening Goat's Foot

Albatrellus ellisii (also called Scaly Yellow Polypore and listed as *Scutiger ellisii*)

This **rough-looking** mushroom has caps that may be over 10 inches wide. They are yellowish-brown, bright yellow or greenish, often a mix of these colors; the dry surface is **hairy or plush** on young specimens, becoming **scaly** as the hairs mat together with age. The pore surface is white when young, turning yellowish or dull greenish with age; it turns **greenish or yellowish-green** when bruised. The pores are large and typically run down the stems, which may be up to 4 inches tall and half as wide. Stems are solid and firm, typically attached to the cap off-center or even at the side; they may be whitish, greenish or colored like the cap. Several specimens may grow together from a fused base. The flesh is firm and white; it may slowly turn greenish to bluish when cut. Spores are white. Greening Goat's Foot grows singly, scattered or in groups under conifers; it is common in the Cascades. It fruits in the fall; specimens may persist for some time.

COMPARE: Goat's Foot (*A. pes-caprae*) is similar in appearance, but its caps a **darker brown to reddish-brown, with no greenish tones**; the scales on cap are **finer**. It is less common in our area.

NOTES: In spite of their unappealing appearance, young specimens mushrooms are edible, but somewhat tough; they should be cook and thoroughly.

Elfin Saddles (several)

Helvella spp.

HABITAT: These unusual-looking mushrooms fruit from the ground near living hardwoods and conifers; they are often found along paths and streams.

DESCRIPTION: Several Elfin Saddles inhabit our area. They have thin-fleshed caps that appear **folded, lobed or saddle-like**; undersides of most are paler than the outsides. Many are known as ***fluted-stalk Helvellas***; stems are wide and heavily ribbed, with numerous pockets or cavities along the ribs, and the interiors are chambered. • Smooth-Stalked Helvella (*H. elastica*) is the most common Helvella in our area. Stems are **smooth** and whitish to cream-colored; they are slender and typically 2 to 4 inches tall. They are hollow and **round in cross-section**; bases may have shallow grooves but are not fluted or ribbed. Caps are brown, tan or grayish-brown and usually less than 2 inches across; undersides are **smooth**. They typically have two lobes that appear to be folded together; edges are rolled inward, giving a pillowy appearance. • Fluted Black Helvella (*H. vespertina*) is the most common of the fluted-stalk Helvellas in our area. Stems are whitish to grayish and may be up to **9 inches** tall, although they are usually shorter. Caps are light to dark **gray or black**; they are irregularly lobed and may seem **wrinkled or brain-like**. They are usually about 2 inches wide but may be up to 4 inches wide; the undersides are smooth and the cap margins are typically attached to the stems. • Fluted Brown Elfin Saddle (*H. maculata*) has caps that are pale to dark brown or grayish-brown, and often **mottled** with paler spots; undersides are **downy**. Caps are saddle-shaped or irregularly lobed, and often wrinkled; they are less than 2 inches wide. The margins are free from the stem and may be rolled upwards on young specimens. The fluted stems are whitish and up to 4 inches tall. • Fluted White Helvella (*H.crispa*) is very similar to the Fluted Brown Elfin Saddle, but its caps are **whitish to cream-colored**; undersides are **darker** than the outsides.

ORE PRINT: White to pale buff; spore prints are seldom taken of *Helvella* species.

ON: Spring through fall.

NAMES: Fluted Black Helvella was formerly listed as *H. lacunosa*.

: See False Morels: Gyromitras (pgs. 56–57); the Saddle-Shaped False ... pg. 57 is another *Helvella* species.

...llas are considered inedible.

...ification feature

Smooth-Stalked Helvella
Fluted Black Helvella
Fluted Brown Elfin Saddle
Fluted White
Helvella

Mountain Cudonia

Pachycudonia monticola (also listed as *Cudonia monticola*)

This saprobe typically fruits in clusters on conifer debris or rotting conifer wood. Caps are **convoluted or wrinkled**, resembling puckered pillows; some may appear saddle-shaped. They are typically less than 1 inch wide and are pinkish-buff to grayish-brown; they have a **leathery** texture, particularly when dry. Stems are typically 2 to 3½ inches tall and about ¼ inch thick; they are **dull brown to brownish-purple**. Spores are probably colorless. Mountain Cudonia fruits in **mountainous areas** in early spring near melting snowbanks, and continues fruiting into summer; they may occasionally appear in fall.

COMPARE: Common Cudonia (*C. circinans*) is similar but **smaller**, with caps that are less than ¾ inch wide and stems up to 2¼ inches tall. Caps are **pale yellowish-brown, pinkish-tan or beige**; they are **less wrinkled** than Mountain udonia, particularly in wet weather. It is found at lower elevations and is most mmon in fall. • Jelly Babies (*Leotia lubrica*) are similar in shape to the Cudonias here, but their caps are **yellowish-brown to buff-colored**, often with a h tint. The caps are typically ½ to 1 inch wide and **sticky** when wet. Stems arly colored, sometimes more yellowish or golden, and are typically 2 to all; like the caps, they are sticky when wet. They are found near both and conifers, typically fruiting in late fall in our area.

species are regarded as inedible; the Cudonias may be toxic, n raw. All species discussed here are somewhat uncommon.

fication feature

Young Common Stinkhorns

Older Common Stinkhorn

Common Stinkhorn

Phallus impudicus

Stinkhorns start their lives encased in a universal veil, appearing like an egg (see pg. 60 for more details). They grow rapidly, rupturing the egg and soon attaining full stature of **6 to 9 inches**. A **volva** (cup-like remnant of the universal veil) remains at the base of the stem, although it may be buried. Stems are white to cream-colored; they are hollow and slightly rough. Heads are covered with **dark, foul-smelling slime** that carries the spores; the tip is often free of slime. Flies strip away the slime, exposing the pale surface below, which is ridged and pitted. These saprobes are found in wooded areas and also appear in gardens, lawns and other cultivated areas, often growing on wood chips. They fruit in **summer**.

COMPARE: Morels (pgs. 26–30) have pitted, ridged caps that are **never covered with slime**; there is **no volva** at the base. They fruit in **spring**. • Dog Stinkhorn (*Mutinus caninus*) has a **pinkish to orangish** stem with a **netlike** texture. There is **no distinct head**, merely a curved stem with brownish slime at the top that is eventually carried away by flies, leaving a bare stem. • Netted Stinkhorn (*Dictyophora duplicata*) is similar to Common Stinkhorn but has a **white net-like skirt** hanging off the bottom edge of the head that encircles the stem loosely, sometimes hanging down to the ground. • The stem of Lizard's Claw Stinkhorn (*Lysurus cruciatus*) splits at the top into several **finger-like projections** that may be cream-colored, brownish, orangish or reddish. Total height is 4 to 6 inches.

NOTES: Stinkhorns are uncommon in our area. They are inedible.

Birch Polypore

Piptoporus betulinus

HABITAT: Found growing **exclusively on birch trees**, stumps and logs, these polypores are more common on dead wood than on living trees. They grow as individual specimens, although there are typically multiple polypores on each tree. They cause brown rot, acting as both parasites and decomposers.

DESCRIPTION: Although this polypore takes several forms and appears in various colors, it is easy to recognize. It looks like a **pillowy growth** that may be shaped like a half-dome, a hoof, a projecting disk, a kidney or a half-bell that may be distorted. The top surface is dull white, gray, tan or brown; it is smooth at first, often developing wide cracks that **expose the pale inner flesh**. The edge of the cap is rolled inward, creating a **thick, rounded overhang** that surrounds the pore surface. The cap may grow to 10 inches across but is usually smaller. There is no stem, although some specimens may have a thick neck at the point of attachment. The underside is whitish to buff, with **small pores** that may become tooth-like with age.

SPORE PRINT: White.

SEASON: Birch Polypore grows from spring through summer; they often persist over winter, appearing as darkened specimens the next year.

OTHER NAMES: Birch Bracket, Birch Conk, Ice Man Polypore, *Polyporus betulinus*.

COMPARE: Tinder Polypore (pg. 200) grows in a similar fashion, but the surface is **banded** and it grows on a **wide variety of trees**. • Several other mushrooms that grow on trees may resemble Birch Polypore at a quick glance, but they have **gills** rather than pores. These include Oyster Mushrooms (pgs. 38–41), White Beech Mushrooms (pg. 40) and Bear Paw Lentinus (pg. 220).

NOTES: Birch Polypore has long been used for medicinal purposes; indeed, it and Tinder Polypore (pg. 200) were found with the "Tyrolean Iceman," a mummified body from the mid-Neolithic era (the body was carbon-dated to between 3350 and 3100 BC) that was discovered in the Italian Alps in 1991. According to a note published in 1998 in the British medical journal *Lancet*, the Iceman may have been using the Birch Polypore as a laxative, to rid himself of an intestinal parasite. Birch Polypores are bitter and generally regarded as inedible. They are somewhat uncommon in our area.

ON LIVE OR DEAD TREES AND LOGS

PRESENT YEAR-ROUND

Tinder Polypore

Fomes fomentarius

HABITAT: These polypores are found growing on living or dead deciduous trees, stumps and logs; they are common in areas with birch trees. They grow as individual specimens, although there may be multiple polypores on each tree. Tinder Polypore causes white rot, acting as both a parasite and decomposer.

DESCRIPTION: This hard, tough-crusted mushroom looks like a half-dome; its surface is minutely hairy or hard and gray, grayish-brown or tan. It grows directly on the woody substrate and has no stem. The top side is **banded or ridged** both in texture and color; it is dull, dry and hard to the touch. The surface underneath is **cream-colored to brownish** and is covered with fine, rounded pores. Caps are generally 2 to 8 inches across. Young specimens may be as tall as they are wide. With age, they become thicker and expand in width, particularly near the bottom; old specimens often look like a **hoof**. They may develop **slight cracks**.

SPORE PRINT: White.

SEASON: Growth takes place in spring and summer; present year-round.

OTHER NAMES: Firestarter Mushroom, Tinder Conk, Hoof Fungus, *Polyporus fomentarius;* called Amadou in Europe.

COMPARE: Willow Bracket (*Phellinus igniarius*; also listed as *Polyporus igniarius* and *F. igniarius*) is similar in shape to Tinder Polypore, but its upper surface becomes blackened and develops **multiple, plate-like cracks**, giving it a **charred appearance**. It grows in the northern part of our area on willow, poplar, aspen, birch and other deciduous trees, and is a common find in the correct habitat. • Birch Polypore (pg. 198) is similar to Tinder Polypore, but it **lacks the banding** and grows only on birch trees. • Artist's Conk (pg. 204) has **white** pores that instantly **bruise brown**.

NOTES: Tinder Polypore has long been used as a firestarter and an antibiotic; see the note on pg. 198 about the Tyrolean Iceman. Willow Bracket is used by the Inupiaq and Yup'ik peoples of Alaska to prepare a chewing mixture called Iqmik. The polypore is burned and its ashes are mixed with tobacco; the ashes amplify the effects of the nicotine, producing euphoria. Iqmik is used by young and old alike, even though it is addictive and causes tooth loss. There is a campaign by health officials to discourage this practice.

Tinder Polypore (top 2 photos)

Willow Bracket

ON DEAD AND DECAYING WOOD

PRESENT YEAR-ROUND

Turkey Tail

Trametes versicolor

HABITAT: Grows on dead wood such as fallen logs, stumps and standing dead trees; typically found on wood from deciduous trees but may occasionally grow on conifer wood. They are decomposers, causing white rot.

DESCRIPTION: These attractive, common shelf mushrooms grow as **overlapping fan-shaped caps**. They may grow in a rosette or in rows, or may cover the wood like a scaly carpet. Individual caps have **concentric bands** of color. The outer band is typically **cream-colored or tan**, and the rest of the bands are shades of gray, blue, brown or reddish-brown. The surface is silky or velvety (a hand lens may be needed to see the hairs, but they can be felt with the fingers); the bands often alternate from smooth to hairy. Caps are **thin, leathery and flexible**; they range from 1 to 4 inches wide. Edges are **ruffled, scalloped or wavy**. The undersides are covered with **fine, round pores** that are whitish, pale gray or yellowish. The caps have no stem, although they may narrow to a neck at the point of attachment.

SPORE PRINT: White to pale yellow.

SEASON: Turkey Tail fruits from spring through fall; the caps are persistent and may be found for several years, continuing growth in successive seasons.

OTHER NAMES: *Coriolus versicolor, Polyporus versicolor.*

COMPARE: Several other shelf-type mushrooms that grow on wood appear similar but are distinguished by various features. • Caps of ***T. pubescens*** (also listed as *T. velutina*; uncommon) are slightly smaller and **velvety to coarsely hairy**; they are cream-colored to buff overall, **lacking the contrasting bands of color** found on Turkey Tail. • Caps of **Hairy Turkey Tail** (*T. hirsuta*) are **thicker** than those of Turkey Tail; the flesh has **two distinct layers** separated by a thin black line (break or cut a cap at the base to see this). They are densely hairy to coarsely velvety, with bands of beige, grayish, yellowish-brown, buff or pale brown; the outer band is often yellowish-brown and hairy. They are common in our area. • ***T. ochracea*** is uncommon. It has thick flesh like Hairy Turkey Tail, but does not ave the two layers. Caps are paler than Turkey Tail, with more subtle zones.

S: Turkey Tail and the lookalikes listed above are tough and inedible. They sed medicinally and are being studied for anti-cancer properties.

Turkey Tail

T. pubescens

Hairy Turkey Tail

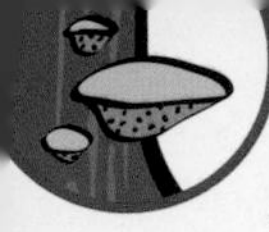

Artist's Conk

Ganoderma applanatum

HABITAT: This common polypore is found growing on living or dead trees, stumps and logs, primarily deciduous but also coniferous; more often found on dead wood than on living trees. They grow as individual specimens, although there may be multiple polypores on each tree. Artist's Conk causes white rot, acting as both a parasite and decomposer.

DESCRIPTION: A tough, woody perennial that grows as a stemless, semicircular shelf, often with irregular, wavy or slightly scalloped edges. Caps range from 2 to **25 inches** across; the body is thick on the side that attaches to the growing substrate, generally becoming thinner towards the edge so it is somewhat wedge-shaped in cross-section. The top surface is **dull, dry and very hard**; it is tan, gray or brownish, often with concentric bands of color. It often develops ridge-like bands as it continues to grow each year; it may also become warty or bumpy and often develops furrows that run from the center toward the edge. The underside is covered with **fine white pores** that instantly turn **dark brown when scratched or bruised**; with age, the pore surface becomes buff-colored and less sensitive to scratches. If the mushroom is cut from top to bottom, layers of pores representing each year's growth will be visible. The mushrooms produce copious amounts of brown spores that are often seen on the growing substrate, or on nearby plants and other objects.

SPORE PRINT: Brown.

SEASON: All year.

OTHER NAMES: Artist's Bracket.

COMPARE: Caps of *G. brownii* are thicker, with a **multi-layered** appearance. The pores are whitish to pale yellow during the growing season, turning brownish when dormant. It is rare in our area. • **Tinder Polypore** (pg. 200) is a tough, dull polypore that is less than 8 inches across and generally much thicker than Artist's Conk; it often appears hoof-like. Its pore surface is **tan or gray** and **does not bruise**.

NOTES: Because it turns dark brown when scratched, Artist's Conk is often used as the medium for scratch art. The cap must be fresh, and the drawings should be done within a few days after removing the cap from the tree. Once the cap dries out, it turns buff-colored; the brown engraved lines remain, creating an unusual piece of art.

ON LIVE OR DEAD TREES AND LOGS

PRESENT YEAR-ROUND

Red-Belted Polypore

Fomitopsis pinicola

HABITAT: This very common mushroom grows on both living and dead trees and is frequently found on stumps and downed wood; it seems to prefer conifers but also grows on deciduous wood. Specimens may grow alone or there may be many on a single tree.

DESCRIPTION: This polypore starts out as a knob, eventually becoming hoof-shaped or sometimes looking like a thick fan. Each year it grows a new band of flesh on the outer edge of the older flesh, which is **hard and woody**. The new band is white to yellowish; there may be beads of moisture on its surface. As the mushroom grows, older portions darken, becoming reddish, then turning reddish-brown, gray and finally blackish; there is typically a **bright or deep red band** near the outer white edge. Younger bands typically have a glossy surface that looks lacquered; on some specimens the entire surface is glossy. The glossy surface will **melt when exposed to the flame** from a match.

SPORE PRINT: White to pale yellowish.

SEASON: Present all year.

OTHER NAMES: *Polyporus pinicola, Fomes pinicola.*

COMPARE: *Fomitopsis ochracea* was first described in 2008. The top surface is **dull** rather than shiny, and **grayish to yellowish-brown**; it **lacks the red band** near the edge. Unlike Red-Belted Polypore, the surface **chars but does not melt** when exposed to a match flame. It is found on both hardwoods and conifers and is fairly common. (Source: *Omphalina*, Vol III, No. 3; March, 2012) • Conifer-Base Polypore (*Heterobasidion occidentale*) often grows as a shelf, with a distinct, irregularly shaped dark cap and a paler pore surface that is often spreading. It may also occasionally appear as a flattened pore surface, sometimes with a small, cap-like edge at the top and sometimes simply a crust-like layer of pores. Caps are **brown to blackish**, often appearing **shingled or layered**; pores are whitish to pale buff. This forest pathogen is found on the undersides of logs, in tree hollows and directly on host trees; it is generally associated with conifers but may also attack hardwoods. It is a notorious and much-feared parasitic tree killer that is common in our area.

NOTES: Red-Belted Polypore has an important role in breaking down woody waste in forests, helping to create material for new soil. It also acts as a parasite on living trees, causing brown rot.

Red-Belted Polypore

Red-Belted Polypore

Fomitopsis ochracea

Conifer-Base Polypore

Lacquered Polypore

Ganoderma oregonense

HABITAT: The Lacquered Polypore grows directly from living or dead trees, as well as from buried roots of trees that have been removed. It fruits singly or in small groups on **coniferous** wood, particularly fir and hemlock. It causes white rot, acting as both parasite and decomposer. It is common west of the Cascades, but less common in the eastern portion of our area.

DESCRIPTION: This species is strikingly beautiful, with a shiny surface that's very colorful. It grows as a shelf-like bracket, frequently near the base of a tree; several individuals may grow in overlapping clusters. It may have a neck-like stalk or may be stalkless. The cap is **semicircular to fan-shaped**, with a somewhat lumpy surface that appears **lacquered**; it may be up to 30 inches across when mature but is typically smaller. It often has concentric zones of color that may be dramatic or subtle. On many young specimens, the outer edge is **white to cream-colored, blending into a yellow zone**; the inner zones are brownish to reddish-brown. Older specimens are mahogany-red, reddish-brown or brownish overall; some have lumpy, ring-like bands. The flesh is spongy on young specimens, becoming firmer with age. The underside is covered with fine whitish or cream-colored pores that turn dull tan with age. The stalk, when present, is colored like the cap. It may be up to 5 inches long and is fairly thick, often appearing knobby and twisted.

SPORE PRINT: Dark rusty brown.

SEASON: Spring through fall.

OTHER NAMES: Western Varnished Conk, *G. sequoiae*.

COMPARE: Members of the *G. lucidum* group are similar in appearance to Lacquered Polypore, but grow from the wood of **deciduous** trees, particularly oak; they are rare in our area. Some mycologists believe the true *G. lucidum* is an Asian species that does not occur in North America.

NOTES: This fungus has been used for medicinal purposes for over 2,000 years in China. It is used to enhance longevity, boost the immune system, reduce blood pressure and treat cancer. Some people are allergic to it.

green = key identification feature

Young Lacquered Polypore
Old Lacquered Polypor

NEAR LIVE, DEAD OR DYING TREES

EARLY SUMMER THROUGH FALL

Dyer's Polypore

Phaeolus schweinitzii

HABITAT: A wood-rotting parasite, this common mushroom is usually found at the base of conifers (rarely deciduous trees) growing from buried roots. It can sometimes be found growing directly from dead or dying wood.

DESCRIPTION: The color and shape of this fungus is quite variable, depending on its age and growing conditions. When young, it is typically spongy and orange to yellowish with a **yellow margin** and a velvety surface; at times it may simply look like a formless blob. It tends to envelop surrounding material as it expands. Single specimens can grow into large rosettes, up to a foot across, with overlapping shelves. With age, it becomes woody and dark brown to black, sometimes with yellow, orange or rust-brown bands of color; it may have lumps on the surface. Underneath is an **olive-gray pore surface** that **bruises brown**. The pores are **large and rough**, becoming angular and almost tooth-like or maze-like with age. The entire mess grows from a stubby, brown stem.

SPORE PRINT: White to creamy yellow.

SEASON: Early summer through fall; grows annually but found year-round

OTHER NAMES: Velvet Top Fungus, *Polyporus schweinitzii.*

COMPARE: Several other mushrooms with similar growth habits and variable appearances are found in our area. Caps of Wooly Velvet Polypore (*Onnia tomentosa;* also listed as *Inonotus tomentosus*) are whitish when young, becoming yellowish-brown, brown or reddish-brown; edges are often paler, and the caps may be subtly zoned. It has **short but distinct stems** that are thick and brownish. Pores are round or angular, becoming tooth-like when old; they are buff-colored to grayish at first, becoming **brownish** with age. It favors spruce trees; uncommon in our area. • Caps of Blushing Rosette (*Abortiporus biennis*; uncommon) are whitish to pale brown; young specimens **ooze drops of red liquid**. Pores are **maze-like** or angular; they are **white to pale pink, bruising reddish-brown**. • Orange Hydnellum (pg. 258) has fused or clustered caps that are very bumpy and orange to brownish with a paler edge. Underneath are white **teeth** that turn brown with age except for the tips, which remain white.

NOTES: Though not edible, the Dyer's Polypore is a favorite of textile dyers because it contains an intense yellow pigment. This same mushroom used with a dye bath or wool treated with iron sulfate produces a beautiful green color.

reen = key identification feature

Young Dyer's Polypore

Mature Dyer's Polypore
Young Blushing Rosette

Wooly Velvet Polypore
Maturing Blushing Rosette

ON DEAD TREES, STUMPS AND LOGS

SUMMER THROUGH FALL

Resinous Polypore

Ischnoderma resinosum

HABITAT: This somewhat uncommon saprobe typically fruits on dead trees, both standing and fallen, as well as on stumps. It may occasionally appear on dying trees in areas where the wood has already succumbed to injury or disease. Although it is generally found on wood of deciduous trees, it occasionally appears on conifers. It may grow singly but is often seen in overlapping clusters.

DESCRIPTION: This mushroom's appearance changes considerably over time, and it may also have varying growth patterns. They usually have well-defined semicircular caps attached directly to the tree, but may also occasionally appear as a flattened pore surface with a small, cap-like edge at the top (as in the bottom right photo). Very young specimens are rounded or lumpy; they are thick, soft and **velvety**, with reddish-brown centers and a white margin. **Amber resin droplets** sometimes appear on cap edges. As the specimens age, they become wider and flatter, often with wavy or scalloped edges. Mature specimens are up to 8 inches wide and roughly 1 inch thick at the base. They are brownish to reddish-brown, often retaining the white margin; the color may be fairly consistent or it may be zoned into concentric rings. Old specimens become wrinkled and develop black, crusty-looking bands interspersed with brownish bands; the surface becomes dry and tough and may develop cracks that radiate from the center to the edges. The underside of young specimens is covered with white pores that **bruise brownish**; with age, the pore surface becomes tan.

SPORE PRINT: White.

SEASON: Summer through fall.

OTHER NAMES: Late Fall Polypore, *Polyporus resinosus.*

COMPARE: Conifer Mazegill (pg. 227) looks similar to mature specimens of Resinous Polypore but is under 5 inches wide and has **slot-like pores and gills** underneath. The cap has concentric bands of color that may be subtle or distinct. Young specimens have bands of orange to rust-brown, while older specimens become dark brown or black in the center; edges are bright yellowish or whitish. It has a **corky** texture.

NOTES: Young, tender specimens of Resinous Polypore are edible when gently stewed; they have a moderately soft texture.

Veiled Polypore

Cryptoporus volvatus (also listed as *Polyporus volvatus*)

Also called the Cryptic Polypore, this round saprobe holds some surprises. From the outside, it looks like a spherical mushroom growing **on a dead conifer**; it may be slightly compressed, appearing somewhat hoof-like, and usually fruits in groups or clusters, often tucked into bark furrows. The outer surface is cream-colored to yellowish-brown, sometimes appearing to have a lacquered layer on the upper half; the surface may be smooth, or may have faint cracks. When a young, fresh specimen is sliced open from top to bottom, the cross-section reveals a fleshy, firm **cap with a thick pore layer beneath it**; the cap margin **extends below like a thick veil**, forming a **hollow space below the tubes**. Bark beetles drill a hole in the underside of the veil and tunnel through the pore layer; when they exit they are covered with spores, spreading them when they lay their eggs on a new host tree. Pores are whitish to buff, turning brown with age. The spore print is cream-colored to pale pinkish-yellow. Veiled Polypore are present from spring through fall, fruiting from the holes where the beetles laid their eggs the previous year. They are common in our area.

COMPARE: Small Puffballs (pgs. 230, 232) appear similar in shape and, often, coloration, but they fruit **from the soil** rather than on trees.

NOTES: Veiled Polypores fruit on recently dead trees, typically appearing the year after they have been killed by fire or bark beetles. They cause white rot of the affected trees.

Cinnabar-Red Polypore

Pycnoporus cinnabarinus (also listed as *Polyporus cinnabarinus*)

It's hard to miss this stunning mushroom in the woods; its bright **orangish-red** coloration draws the eye. It grows as a stemless semicircular or kidney-shaped cap that is attached to fallen or dead deciduous trees, particularly oak; it is occasionally reported on conifers. It typically is not found on very old, rotten wood. This uncommon species is most often found in open areas such as wood edges and powerline cuts. Caps are up to 5 inches across; they are up to ½ inch thick with a thinner edge and are **tough and leathery**. They grow singly or in overlapping clusters. The surface is finely hairy on young specimens, becoming hairless but rough-textured, wrinkled or pockmarked with age; the color may fade to yellowish-orange. The underside is covered with **fine, bright reddish-orange pores** that are rounded or somewhat angular. Its spore print is white, and it grows from summer through fall in our area.

COMPARE: *Pycnoporellus fulgens* (also listed as *Polyporus fibrillosus* in older texts) has a **yellowish-orange cap** and **large pores** that are pale orangish to apricot-colored.

NOTES: Both species discussed here should be considered inedible.

Blue Cheese Polypore

Postia caesia group (also listed as *Tyromyces caesius* and *Oligoporus caesius*)

This soft, watery polypore is a saprobe that prefers the wood of deciduous trees but may be found on conifer wood. It grows singly or in small groups that are often overlapping. The cap is roughly semicircular with wavy edges but may also be irregularly lumpy; it is up to 3 inches across and has no stem. The surface is **dirty white to grayish** and is covered with fine hairs that may be grayish-blue; it develops **bluish-gray or bluish tones** with age or handling and is not zoned. The bottom surface is whitish to gray, becoming grayish-blue or grayish-purple with age or handling; pores are moderately coarse and angular, developing a tooth-like appearance with age. The flesh is spongy and whitish, bruising grayish-blue; it has a pleasant fragrance. Its spore print is pale blue; it grows from summer through fall and is fairly common in our area.

COMPARE: White Cheese Polypore (*T. chioneus*; also listed as *T. albellus*) is similar, but both surfaces are **white**, lacking the grayish or bluish tones; it grows on dead wood of conifer and deciduous trees.

NOTES: These polypores are not regarded as edible; some say they have a soapy taste.

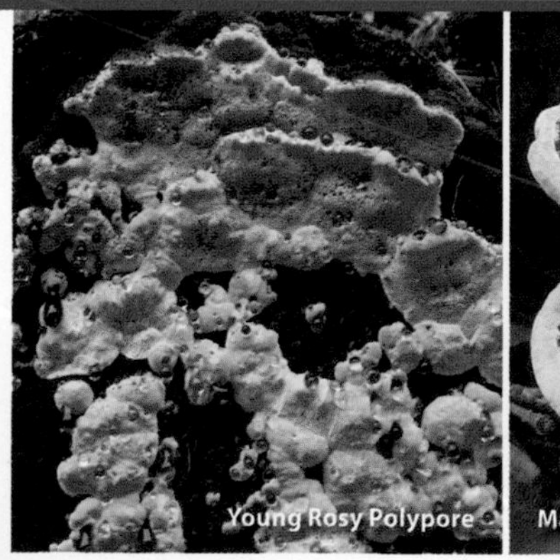
Young Rosy Polypore

Mature Rosy Polypore

Rosy Polypore

Rhodofomes cajanderi (also listed as *Fomitopsis cajanderi*)

Young Rosy Polypores don't look like a shelf fungus. This species starts out as blobs of **pinkish pore masses**; **reddish droplets** are present on the surface in damp weather. The brackets that follow are hoof-shaped at first, soon becoming fan-shaped; the upper sides are pinkish-brown, dark reddish-brown or blackish, typically with a **pale pink margin**. Mature brackets are typically about 4 inches wide and up to ¾ inch thick; the surface may be smooth or rough, and may have small irregular bumps on it. The fine pore surface below is **rose-pink to pinkish-red** at first, becoming reddish-brown with age. Young specimens are fairly soft, but the flesh soon becomes hard and **corky or woody**. Spores are white. This common species fruits primarily on conifers, singly or in clusters that may be overlapped. Its growth season is in fall, but the polypores are present year-round.

COMPARE: *R. roseus* (also listed as *F. rosea*) may be nearly 5 inches wide and 1¼ inches thick; they are often **hoof-shaped at maturity**, but may also be fan-shaped. Pores of young specimens are **pale pink**. Other differences are microscopic. • ***Leptoporus mollis*** (also listed as *Polyporus mollis*) is a soft, irregularly shaped whitish, pinkish or pale salmon-colored shelf with a white to pale reddish-purple pore surface below. The pore surface is thick and **extends below the shelf** for some distance. This species is rare in our area, found on dead conifers.

NOTES: The species here are not known to be edible. Rosy Polypore is bein studied for medicinal purposes.

Agaricon

Laricifomes officinalis (also listed as *Fomitopsis officinalis*)

If you find a good-size Agaricon, you won't have any question about its identity. They are **multi-layered columns** that can be **12 to 18 inches wide**; very old specimens may be nearly **4 feet long**. Young specimens are pillowy and white, and soft enough to press a finger into. They become hoof-like as they grow, developing a hard crust with a **whitish** pore surface underneath; a spore print of the fresh pore layer will be whitish. Additional layers are added at the bottom each year; the outer surfaces are white to yellowish at first, turning grayish to yellowish-brown with age. The fruitbody **hangs free of the host tree except at the top**. The surface may develop cracks over time, and algae often covers the older layers. Flesh in older portions is corky or chalky, becoming crumbly when very old. They are perennial and may live for decades if not disturbed. They grow as individual specimens, although several may be found on the same tree. They are found on living or dead conifers, particularly larch and Douglas fir; an alternate common name for them is Larch Polypore. They are not common in our area.

COMPARE: Young specimens of Tinder Polypore (pg. 200) are hoof-like, similar to young Agaricon, but the pore surface underneath is **pale brown or gray**. Tinder Polypore may also appear to grow in long columns, but these are composed of maller, individual fruitbodies, each of which is **attached to the host tree** rather an hanging free.

TES: Agaricon is not edible, but has been used medicinally for centuries.

reen = key identification feature

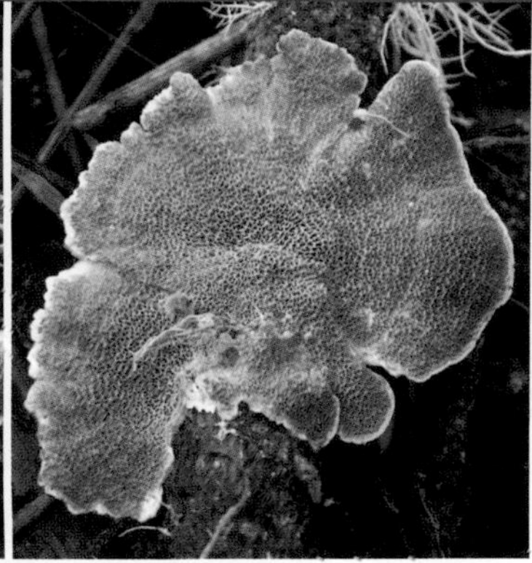

Purplepore Bracket

Trichaptum abietinum

This **tough, thin** polypore is common worldwide in temperate northern conifer forests, and is found on dead or dying **conifers**. Individual brackets are generally **fan-shaped** with irregular edges; they are typically less than 1½ inches across, although several may fuse together to form a unit up to 4 inches across. Purplepore Bracket is usually found in **colonies of overlapping shelves**; individual caps may project an inch or more from the wood. It may also grow as a flat crust with just a slightly folded-over edge at the top; when found on the underside of a dead tree, it is often entirely flat, with no cap-like edge. The top surface is whitish to pale gray and coarsely hairy or fuzzy; it often has ring-like zones of color, and the **outer edge is purplish** on young specimens. Older specimens are often covered with green algae. The underside of young specimens is covere with **purplish pores** that are round to angular; with age, the pores turn browni and become **ragged**, appearing almost tooth-like. Spores are white. Its gro season begins in late summer to early fall, but the brackets are slow to dec may be found all year.

COMPARE: Violet-Toothed Polypore (*T. biforme*) is similar, but it fruit and dying **hardwoods**. Individual caps may be over **2 inches** ac frequently **narrower at the base**, appearing petal-like.

NOTES: *Abietinum* refers to *Abies*, which is the genus for fir sp host for this saprobe.

ON DEAD AND DECAYING WOOD

FALL THROUGH SPRING

Bear Paw Lentinus

Lentinellus ursinus

HABITAT: This saprobe gets its nutrients from decaying wood. It may grow singly but is usually found in overlapping clusters on dead conifers and hardwoods.

DESCRIPTION: Bear Paw Lentinus gets its species name from *ursa*, the Latin word for bear, due to its brown color and **hairy surface**. Caps are fan-shaped, shell-shaped or kidney-shaped, and up to 4 inches wide; edges are wavy and may appear irregularly lobed. They are hygrophanous (pg. 11), becoming darker when moist and paler when dry. The surface is generally brown, reddish-brown or brownish-black, fading to tan in dry weather; the outer edge is typically lighter in color. These mushrooms are **stemless**; the caps fan out from a hairy base that is attached to the decaying wood on which the mushrooms are growing. Gills are **closely spaced** and white, buff-colored or pale pinkish-brown, with distinctly **serrated** edges; they radiate up and outward from the point of attachment.

SPORE PRINT: White.

SEASON: Bear Paw Lentinus fruits in spring, and again from fall through winter.

OTHER NAMES: *L. ursinus* is the name of a European species that may be somewhat different from the species found here; a new name may be determined for the North American version in the future.

COMPARE: Several similarly sized *Lentinellus* species are found in our area. Fox Lentinus (*L. vulpinus*) has yellowish-tan caps with **short stems** that **fuse with neighboring stems** to form a thicker base. They grow in overlapping clusters on decaying hardwood. ***L. montanus*** is similar in color to Bear Paw Lentinus and also lacks a stem, but its gills are more **widely spaced**. It fruits on conifers at higher elevations in spring, sometimes near snowbanks. Other differences are icroscopic. • The Shoehorn Oyster (*Hohenbuehelia petaloides*) has a **smooth, lled cap** and a wide, off-center stem that gives it a funnel-like appearance. own to grayish-brown caps are moist to gelatinous. It fruits on rotting od logs, on buried wood and in lawns or areas with woody debris; it ears in planted beds or with potted plants. • Hairy Panus (pg. 223) has sh-brown to pinkish-brown caps, but it has short stems; gill edges not serrated.

species are said to have an extremely bitter or hot taste and for the table. Those discussed here are uncommon in our area.

ion feature

Bear Paw Lentinus

Fox Lentinus

Shoehorn Oyster

Split Gill

Schizophyllum commune

This small mushroom acts as both a parasite and decomposer, getting its nutrients from the wood of decaying or dead deciduous trees; it may also grow on processed lumber. Although small and easily overlooked, it has intriguing features when viewed closely; a hand lens is helpful. Caps are **fuzzy** and white to grayish above. They are up to 1½ inches wide and are fan-shaped or irregularly lobed; edges are minutely **scalloped**. They grow scattered, layered or in rosettes. The underside is pinkish-gray, with **doubled or split gill-like structures** that fan out from the center to the edge. These "gills" are really a folded pore surface; they pull together in dry weather to protect the spores within but open to release them when moisture is present. In fact, the entire mushroom will curl up and appear even smaller when dry but rehydrate and regain its shape when wet. This tough little shelf can last for many seasons. Its spore print is white; it is found year-round.

COMPARE: Various Creps (pg. 224) appear similar, but they have **true, knife-edged gills** rather than split gill-like folds. Cap edges may be wavy but are **not scalloped**. Creps are inedible.

IOTES: Many experts call Split Gill the most common and widespread mush-om in the world. Although it is a traditional food in certain cultures, it is not ommended. It is small and tough, and has been known to infect humans with promised immune systems. It is being studied for possible medicinal uses.

en = key identification feature

Hairy Panus

Lentinus strigosus (also listed as *Panus rudis, Panus neostrigosus*)

This mushroom, which is less than 4 inches across, has several different forms, from an almost stemless shelf to a short-stemmed funnel. Caps are pinkish-tan, purplish, reddish-brown or orangish, and **hairy to velvety**, with rolled-under edges. Stems are also hairy and less than 1 inch long; they may be off-center. Gills are closely spaced and **run down the stem**; they are colored like the cap when young, turning white with age. Spores are **white**. This saprobe gets its nutrients from rotting hardwood, especially cut or fallen logs and stumps. It grows singly, in loose groups, or more often in tight clusters, fruiting from spring through fall.

COMPARE: Smooth Panus (*Panus conchatus*) is up to 6½ inches wide, with stems up to 2 inches tall. Caps are **smooth** and more purplish, especially when young. • Styptic Panus (*Panellus stipticus*) is generally 1 inch across or less. The semicircular cap fans outward from a short stem near the inside edge. Caps are velvety and tan or buff-colored. Gills are attached to the stem and **do not run down it**. They are light brown and forked, with numerous **cross-veins**. Gills of young, fresh specimens glow in the dark (called bioluminescent). • Orangish specimens of Hairy Panus may be mistaken for a faded Mock Oyster (pg. 225), but Mock Oyster is **stemless** and more **brightly colored**; it has a **pink to tan** spore print.

NOTES: Hairy Panus and Styptic Panus shrivel up in dry weather, re-hydrating when wet. All the species noted above are inedible, and uncommon. Styptic Panus is used in traditional Chinese medicine as a blood thickener and purgative.

Peeling Oysterling

Creps (several)

Crepidotus spp.

These small, **stemless** caps grow in loose groups on well-rotted deciduous wood, especially fallen logs and branches; they resemble tiny Oyster Mushrooms (pgs. 38–41) and are sometimes called Oysterlings. Caps are typically fan-shaped, but may be nearly circular when growing under a log. Gills are **crowded** and fan out from the point of attachment, which often has fuzzy mycelium (root-like fungal filaments) at the base. Gills are white at first; spores are brown, coloring the gills and often the caps of surrounding specimens. Creps fruit from spring through fall; common. • Peeling Oysterling (*C. mollis*; pictured above) is larger than most Creps, up to **2½ inches** wide. Caps are tan to beige when moist, turning pale grayish-beige when dry; **minute brown scales** decorate the top. The cap surface is **gelatinous** and the flesh is soft, giving it the alternate name of Jelly Crep. • The Flat Crep (*C. applanatus*) is less than 2 inches wide, with white caps that become brownish with age; cap surfaces may be smooth or have scattered fibers. • Caps of Little White Crep (*C. epibryus*) are **bright white**; they are generally less than 1 inch wide and often **nearly round**. They **curl inwards from the edges**, often forming a half-dome. The cap surface is silky to downy, becoming smooth with age.

COMPARE: Yellow-Gilled Crep (*C. crocophyllus*; uncommon) has buff, yellowish or orangish caps up to 2 inches wide, overlaid with brown fibers that may be sparse or heavy. Gills of young specimens are **yellowish to orange**, turning brown with age.

NOTES: These small Oysterlings are not edible.

Mock Oyster (also referred to as Orange Mock Oyster)

Phyllotopsis nidulans

These saprobes are usually seen in dense, overlapping clusters, but may also be found singly or in loose groups; they fruit on dead and rotting wood of deciduous trees and conifers. Though small, these **fuzzy** little shelves are easy to spot because of their **yellowish-orange to orangish-buff** color. Caps are typically 1 to 3 inches across and fan-shaped. Gills are closely spaced and the same color as the caps; they radiate out from the **stemless** connection point to the wood. Often the edge of the cap is rolled under, especially when young. The cap surface fades to dull tan with age, but remains fuzzy at every stage. They have a **foul odor**, and are also called Smelly Oyster. Their spore print is **pink to tan**; they grow from early summer through fall and, rarely, in spring.

COMPARE: Yellow-Gilled Crep (pg. 224) have similarly colored caps, but they are overlaid with **fine brown fibers**; its spore print is **brown**. • Some *Panus* species (pg. 223) and *Lentinellus* species (pg. 220) grow on wood and have densely **furry** caps, but they are not orangish like the Mock Oyster. • Chicken Mushroom (pgs. 36–37) is a prime edible shelf mushroom that is bright orange, but the underside is covered with **tiny pores** rather than gills and the top sides are **smooth** rather than fuzzy or hairy.

NOTES: You are not likely to confuse this inedible fungus with something tasty because of its strong, unpleasant odor. It is uncommon in our area.

Indian Paint Fungus

Echinodontium tinctorium

This saprobe typically looks like a **thick, hoof-shaped chunk of wood** that is cracked and burned. Indian Paint Fungus grows on **hemlock and fir** trees, typically singly; they generally fruit on living trees from a wound or underneath a dead branch, but occasionally appear on downed wood. Caps are often up to 10 inches wide and almost half as thick, with a **dry, black surface** that develops radial cracks with age; moss often grows on the caps of older specimens. The cap edges may be paler and brownish. The surface underneath is very rough, with dark-tipped **spine-like or tooth-like projections** that carry the spores. The flesh inside the cap is hard and woody; it is **bright orange to reddish**, making quite a contrast with the dull exterior. Its spores disperse during cool, damp fall weather, spreading into the pith of the living tree; they remain dormant—sometimes for generations—until the tree is injured, then they begin to develop into the fungus. Spores are reportedly white, but spore prints are not taken from this species. It is perennial, found year-round, and is common in our area.

COMPARE: Chaga (pg. 263) has a similarly blackened, rough exterior, but it fruits on **birch** trees; it typically appears as a bulging canker, but may sometimes project outward.

NOTES: The colorful inner material was used by Native peoples to make a body paint; it was also powdered and used medicinally as a skin salve and perhaps other uses. Today, textile dyers use it to color yarns.

Conifer Mazegill

Gloeophyllum sepiarium (also listed as *Daedalea sepiaria*)

This woody, fan-shaped to irregularly shaped saprobe grows on dead conifers, as well as construction lumber and, occasionally, on hardwoods; it may appear singly but often fruits in overlapping shelves or rosettes. From the top it looks like many other shelf mushrooms, but the underside is covered with a series of **irregularly shaped gills and elongated pores** that looks like an intricate **maze**. Gills are tan to brownish, with pale edges. Individual caps are subtly zoned and yellowish-brown when young, becoming reddish-brown or dark brown; they have a bumpy, **hairy to velvety** surface and may be up to 4½ inches across and 3 inches from front to back. There is no stem; the maze fans out from the cap's point of attachment to the wood. Spores are white. This common species is present year-round; specimens get darker over time. It causes brown rot of the wood.

COMPARE: Two other shelf mushrooms have similar appearances. • Gilled Polypore (*Lenzites betulina*; also listed as *Trametes betulina*) has similar elongated, gill-like pores that are **white**. The cap surface is hairy to velvety and has **distinct bands of varying colors**, often including green from algae growth on old specimens. It fruits on **hardwoods** including birch (*Betula* is Latin for birch) and is uncommon in our area. • Oak Mazegill (*Daedalea quercina*) is up to **8 inches** wide, with a **tough, woody** texture and caps that are rough but **not hairy**; it fruits on hardwoods, particularly oak, and is rare in our area.

NOTES: All of the mushrooms listed above are inedible.

FROM THE SOIL NEAR LIVE TREES

SPRING THROUGH FALL

Common Earthball

Scleroderma citrinum

HABITAT: These common fungi fruit from the ground, singly or in groups, near living conifers and hardwoods; they are mycorrhizal and have a symbiotic relationship with the trees. They are fond of mossy wooded areas and grassy lawns; they occasionally grow directly on rotted wood.

DESCRIPTION: This small sphere could almost be mistaken for a Puffball, but it has a **yellowish to tan** exterior decorated with **dark, scaly pyramids** that protrude above the surface, creating a **rough** texture; the surface may appear cracked around the pyramids. This surface is a **thick, tough skin** surrounding the mass of spores. The sphere is typically 1 to 3 inches across; as it grows, it often flattens out slightly and may become oblong or slightly lobed. The interior is initially white like a Puffball, but much **firmer**. As it matures, the interior darkens, turning **purplish** to purplish-brown from the inside out, and, finally, **blackish to dark brown**; the skin becomes thinner but is still tough. Like a Puffball, it develops a hole or cracks at the top through which the ripe, powdery spores are eventually released. Earthballs have **no stem** but are attached to the ground or wood by a cluster of rhizomorphs (thick root-like strands).

SPORE PRINT: Spores are black to dark brown; spore prints are not taken.

SEASON: Spring through fall.

OTHER NAMES: Pigskin Poison Puffball, Hard Puffball, *S. aurantium*, *S. vulgare*.

COMPARE: Several Earthballs have **smooth** skin that often breaks up to form a **finely crackled-looking surface**, like dried mud. The Smooth Earthball (*S. cepa*) is probably the most common in our area. It is less than 2 inches wide and often fairly flattened. The top cracks into several lobes that **fold back like a star** to release the spores. • Leopard Earthball (*S. areolatum*) are often somewhat pear-shaped, and less than 2 inches wide. The yellowish-brown skin develops fine cracks with **dark, dot-like scales**, starting at the top and eventually covering the entire surface. Its skin is thinner than the other Earthballs listed here, but is still tough. • Small edible Puffballs (pg. 232) appear similar to some Earthballs, but their interiors are **soft and white**, becoming **yellowish**; their skins are **thin** and are not tough like those of Earthballs. Puffballs never have the firm, dark centers found in maturing Earthballs.

NOTES: Earthballs are **toxic**, causing gastrointestinal problems, chills and other unpleasant symptoms.

Common Earthball
Smooth Earthball

FROM THE SOIL NEAR LIVE TREES

LATE SPRING THROUGH FALL

Smoky Puffball

Gastropila fumosa

HABITAT: This common mushroom is found at higher elevations in the mountains, where it appears under spruce and fir. It fruits singly or in loose groups, and is often partially or mostly buried by duff.

DESCRIPTION: Young specimens that are emerging from the duff are whitish and smooth to minutely hairy. After exposure to light, the surface darkens, becoming light to medium gray or brownish; the skin is **thick and hard**, and is often wrinkled or cracked on maturing specimens. Smoky Puffballs are 1 to 3 inches wide and may be fairly round, but are more often slightly flattened or cushion-like; the base is pleated and attached to a **cord-like rhizomorph** that acts like a root. Growing specimens have a **foul odor** that has been likened to a wet dog wearing dirty socks; it is also compared to sour milk or diesel oil. The interior spore mass is soft and white in young specimens, becoming yellowish to yellowish-brown before maturing to a dark brown powder.

SPORE PRINT: Spores are brown; spore prints are not taken.

SEASON: Late spring through fall.

OTHER NAMES: *Calvatia fumosa, Handkea fumosa.*

COMPARE: Small Warted Mountain Puffball (*Lycoperdon subcretaceum*; also listed as *G. subcretacea, C. subcretacea* and *H. subcretacea*) is found in similar habitat, and is similarly sized, with thick, hard skin. Its whitish surface is covered with **pointed warts** that are white at first; the tips of the warts turn **grayish-brown to smoky gray**. Individual warts fall off over time. The skin may crack along the wart bases, and the outer layer of skin eventually flakes off, revealing an inner layer that is yellowish to brownish. The base has **white mycelium** (root-like fungal filaments) rather than a cord-like rhizomorph, and the developing mushrooms **lack the foul odor** of Smoky Puffballs. It is much less common than Smoky Puffball.

NOTES: The hard shell is reportedly chewed by rodents, releasing the spores. Smoky Puffball is not collected for the table; the odor of young specimens makes it unappealing. Some sources say that Small Warted Mountain Puffball is edible when the inner mass is still white and soft, but it is not known as a desirable species.

Smoky Puffball

Small Warted Mountain Puffball

Gem-Studded Puffball

Lycoperdon perlatum

HABITAT: This saprobic mushroom grows **from the ground**, usually in large groups or clusters but also singly or scattered. It is common in conifer and mixed-wood forests but is also found in grassy urban areas.

DESCRIPTION: The Gem-Studded Puffball has a generally **spherical top** that may be up to 3½ inches in diameter but is usually smaller. Rather than a true stem, it has an **elongated sterile base** that varies from 1 to 2 inches tall, making the mushroom look like an upside-down pear; however, it often grows in tight clusters so only the spherical tops are visible. The outer skin is white, cream-colored or tan and is covered in **minute spines** that may disappear with age, leaving a slightly rough surface. As with other Puffballs, the outer skin encases the interior spore-producing flesh. Initially smooth, white and edible, the flesh becomes yellowish to olive-brown and inedible, finally turning into a brown powder. Each sphere develops an opening at the top to release, or puff out, the spores.

SPORE PRINT: Spores are brown; spore prints are not taken.

SEASON: Late spring to fall.

OTHER NAMES: Warted Puffball, Devil's Snuff-Box, *L. gemmatum.*

COMPARE: The slightly smaller Pear-Shaped Puffball (*L. pyriforme;* also listed as *Morganella pyriformis*) grows in dense clusters from **decaying wood.** Its whitish to whitish-brown skin is **smooth** or slightly granular; it lacks the overall spines found on Gem-Studded Puffball, although scattered small spines may be present on the top of young specimens. It is 1 to 2 inches high and wide. • Dusky Puffball (*L. nigrescens;* also listed as *L. foetidum*) is **brownish overall**; it is pear-shaped and less than 2 inches wide. The surface is covered with **fine, dark spines** that lean together, forming pyramids.

NOTES: The Puffballs listed here are edible when young, when the inner flesh is *completely white*. They can be mistaken for various cap-and-stem species in the button stage, including **deadly** Amanitas (pgs. 60–65), various Agaricus (pg. 84) or the egg stage of Stinkhorns (pg. 197). Small puffballs growing from the ground should always be cut in half and inspected as described on pg. 49 to make sure they are not overripe or young examples of another species such as an Amanita button (pg. 60); also see Earthballs, pg. 228. The ripe spores should not be inhaled, as they can cause respiratory distress.

Gem-Studded Puffball
Pear-Shaped Puffball

Earthstars (several)

Geastrum spp.

HABITAT: Earthstars grow from the ground singly or in groups near hardwoods and conifers. They are saprobes, getting their nutrients from leaf litter and dead wood; often found in large numbers near the stumps of dead trees.

DESCRIPTION: Earthstars begin their lives as small, smooth, tan egg-shaped balls that have a pointed beak at the top. The skin splits and unfolds into a **star-shaped base** surrounding the central sphere, which is a tough skin encasing the spore mass, much like a Puffball (pgs. 230, 232). The star may be hidden by the dirt and debris it collects. With age, the sphere turns darker brown and the beak at the top opens to release the ripened spores. There are numerous species, each distinguished by slight variations. • Rounded Earthstar (*G. saccatum*) is the most common; it is less than 2 inches across, including the opened rays of the star. The sphere nestles in the bowl-shaped base of the star, which is buff-colored on the side facing up. The spore beak sits in a **depressed ring** that is slightly fuzzy and colored differently than the rest of the sphere. • Collared Earthstar (*G. triplex*) may be nearly **5 inches** across when fully opened. The star's rays are pale pinkish, tan or pinkish-brown on the side facing up. The rays often fold under and crack into layers; the top layer forms a **collar-like rim** around the base of the sphere. The area around the spore beak is pale and slightly fuzzy; it may be slightly depressed but not as much as Rounded Earthstar. • Rosy Earthstar (*G. rufescens*) is up to 3½ inches across when fully opened. The star's rays are **pinkish to pinkish-brown** on the side facing up. The outer surface of the sphere is **slightly downy**. It is rare in our area.

SPORE PRINT: Brown.

SEASON: Summer through fall.

OTHER NAMES: Some Native American tribes traditionally called them Fallen Stars and thought their appearance foretold of celestial events.

COMPARE: Giant Hygroscopic Earthstar (*Astraeus pteridis*) is up to **6 inches** across when fully opened; its rays have a **broken, linear pattern of dark brown and tan**. It is **hygroscopic**, absorbing moisture from the air. In dry weather, the rays curl up to protect the interior but open when it rains to let the drops hit and disperse the spores. The rays can open wide enough to push the brown spore mass off the ground to give the spores a chance to be carried farther by wind.

NOTES: The species listed here are inedible but are fascinating and beautiful.

Rounded Earthstar
Collared Earthstar
Giant Hygroscopic Earthstar

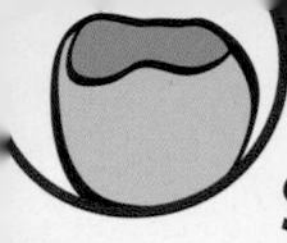

ON DECAYING WOOD AND WOODY DEBRIS

EARLY SPRING TO EARLY SUMMER

Small Black Cups (several)

Various genera

HABITAT: With the exception of *Helvella corium*, the small species below are all saprobes that are found on rotting coniferous wood, which may be exposed or buried; Jellylike Black Urn may also fruit on decaying deciduous wood.

DESCRIPTION: Black Snowbank Cup Fungus (*Donadinia nigrella*) are found at mid to high elevations **near or in melting snowbanks**. They fruit singly or in small groups on buried wood, wet sticks and other woody debris. The thin-fleshed cups are shaped like shallow bowls and typically less than 1 inch wide; they are black to brownish-black, with fine hairs on the outside. The cups are perched on **thin black stems** that are up to **2¼ inches tall** and often curvy. • Caps of Hairy Black Cup (*Pseudoplectania nigrella*) are less than 1 inch wide and may be rounded in outline or **irregularly shaped**; the cap edges and outsides are covered with fine hairs that create a **wooly, felt-like** surface. These all-black mushrooms grow singly or in clusters on decayed wood and mossy areas, with **little or no stem**. • Jellylike Black Urn (*Plectania melastoma*) are usually less than 1 inch wide and tall. Edges are typically rolled inward, sometimes causing the cup to appear like an **open sphere**; however, the sides are often pushed in, creating an oblong opening at the top. Insides are black to brownish-black; outsides are black and hairy, with **orangish granules** at the top of young specimens. The cups may narrow to a short, stem-like base, or may be attached directly to decaying sticks and other woody debris, typically from conifers but occasionally from hardwoods. • Caps of *Pseudoplectania melaena* are bowl-shaped to **saucer-like**. They are typically about 1 inch across but may be up to **3 inches**. Insides are olive-brown at first, darkening to black; outsides are black, with a **felt-like** texture. A short stem, less than 1 inch tall, is usually present.

SPORE PRINT: Spore prints are generally not taken for these small cups.

SEASON: Early spring through early summer.

OTHER NAMES: Black Snowbank Cup Fungus is also listed as *Plectania nannfeldtii*. *Pseudoplectania melaena* is also listed as *Pseudoplectania vogesiaca*.

COMPARE: *Helvella corium* are mycorrhizal, associating with **willows and aspens**. Caps are cup-like and often folded together; they are up to 1 inch wide and black, with **pale hairs** at the top outside edge. Stems are up to 1½ inches tall and moderately thick. They are black at the top and whitish at the base.

NOTES: None of the species listed here are collected for the table.

Black Snowbank Cup Fungus
Hairy Black Cup
Jellylike Black Urn
Pseudoplectania melaena
H.corium

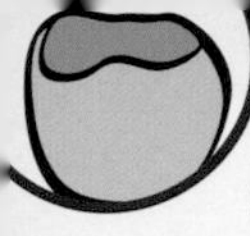

FROM THE SOIL OR DOWNED WOOD

EARLY SPRING THROUGH FALL

Orange to Red Cups (several)

Various genera

HABITAT: Varies by species; please see individual accounts below.

DESCRIPTION: The cups listed in this paragraph may be bowl-shaped, saucer-like or nearly flat. • **Snowbank Orange Peel Fungus** (*Caloscypha fulgens*) fruits at **higher elevations in spring**, shortly after snowmelt. They are up to 1½ inches across; edges may be wavy and are often pushed together, making the openings appear lobed or elongated. Upper surfaces are bright yellowish-orange to orangish; undersides are dull orangish, **overlaid with greenish tones**. With age or handling, the cups turn bluish-green. Cups are usually stemless. They are found primarily under conifers, where they fruit from mossy ground, pine-needle duff or buried wood. • **Orange Peel Fungus** (*Aleuria aurantia*) are bright orange on the upper surface; undersides are **pale sherbet-orange to whitish**, with a **powdery** or granular surface. Cups may be **nearly 4 inches across**, although they are typically smaller; there is no stem. They fruit scattered or in tight clusters from bare soil, in sandy or grassy areas, and in disturbed areas; most common in **fall**, but also found in spring and summer. • **Scarlet Cup Fungus** (*Sarcoscypha coccinea*) are **bright red** on the upper surface, with a **frosted-looking** underside. Cups are up to 2 inches across. Stems are whitish and may be very short, or up to **1½ inches long**; when present, long stems may bend around surrounding woody material. Scarlet Cup Fungus appears in early spring, fruiting on downed hardwood branches and sticks, particularly those that are mossy or lightly covered with earth.

SPORE PRINT: Spore prints are generally not taken for these small cups.

SEASON: Early spring through fall.

OTHER NAMES: Scarlet Cup Fungus is also called Ruby Elfcup.

COMPARE: **Eyelash Cup** (*Scutellinia scutellata* group) are orangish to reddish, with **dark, long, bristle-like hairs around the edges**; they are less than ¾ inch wide and shaped like very shallow cups to nearly flat discs. Several very similar *Scutellinia* species in this group require a microscope to tell apart. • **False Eyelash Cup** (*Melastiza chateri*) is slightly larger than Eyelash Cup, with **short, soft, finer hairs** around the margin; other differences are microscopic.

NOTES: Snowbank Orange Peel Fungus is reportedly mildly toxic. Orange Peel and Scarlet Cup Fungus are reportedly edible but poorly regarded. The others here are not known to be edible.

Snowbank Orange Peel Fungus
Scarlet Cup Fungus
Eyelash Cup

FROM THE SOIL AND GROUND DEBRIS

SPRING

Pig's Ear

Gyromitra ancilis

HABITAT: This common saprobe fruits singly or in clusters from the ground near old conifer stumps, and on woody debris; it first appears shortly after snowmelt.

DESCRIPTION: Pig's Ear has a **stub-like stem** underneath, but it does not elevate the fungal body much above the ground. Young specimens are shaped like shallow bowls or cups, but they soon become more flattened, lumpy and irregular, with wavy or curled-under edges. The top surface is brown, ranging from yellowish- to reddish- to chestnut-brown; it may be fairly flat but usually looks **wrinkled, puckered or gathered**. The body is typically 2 to 3 inches across, but may be larger; the flesh is fairly thick. Undersides are cream-colored, pale gray or whitish; they may be smooth or slightly hairy. The flesh on the underside appears to be gathered together to join with the short, thickened stem.

SPORE PRINT: Whitish.

SEASON: Spring.

OTHER NAMES: *Discina ancilis, Discina perlata, G. perlata.*

COMPARE: Several cup mushrooms, particularly Gyromitra species, are similar, with a few visual variations to distinguish them from Pig's Ear; microscopic analysis is the best method of separating these species. Note that these species may be listed under a different genus; alternate names are in parentheses. • Young and fresh ***G. melaleucoides*** (*Peziza melaleucoides*) are dull brownish-gray on the top surface; undersides are paler and **waxy-looking** when moist. Both sides have **fewer wrinkles or folds**; the stems may be slightly longer. • ***G. leucoxantha*** (*Discina leucoxantha*) is **bright orangish-brown to yellowish** above; undersides are **whitish and downy**. It is found under **hardwoods** as well as conifers. • ***G. olympiana*** (*Discina olympiana*) is **yellowish-tan** and brighter than Pig's Ear, but not as bright as *G. leucoxantha*. • **Veined Cup** (*Disciotis venosa*) is more **cup-like and erect** than the Gyromitras listed above. The top surface is reddish-brown to dark brown, with **raised wrinkles** radiating out from the center. Undersides are whitish to buff-colored, with **small, dark scales** around the top edge; the undersides become ribbed as they join with the **short, stout stem**, which is often buried. Also called Bleach Cup because it has a **bleach-like odor**. It prefers damp areas. It is uncommon in our area.

NOTES: Pig's Ear and Veined Cup are considered edible when well cooked. Edibility of the other species above is unknown; they are best avoided.

Pig's Ear
G. melaleucoides
Pig's Ear, underside
Veined Cup

Black Jelly Jug

Black Rubber Cup, showing jelly-like flesh

Black Jelly Jug

Urnula padeniana (also called Giant Gel Cup, *Sarcosoma mexicanum*)

Young specimens of this common mushroom have **wide cups that taper into a cone-shaped base**; they look like a slightly curved, upside-down wedge with a bowl-shaped top. They are often 4 inches wide and tall, sometimes larger. The upper surface is **wrinkled or lumpy** and dark gray to black; it is dull when dry, becoming glossy in wet weather. The lower surface is similarly colored and velvety; the center is heavily wrinkled where it joins the base. The base, or stem, is usually wrinkled or ribbed. The flesh is **rubbery**, with a **jelly-like center**. With age, the jelly-like mass deteriorates, causing the base to become thinner; the cup becomes flattened, so the entire specimen appears more like a **lumpy, cushion-like disc** than like a cup. Spores are not collected from this species. Black Jelly Jug is found in spring soon after snowmelt, appearing singly or in clusters; it fruits on or near rotten conifer wood or conifer duff from low to high elevations.

COMPARE: Black Rubber Cup (*Pseudosarcosoma latahense*) is similar in shape and has similar rubbery flesh, but it is typically **less than 2 inches across** and the jelly-like center is **less gelatinous**. It is **purplish-brown** at first, turning black with age. The underside is grayish to black and covered with fine, matted hairs. Other differences are microscopic. Black Rubber Cup is often found at higher elevations; it is somewhat uncommon.

NOTES: It is unknown if these homely-looking mushrooms are edible. Surprisingly, they are related to Morels (pgs. 26–30), a highly sought edible.

White-Footed Elfin Cup

Helvella leucomelaena

These cup mushrooms must be seen from the side to be appreciated. The cups are up to 2¾ inches wide and are **dark grayish-brown to blackish** inside. The color extends to the top edge of the underside, but changes to white as the cup merges with the white, **fluted** stem. Ribs on the stem **extend around the bottom of the cup**. The total height is 2 inches or less. Spores are not collected from this species. White-Footed Elfin Cup are found in coniferous woods, fruiting from needle duff, moss or leaf litter; they also appear along paths and roads, growing from hard-packed soil or grassy areas. Found from spring through early summer; common in our area.

COMPARE: Cups of Brown Ribbed Elfin Cup (*H. acetabulum*) are **lighter** in color and more **brownish**, ranging from buff-colored, grayish-brown to tan; they are up to **3¼ inches** wide. The ribs on the stem are more numerous and more pronounced; they extend farther up, often **branching** around the underside of the cup. The total height is typically 3 inches or less. They are found in coniferous, hardwood or mixed forests. • *H. solitaria* are up to 2¼ inches wide and tall. Stems are thinner, with a **more abrupt connection** to the cups. Cups are grayish-brown to dark brown and are often compressed in from the sides, appearing elongated or, sometimes, lobed. Found in coniferous, hardwood or mixed forests.

NOTES: These species are not collected for the table; some may be mildly toxic.

FROM THE SOIL

SPRING THROUGH FALL

Worm Corals (several)

Various genera

HABITAT: These species grow **directly from the ground**; they are often found in grassy or mossy woodland spots, primarily near conifers.

DESCRIPTION: Golden Fairy Club (*Clavulinopsis laeticolor*) is the most common of the species listed here. It is **yellowish-orange to orangish** and typically less than 2 inches tall. The upper portion is up to 3⁄16 inch wide and often somewhat flattened, with a blunt, **squared-off tip**; there may be a groove or fold running from the top towards the base. It is club-shaped and typically unbranched, but may fork once. The club narrows towards the base, which is whitish and often surrounded with fine white mycelium (root-like fungal filaments); the club often curves a bit, particularly towards the base. It grows in loose clusters rather than tight bunches. • Purple Club Coral (*Alloclavaria purpurea*) is spindle-shaped and **purplish**, ranging from lavender, dull smoky purple, pinkish-purple to pale brownish-purple. It typically grows in **fairly tight clusters**, usually near conifers. Individual spindles are 1½ to 4¾ inches tall and very **slender**, with narrowed tips; the tips are unbranched. • Fairy Fingers (*Clavaria fragilis*) are **white**, turning yellowish from the top down as they mature. They fruit in clusters; individual clubs are 2½ to 6 inches tall and generally fairly thin. The spindle-shaped bodies are often wavy or curved, and may be somewhat flattened; they have a brittle, fragile texture. • Rosy Club Coral (*Clavaria rosea*; rare) are **pinkish**, ranging from rose-pink to reddish-pink, and up to 2 inches tall. They are cylindrical; the tops may have a few small teeth or may be flattened. Found singly or in small groups.

SPORE PRINT: White.

SEASON: Spring through fall.

OTHER NAMES: Purple Club Coral is also listed as *Clavaria purpurea*. Fairy Fingers is also listed as *Clavaria vermicularis* and is also called White Worm Coral.

COMPARE: Spindle-Shaped Yellow Coral (*Clavulinopsis fusiformis*) is similar to Golden Fairy Club, but it is **bright yellow** rather than orangish. It is up to **6 inches** tall, and grows in **tight bunches**. This species is common in the eastern part of the U.S. but is rare in our area. • Egg Yolk Club (pg. 252) is similar to Golden Fairy Club, with a top that is egg-yolk yellow, but it is **distinctly bicolored**; a greater portion of its lower part is white. It is uncommon in our area.

NOTES: Although some worm corals are edible, they are too insubstantial to be of interest for culinary uses; some may be bitter.

Golden Fairy Club

Purple Club Coral

Fairy Fingers

Rosy Club Coral

Crested Coral

Clavulina coralloides

HABITAT: This mycorrhizal species fruits from the soil near hardwoods and conifers; may also be found on rotted wood. It appears singly or in small groups.

DESCRIPTION: This common coral fungus consists of a **thick, fleshy base** with numerous **thick, erect branches**, each of which often branches repeatedly to form a fairly dense cluster. The tips of each branch are often flattened, and appear **jagged or fringed**, with several small points or spikes that make them appear **crest-like**. The multi-branched clusters are typically 1½ to 3 inches high and wide; they are **dingy whitish**, becoming yellowish or pale tan with age. The flesh is whitish and brittle to tough.

SPORE PRINT: White.

SEASON: Summer through fall.

OTHER NAMES: Crested Coral is also listed as *Clavulina cristata*, *Clavaria cristata* and *Clavaria coralloides*.

COMPARE: White Coral (*Ramariopsis kunzei*) is a multi-branched coral that is similar in size to Crested Coral, but the tips of its branches are **blunt** and not crest-like, lacking the small points or spikes; it is a **brighter white** overall. The branches around the edges may curve outward, giving it a rounded outline. It is uncommon in our area. • Gray Coral (*Clavulina cinerea*) is very similar to Crested Coral and is whitish when young, but it soon becomes dull **grayish**, ranging from ash-colored to lilac-gray to brownish-gray; the branch bases are whitish. Its branch tips may be flattened and are often forked, but are rarely crest-like. Common in our area. • Wrinkled Coral (*Clavulina rugosa*) is much less complex-looking than the other corals discussed here. It is white, with one to three undivided branches that have rounded or blunt tips. Branch surfaces have **wrinkles, grooves or brain-like swellings** that run lengthwise. Wrinkled Coral lacks the fleshy base of Crested Coral; instead, several branches merge together to form a stem-like base. It is uncommon in our area.

NOTES: Crested Coral is edible when fresh and whitish, but has little flavor; specimens which are yellowed should not be eaten due to potential confusion with Yellow-Tipped Coral (*Ramaria formosa*), a **toxic** species that appears somewhat similar but has **salmon-colored branches with yellow tips**. The others here are edible but not generally sought out for the table.

Crested Coral
White Coral
Wrinkled Coral

Gray Coral

FROM THE SOIL NEAR LIVE TREES

SUMMER THROUGH FALL

Club-Shaped Corals (several)

Clavariadelphus spp.

HABITAT: The species listed here are thought to be mycorrhizal; they are found scattered or in loose clusters near conifers, fruiting from forest duff or soil. *C caespitosus* and *C. occidentalis* also fruit in mixed forests.

DESCRIPTION: The club-shaped mushrooms described here are firm to somewhat tough; most have a wrinkled surface that may look veined. Chemical tests are often used to positively identify some of these species. • Flat-Topped Coral (*C. truncatus*) is the most common club-shaped coral in our area. They have a **flattened** (truncated) top that may be level or depressed in the center; edges are generally softly rounded but may also be somewhat abrupt, giving the impression of a small, solid trumpet. They are up to 6 inches tall; tops may be 3 inches across. Tops are **yellowish-orange**. Stalks are heavily wrinkled, especially towards the top; they are **pinkish-tan to pale orangish-brown**, tapering to a whitish base that is often surrounded by white mycelium (root-like fungal filaments). • *C. caespitosus* is **pinkish-brown, purplish-brown or grayish-red**, becoming brown with age. It is up to 6 inches tall and grows in **tight clusters** (referred to as cespitose). The stalks are generally cylindrical, with a rounded or slightly pointed top; some may appear broad and laterally compressed. • Strap-Shaped Pestle (*C. sachalinensis*) is **yellowish-orange to dull buff overall**, and less than 3 inches tall. Young specimens are cylindrical, becoming **club-like** with age; the tops may be blunt or rounded, occasionally appearing lobed. *C. ligula* is visually identical; microscopic examination is required to separate the two. • *C. occidentalis* is pale yellow when young, becoming pinkish-buff to grayish-orange. It is up to **9¾ inches** tall, with a **broad top** that is laterally compressed. • *C. mucronatus* is **white** when young, becoming pinkish-buff with age. It is typically shaped like a **very narrow, elongated cone** with a rounded top that has a **sharp point** in the center; it is less than 3½ inches tall. Rare.

SPORE PRINT: Most species listed here have white spores; those of Strap-Shaped Pestle and *C. mucronatus* are darker, typically buff-colored.

SEASON: Summer through fall.

OTHER NAMES: None noted.

COMPARE: Worm Corals (pg. 244) are smaller and more cylindrical.

NOTES: Flat-Topped Coral is a good edible, with a sweet flavor. The others listed here are reportedly indistinct in flavor and are not sought out for the table.

Flat-Topped Coral
Strap-Shaped Pestle
C. caespitosus
C. mucronatus

Pale Yellow Spring Coral

Ramaria rasilispora

This common coral fruits from the soil in conifer woods, typically at elevations of 2,500 feet or higher. Specimens are often partially buried, and should be dug up completely to assist in identification. It is cauliflower-like, with a thick central stem base that branches several times. The base is **white throughout** and does not stain when bruised; it may be 3 inches tall and nearly as wide, and it tapers towards the bottom. The branches are white and thick when young, elongating with age. Developed specimens have numerous smaller, crowded branches with toothy tips that are **pale yellow to yellowish-brown**; the entire body is up to 8½ inches across and 6 inches tall. Spore prints are not taken; many identification characteristics are based on reaction to chemicals and on microscopic features. Pale Yellow Spring Coral is most common in spring, fruiting into early summer.

COMPARE: Two subspecies of *R. rasilispora* have been identified: *R. rasilispora* var. *rasilispora*, described above, and ***R. rasilispora*** **var.** ***scatesiana***, which is slightly paler and also fruits in **fall**. • **Big-Base Goldie** (*R. magnipes*) is common in our area. It has a **thicker** central stem that may **stain brown**; branch tips are **brighter yellow**, changing to **reddish** when bruised. Other differences between all species here are microscopic.

NOTES: The corals above are popular edibles, but may be slightly bitter when cooked. Big-Base Goldie has a strong laxative effect on some people, so eat only a small amount the first time.

Perma Pinky

Ramaria rubripermanens

This distinctive, cauliflower-like coral has a massive stem base that may be up to **4½ inches tall and 3½ inches wide**; it is **white throughout** and does not darken with age. The branches are white when young, darkening slightly with maturity. Young specimens have numerous smaller, short branches with **stiff, spiny tips** and aborted branches that are **pinkish, purplish-brown or dark wine-colored**; the branches elongate with maturity and the tips become toothy or crest-like. The entire body is up to 4 inches across and 8 inches tall. Spore prints are not taken; many identification characteristics are based on reaction to chemicals and on microscopic features. Perma Pinky fruits primarily in spring, and occasionally in fall.

COMPARE: Two related species have microscopic differences but are very similar in appearance to Perma Pinky; physical differences are somewhat subtle. • Pale Pinky (*R. rubrievanescens*) has **pale pink tips** on the branches that fade rapidly, and its stems **darken to brownish-violet** with age and bruising. It fruits **only in fall**. • Stems of Wine-Tipped Coral (*R. botrytis*) bruise **pale yellow to light brown**. Its branch tips are **reddish to purplish**; the color extends a short distance down the branches. It fruits in **late summer to fall**.

NOTES: The species discussed here are considered choice edibles, particularly when young; the thick, fleshy stems yield a good quantity of edible material that is said to have a nutty taste. All are fairly common in our area.

Egg Yolk Club

Neolecta vitellina

This uncommon but beautiful species is easy to spot, sticking up above the moss and needle duff it favors. It is club-shaped to spatula-shaped and often somewhat irregular, with a wrinkled or pleated appearance; fungi of this sort are often called earth tongues. The top is broader than the base and may be somewhat flattened; total height is up to 1½ inches tall. The top is bright **egg-yolk yellow**; the bottom portion is **white**, and the base may be surrounded with white mycelium (root-like fungal filaments). The surface of the club may be smooth or lightly velvety. The spores are apparently colorless. It is found from summer through fall, often in ravines or on sloped areas.

COMPARE: Some Worm Corals (pg. 244) are similar in shape, but none in our area have the distinct bicolored combination of egg-yolk yellow on top with a white base. • Irregular Earth Tongue (*N. irregularis*) is somewhat club-shaped but very **irregular**, with flattened lobes or branches at the top; it is often twisted. It is **deep yellow to yellowish-orange** and up to **2¾ inches** tall. Other differences are microscopic. It is more common in the eastern part of North America and rare in our area.

NOTES: Edibility of Egg Yolk Club is uncertain; it is too rare and small to be of much use as an edible. Some report that Irregular Earth Tongue is worth seeking for the table, while others ignore both species when foraging for edible mushrooms.

Stuntz's Red Coral

Ramaria stuntzii

This sturdy, brightly colored coral looks like a cauliflower that has been partially dipped in scarlet dye. The lower part of its thick, solid stem is white, becoming pale orange to reddish-orange before dividing into multiple short branches that are **orangish-red, pinkish-red or scarlet**. With age, the branches fade to pinkish-orange and the tips become darker. The entire body is up to **5½ inches wide and 6½ inches tall**; younger specimens are somewhat shorter and more compact. Spores are orangish-yellow. These mycorrhizal mushrooms are fairly common in our area. They are found singly, in scattered groupings or in fairy rings under conifers, primarily Western hemlock; they fruit in fall.

COMPARE: Carmine Coral (*R. araiospora* var. *araiospora*) is **smaller**, typically less than 3 inches across and 6 inches tall. The stem base is **more delicate** than that of Stuntz's Red Coral; it is up to 1½ inches tall and about half as wide and is white, pale yellow or pale pinkish. Multiple branches split off from the base, forking repeatedly. Branches are **bright red** with **red tips that fade to orange or yellow** with age. Crimson Coral (*R. araiospora* var. *rubella)* is very similar to Carmine Coral, but its branches are more **reddish-blue to magenta**. Branch tips are bright pink to red; the tips fade somewhat with age but **remain pink** rather than becoming orange or yellow. Other differences are microscopic. Both are found in fall.

NOTES: These colorful corals are considered good edibles; they reportedly have a mild cabbage-like taste. All discussed here are a fairly common find.

Witches' Butter and Jelly Fungi (several)

Various genera

HABITAT: These jelly-like fungi grow on dead and decaying wood, including fallen logs, sticks and branches. They appear singly or in colonies.

DESCRIPTION: Several types of jelly-like fungi are often seen on wood. They are **gelatinous** when fresh and moist; they shrivel in periods of dry weather but are revived by rain. • Two common types are **brightly colored** and **irregularly lobed**; they become darker when dry. Lobes may be flattened and folded, or more swollen and brain-like; clusters are typically 1 to 3 inches wide and up to 1 inch high. Orange Jelly (*Dacrymyces chrysospermus*) is typically **bright orange**, tapering and becoming **white** at the point of attachment; it fruits on **coniferous** wood. Witches' Butter (*Tremella mesenterica*) tends to be **yellowish** to yellowish-orange and lacks the white at the point of attachment; it grows on **deciduous** wood. Other differences between the two are microscopic. • Small Staghorn (*Calocera cornea*) are egg-yolk yellow to orangish-yellow when fresh, becoming darker with age. They are up to ¾ inch high and **cylindrical or awl-shaped with rounded tips**; they typically grow upright. The surface is smooth, and gelatinous to sticky in damp weather. These saprobes are usually found on rotting hardwood but may also fruit on conifers, generally from summer through fall; common. • Golden Jelly Cone (*Heterotextus alpinus*) are **cup-shaped to top-shaped** (like an upside-down cone with a rounded top), with a very short, **stem-like point of attachment**. They are amber to yellowish-orange and somewhat **translucent**. This common spring species fruits at higher elevations on conifer wood, often shortly after snowmelt.

SPORE PRINT: Varies between species; not used for identification.

SEASON: Various species here are found throughout the year.

OTHER NAMES: Orange Jelly is also listed as *D. palmatus*; Witches' Butter is also referred to as *T. lutescens*. Golden Jelly Cone is also called *Guepiniopsis alpinus*.

COMPARE: Small Staghorn somewhat resembles a small specimen of Golden Fairy Club (pg. 244), but Golden Fairy Club grows from the ground and may be nearly 2 inches tall; it has a brittle texture.

NOTES: Orange Jelly and Witches' Butter are sometimes cooked in soup. The others listed above are generally considered inedible.

Witches' Butter
Small Staghorn
Golden Jelly Cone

Hawk-Wing

Sarcodon imbricatus

HABITAT: This common mycorrhizal species is found singly or in clusters under conifers and hardwoods; it may grow in a ring and is often found in duff or mossy areas.

DESCRIPTION: This large mushroom is fairly distinct in appearance, with widely convex caps that may be over 9 inches wide at maturity. The center of the cap is depressed; the edges are rolled under, and may be somewhat wavy or lobed. Caps are pale brown to warm buff and decorated with **large, dark brown to blackish-brown scales** that often curve upward, somewhat resembling wood shavings. The large, curved scales are concentrated in the center of the cap; towards the cap edges, the scales become smaller and flatter. The depression in the center deepens over time, and may extend into the stem; old specimens may appear vase-like. The underside is covered with **fine pale-brown teeth** that are up to ½ inch long and may run down the stem slightly; the teeth darken with age. Stems are typically 2 to 3 inches tall and may be nearly half as thick; they are often attached to the caps slightly off-center. They are whitish at first, becoming pinkish-buff; white mycelium (root-like fungal filaments) is often visible at the base. There is no ring.

SPORE PRINT: Brown.

SEASON: Late spring through fall.

OTHER NAMES: *S. imbricatus* is also called Scaly Tooth and Shingled Hedgehog.

COMPARE: Bitter Tooth (*S. scabrosus*) has **smaller scales** that don't dramatically curl upwards like those of Hawk-Wing. The stem is **dark at the base**, ranging from blackish-olive, dark bluish-green or greenish-black. It is very bitter and is not eaten. • Tooth Mushrooms (pg. 258) **lack the dark scales** on the cap; they are usually smaller and have a less-distinct "cap-and-stem" shape.

NOTES: Hawk-Wing is edible when young but may be somewhat bitter; it becomes more bitter with age. It may cause indigestion for some people. Mature specimens of the Sarcodon species here are used to dye wool; Hawk-Wing produces green to grayish-green hues, while Bitter Tooth produces more bluish hues.

FROM THE SOIL NEAR LIVE TREES

SUMMER THROUGH FALL

Tooth Mushrooms (several)

Hydnellum spp.

HABITAT: These mycorrhizal mushrooms fruit under conifers. They often envelop surrounding debris as they grow, and may be attached to sticks or plants.

DESCRIPTION: Hydnellum are shaped like **short, inverted cones** that narrow down to a stubby stem; caps expand and become flatter with age. Species listed here are common in our area and are typically 3 to 6 inches across, with irregular edges. The cap surface is **velvety** on young specimens; over time, numerous **fan-like projections or knobs** may develop on the surface. Undersides are covered with short spore-bearing **teeth** that extend slightly down the stem. Flesh is firm and tough; when cut vertically, the flesh of some species appears **zoned**, similar to the rings on a cut log. • Caps of Blue Tooth (*H. caeruleum*) are **pale blue** at first, becoming **brownish at the center**; with age, the entire cap is orangish-brown to tan. Teeth are whitish to bluish, becoming brownish with pale tips. Stems are orange to brownish. The flesh is zoned; the cap zones are **bluish**, with zones of rusty brown to reddish-orange below. • Caps of young Orange Hydnellum (*H. aurantiacum*) are **bright orange with paler edges**; older specimens are reddish-brown overall. Teeth are white, turning grayish-brown with white tips. Stems are orange, aging to reddish-brown. Flesh is whitish to pale orange and often zoned in the caps, darkening to orangish-red in the stems. • Caps of Sweet Spine (*H. suaveolens*) are whitish at first, turning tan or **pale violet-gray** from the center outward; edges remain pale. Teeth are whitish to pale bluish, eventually turning grayish-brown. Stems are **bluish-violet to bluish-black**. The flesh has white and blue zones in the cap, becoming **dark blue** in the stem area. This species has a **sweet, anise-like odor**. • Caps of Strawberries and Cream (*H. peckii*) are **pinkish to whitish** when young and often dotted with **drops of red liquid** that leave a potholed surface when they evaporate. Mature caps are dark reddish-brown with a **pink edge**. Teeth are **pinkish**, becoming brownish. Stems are colored like the cap. The flesh is **pinkish to brownish** in the cap, becoming darker in the stem area.

SPORE PRINT: Brown.

SEASON: Summer through fall.

OTHER NAMES: Stipitate Hydnums (meaning, having a stem and teeth).

COMPARE: Caps of Hawk-Wing (pg. 256) are covered with dark, curved scales.

NOTES: *Hydnellum* species are inedible but are used by dyers.

Blue Tooth
Orange Hydnellum
Blue Tooth
Orange Hydnellum
Sweet Spine
Strawberries and Cream

FROM THE SOIL NEAR LIVE TREES

LATE SUMMER THROUGH FALL

Blue Chanterelle (several)

Polyozellus spp.

HABITAT: These uncommon to rare mushrooms are mycorrhizal, fruiting in association with conifers. They typically appear in large clusters.

DESCRIPTION: Three Blue Chanterelle species are found in our area. All are **blue to purplish** mushrooms with many **spoon-shaped to fan-shaped caps** that fruit in **tight clusters**; caps are slightly zoned and edges are **wavy**. The upper surfaces are **wooly** on young specimens; with age, all darken to **blackish**, making exact identification challenging. Like common Chanterelles (pgs. 42–44), the undersides have **blunt-edged folds or ribs** rather than true, knife-edged gills. Many differences between the species are not visible to the eye, and a microscope is sometimes needed to positively identify specimens. • *P. atrolazulinus* is the most common in our area. The cluster of caps is up to 6 inches tall and 7¾ inches across; individual caps are up to 4 inches tall and 3 inches wide. Caps are **bright blue** at first, becoming **dark blue** and, finally, blackish. Undersides are **pale grayish-purple**. Flesh is **dark purplish-blue to blackish-green**. • *P. marymargaretae* are similar in size and color to *P. atrolazulinus*, although individual caps may be somewhat wider and undersides are more **bluish**. The flesh is **deep blue**. • *P. purpureoniger* are larger, fruiting in clusters up to 8 inches tall and **12 inches** across. Individual caps are up to **6 inches tall and wide** and are **royal purple** when young, becoming **brownish** and, finally, blackish. Undersides are **dark purple**, becoming purplish-gray. Flesh is **straw-colored to light gray**.

SPORE PRINT: White.

SEASON: Late summer through fall.

OTHER NAMES: Many sources list these as *P. multiplex*; see below.

COMPARE: The Black Chanterelle (*P. multiplex*) was identified in 1899. Specimens found in our area were assumed to be *P. multiplex* until recent study revealed that there is a complex of five closely related species. The three described above are found in our area; the other two, including *P. multiplex*, are found in eastern North America but not in our area. • The more-common Chanterelles (pgs. 42–44) are yellowish, golden or whitish and do not grow in tight clusters.

NOTES: Blue Chanterelles are edible but not as choice as the more familiar Chanterelles on pages 42–44. Textile dyers use Blue Chanterelles to produce violet, green and blue tones in various fibers.

P. atrolazulinus (both photos)

Common Deer Truffle

Elaphomyces granulatus group

This widely distributed truffle is found under conifers and hardwoods, typically 2 to 3 inches below the surface but sometimes deeper. They are typically 1 to 1½ inches across and roughly spherical to oval. The outside is surrounded with yellowish mycelium (root-like fungal filaments); the surface beneath the mycelium is yellowish-brown and **rough or granular**, covered with **firm, fine warts**. The skin is thick and rind-like; when cut, it reveals a yellowish layer on the outside, with a thick whitish to grayish inner layer that may have darker zones but does not appear mottled or marbled. The interior is stuffed with cottony material that is whitish to grayish and may appear somewhat chambered, separated by pale bands; the inner material turns blackish and powdery when fully mature. The odor has been described as metallic or medicinal. Common Deer Truffles are found year-round, often in areas that have numerous rodent burrows.

COMPARE: Marbled Deer Truffle (*E. muricatus* group) is similar, but the thick skin appears **mottled or marbled** in cross-section. The outer surface is orangish-brown and appears **pimpled** or somewhat **spiny**. The interior spore mass is dark brown, grayish or purplish when mature. • ***Scleroderma*** **spp.** (pg. 228) are also rounded, with rough exteriors and interiors that become powdery and dark, but they grow **aboveground** rather than below the surface.

NOTES: Common Deer Truffle is said to be edible, but is a poor substitute for a choice truffle.

Chaga

Inonotus obliquus

Also called the Clinker Polypore or Birch Conk, this unusual, homely fungus would generate no notice at all if it were not used to make a highly regarded medicinal tea. It typically grows as a **bulging canker** on living trees, primarily **birch**; it may also grow as a snout-like or irregular projection rather than a bulge. Chaga may be a foot or more across. The surface is **black and heavily cracked**, often with brownish areas showing between the cracks; it looks **charred or burned**. The interior is yellowish-brown, with a **corky** texture. At this stage the fungus is sterile and does not produce spores. The fertile stage comes only after the host tree has died and a layer of tubes develops under the bark. These spore-producing tubes are quickly attacked and destroyed by beetles. Chaga grows in the fall but is present year-round. It is a parasite that will eventually kill the host tree in less than a decade. It is somewhat uncommon in our area.

COMPARE: The unusual burned appearance and birch tree habitat make this a distinct fungus.

NOTES: Chaga is widely used in Slavic countries, Eastern Europe and some parts of Asia to make a tea that is believed to both prevent and cure cancer. It is rich in antioxidants and is also used to fight viruses, to cure disorders of the digestive system and as a general health tonic. A hatchet is generally needed to remove it from the host tree; the entire fungus is then pounded or ground and the resulting material is steeped to make tea.

Crown Fungus

Sarcosphaera 'coronaria'

These common mushrooms are roughly spherical at first, somewhat resembling a truffle, but they are **hollow inside** and are actually a cup mushroom. They are 2 to 4 inches across and may be slightly flattened, rounded or lobed; young specimens are often mostly buried in duff or soil, emerging at least partway as they develop. The outer surface is whitish to cream-colored, typically dusted with clinging dirt or duff. The top is soft and often slightly depressed; it **breaks open in ray-like segments** to form a roughly crown-shaped cup with a smooth inner surface, which may be whitish at first but soon becomes **pale violet, violet-gray or pinkish**. Crown Fungus often fruits in groups that can be fairly large; they are found in hardwood and coniferous forests, park areas, and along paths and roads, most commonly at elevation. They often appear near melting snow in early spring, continuing through summer.

COMPARE: Several *Peziza* species are found in our area. Some of these cup fungi may have violet tones but are generally brownish to tan, inside and out; they are shaped like **open cups with smooth edges** that may be puckered, ruffled or wavy but are not jagged and crown-like.

NOTES: Crown Fungus are reported to be toxic when raw; members of the genus are known to hyperaccumulate arsenic. Some sources list them as edible when well cooked, but we do not consider them worth the risk and do not recommend eating them.

Carbon Antlers

Xylaria hypoxylon (also referred to as Candlesnuff Fungus)

These saprobes are usually 1 to 3 inches tall and less than ⅜ inch thick, with a tough, wiry texture. The stalks are cylindrical to narrowly club-shaped at first, and coated with **whitish** or grayish powder. As they mature, many stalks develop thin **antler-like forks** near the top; the antlers are often flattened and may have multiple prongs. Fully mature specimens are **jet black** and covered with **small pimple-like bumps** that have tiny pores (visible with a hand lens) which contain the mature, black spores. They fruit on rotting logs and stumps, buried wood and other woody debris, typically from hardwoods but occasionally conifers. They appear in clusters that may be loose or dense, fruiting from spring through fall. They are common west of the Cascades but uncommon on the east side.

COMPARE: Other Xylaria are occasionally found in our area, but they are less branched, smaller or thread-like.

NOTES: Carbon Antlers are tough and inedible, but are very interesting to study. The powdery whitish coating contains asexual spores.

Fluted Bird's Nest

White Barrel Bird's Nest

Bird's Nest Fungi (several)

Various genera

Although tiny, these unusual fungi are charming. They are easiest to identify in the mature stage, when they look like **tiny, cup-like nests** ½ inch or less across, with even tinier **flattened spheres inside**. A dome-like lid covers the top of young specimens. The lid falls away to reveal the interior with two to numerous "eggs" that are usually less than 1⁄16 inch wide. The "eggs," which contain the spores, are ejected when the cups are struck by raindrops. Bird's Nest Fungi fruit singly, scattered or in dense clusters on downed branches, woodland debris and manure. Several varieties are common in our area, fruiting from spring through fall. • Fluted Bird's Nest (*Cyathus striatus*) is cone-shaped. The outside is grayish-brown to brownish and covered with **coarse, shaggy hairs**; the interior is **ribbed** and tan, gray or dark brown. Eggs are grayish to brownish. • White Barrel Bird's Nest (*Nidula niveotomentosa*) is cylindrical, flaring slightly at the top. The outside is **white** and **fuzzy-hairy**; the interior is tan to golden brown. The tiny eggs are brownish and **embedded in a gelatinous substance**. • White-Egg Bird's Nest (*Crucibulum crucibuliforme*) is cup-shaped, becoming cylindrical. The outside is **yellowish to tan** and often **velvety**; the inside is smooth and tan to pale grayish. Eggs are **white**.

COMPARE: Other than additional Bird's Nest species (including those in the *Nidularia, Mycocalia* and *Sphaerobolus* genera) nothing resembles these fungi.

NOTES: Bird's Nest are best appreciated when viewed with a hand lens, and make splendid subjects for macro photography. They are inedible.

Fuzzy Truffle

Geopora cooperi

This fairly large truffle is up to **3 inches** wide and generally spherical but lumpy. The outer surface is tan to dark brown, with a fuzzy coating of fine hairs; **fine warts** are often present on the surface. When cut open, it looks somewhat brain-like, with numerous, **convoluted folds and chambers**; the folds are whitish, highlighted with brown edges and streaks. The folds are coiled together but not fused; they usually can be pulled apart. Descriptions of its odor range from radish-like, garlicky or mild, to sour like fermented cider; it has a mild taste and is edible but not as highly regarded as the true truffles in the *Tuber* genus. Fuzzy Truffle generally fruits partially or completely underground, primarily near conifers but also found near willow and aspen; it can be found from spring through fall. It is often found at elevation and is common in our area.

COMPARE: Less-common *Hydnotrya* species may also have heavily chambered flesh, but they may also be mostly hollow, with large, simple folds. They are **less than 1½ inches** across and often somewhat flattened. The exteriors are **smooth or very lightly velvety but not warty**. They may be buried in soil, but are often found **inside rotted logs** or other woody debris on the forest floor.

NOTES: Squirrels and rodents often nibble on Fuzzy Truffle, helping to disperse the spores.

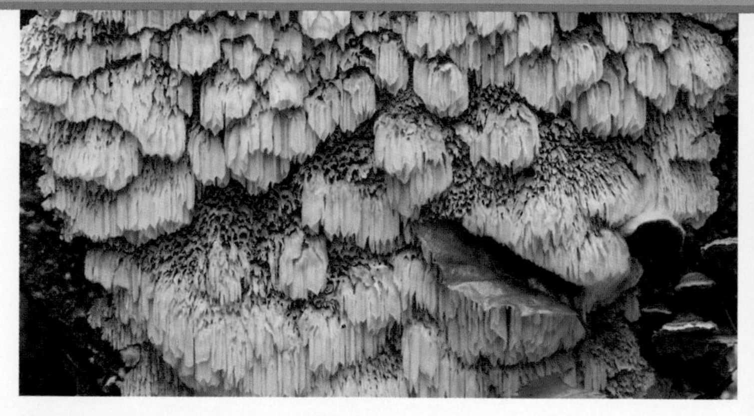

Orange Sponge Polypore

Pycnoporellus alboluteus

This unusual-looking but common polypore is a saprobe that grows in **flat, spreading clusters**, typically on the undersides of fallen logs; it is often found on spruce but also appears on other conifers and, occasionally, aspen. It has no cap, but the upper edge may hang away from the log, revealing the **spongy, bright orange** top surface that is often covered with fine hairs. The pores on the underside are **angular and very coarse**, with whitish tubes up to ¾ inch long; the open ends of the pores split or erode, giving the pore surface an irregular, **tooth-like** appearance. The fruiting body may be up to 3 feet wide, although it is usually smaller; it can be peeled away from the growing surface in a thick layer. Its spores are white. Orange Sponge Polypore is typically found in montane regions; it starts fruiting during snowmelt, but persists into fall. It is inedible.

COMPARE: *P. fulgens* is an orangish to orangish-brown bracket that also has coarse, angular teeth at the ends of long tubes, but it is **firm** and **shelf-like with a fan-shaped body** rather than spongy and flat; at times, the fruiting body looks **bent** because it grows flat on a vertical surface for a short distance before extending outward. The top surface may be zoned with bands of various orange to brownish-orange shades; the edge is often whitish. Other differences are microscopic. It is an uncommon annual that grows from spring through fall.

NOTES: Both of these species cause brown rot of wood.

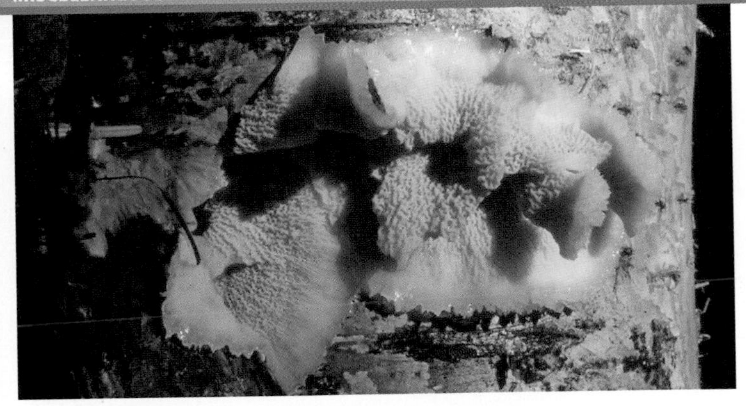

Trembling Crust

Phlebia tremellosa

Although it usually has a **folded-over, cap-like edge at the top**, the bulk of this common saprobic fungus grows as a clinging, irregularly shaped mass that is anywhere from 2 to 9 inches across. It is found on dead trees, logs and stumps, most commonly hardwoods but also occasionally on conifers. It may grow singly, but often appears in overlapping, shingled groups. The cap, or upper edge, is whitish, yellowish or pale pink with a **wooly** texture. The spore-bearing underside (the side facing out) is translucent, with a **waxy to gelatinous** feeling and a **rubbery** texture. It may be pale orange, brownish-orange, pinkish or deep orangish-red; dried specimens are dark red. The surface often appears wrinkled or ridged, and is covered with **pore-like pockets arranged in irregular rows** that radiate from the center outward. Spore prints of this species are generally not taken. It is found from early summer to late fall.

COMPARE: Other *Phlebia* species found in our area grow as simple, spreading crusts, with no cap-like or projecting edges.

NOTES: Trembling Crust and other Phlebia are inedible. Although Phlebia may appear to have pores like Boletes and other pored mushrooms (pgs. 31–33, 66–69, 174–193) and some shelf fungi (pgs. 198–219), the entire underside of *Phlebia* species carries the spore-bearing structures called *basidia*. In contrast, basidia are found only inside the tubes of Boletes and other pored mushrooms; the ripe spores are ejected from the tube openings (the pores).

Pig's Ear Gomphus

Gomphus clavatus

Found on the ground near conifers, these mushrooms are somewhat funnel-like, with a flared-out top and narrower base. The base may be fairly broad and neck-like, or it may be much narrower, appearing like a stem. Pig's Ear Gomphus may grow alone, scattered or in groups; several individuals may fuse together at the base. They are up to 4 inches tall; mature specimens may be up to 6 inches across at the top. Outsides are lilac or purplish-brown, fading to yellowish-tan. The upper portion is covered with **shallow, wrinkle-like veins** that descend a good distance down the base; the upper margin is wavy or ruffled. The top has a **cup-like depression** that becomes more funnel-like with age; the interior surface is smooth, sometimes with a few small scales, and **pale brown to lilac-colored**. Flesh is solid and thick; it is whitish to buff-colored. The base may bruise faintly rust-colored. The spore print is brownish-yellow. Pig's Ear Gomphus is common in our area, and is found from late summer through fall.

COMPARE: Scaly Vase Chanterelle (pg. 44) appears somewhat similar, but its interior is **yellowish-orange, orange or reddish-orange** and scaly; the outside is wrinkled and yellowish-tan to yellowish-red.

NOTES: Pig's Ear Gomphus is edible; some consider it choice while others find it bland or mediocre. It is often infested with insect larvae, making it difficult to prepare. Scaly Vase Chanterelle can cause digestive problems and should be considered inedible. Pig's Ear Gomphus is also referred to simply as Pig's Ear.

Jelly Tooth

Pseudohydnum gelatinosum

These unusual saprobes are found singly, scattered or in small groups on rotting conifer wood, including stumps and logs; they also fruit from woody debris and duff under conifers. The entire fruiting body is **pale and translucent**, with a **rubbery, gelatinous texture**. Caps are fan-shaped to broadly tongue-like; they are typically 1 to 3 inches across, and often have wavy or irregular edges. The tops are white, grayish or brownish, with a dull, rough texture. A thick stem flows smoothly from one edge of the cap. The stem is colored like the cap or paler; it is similarly roughened, and is typically about as tall as the cap is wide. **Short, soft, pointed spines** cover the underside of the cap; they are translucent and white to pale gray. Spores are white. Jelly Tooth can be found from early fall into early spring; it is a common find. They are sometimes called Cat's Tongue, due to their roughened texture.

COMPARE: Jelly Fungi (pg. 254) are also soft, gelatinous and translucent, but they **lack the rudimentary cap-and-stem shape** of Jelly Tooth, and have **no spines**.

NOTES: Jelly Tooth are edible but have almost no flavor; however, their rubbery, gelatinous texture is interesting. Some people eat them raw with cream and honey (or sugar); others marinate them for use in salads.

Helpful Resources and Bibliography

Information on mushrooms is readily available in books, magazines and on the Internet; note, however, that some websites are less reliable than others. Here is a list of some websites and books that provide reliable information that may be of interest to readers.

WEBSITES

Mycological societies

North American Mycological Association (namyco.org)

For a listing of NAMA-affiliated mycological societies in each state, consult the state-by-state list at http://www.namyco.org/clubs.php

University or independent websites

American Mushrooms, David Fischer (americanmushrooms.com/basics.htm)

Fungi magazine, Britt Bunyard (fungimag.com)

Mushroom Expert, Dr. Michael Kuo (mushroomexpert.com)

Mushroom Observer, N. Wilson and J. Hollinger (mushroomobserver.org)

MykoWeb: Mushrooms and Other Fungi on the Web (mykoweb.com)

Pacific Northwest Key Council (svims.ca/council/keys.htm)
The Pacific Northwest Key Council was formed in 1974 by Kit Scates of Post Falls, Idaho and Dr. Daniel E. Stuntz of the University of Washington to promote the study of Pacific Northwest fungi through educational and scientific activities. Their project was a response to the lack of information on mushroom identification available to the amateur at the time. The group of both amateur and professional mycologists continues to be active, drawing their members from the northwest region including Washington, Oregon, Idaho, western Montana and southern British Columbia. Mostly their work has consisted of developing Keys based when possible on macroscopic characteristics of the regional mycoflora.

Pictorial Key to Mushrooms of the Pacific Northwest
(www.alpental.com/psms/PNWMushrooms/PictorialKey/index.htm)

Urban Mushrooms (urbanmushrooms.com)

BOOKS

Arora, David. *Mushrooms Demystified*. Berkeley: Ten Speed Press, 1986.

—*All That the Rain Promises and More…* Berkeley: Ten Speed Press, 1991.

Desjardin, Dennis E., Michael G. Wood and Frederick A. Stevens. *California Mushrooms*. Portland: Timber Press, 2015.

Kroeger, Paul, Bryce Kendrick, Oluna Ceska and Christine Roberts. *The Outer Spores: Mushrooms of Haida Gwaii*. Sidney, BC: Mycologue Publications, 2012.

Kuo, Michael. *Morels*. Ann Arbor: The University of Michigan Press, 2005.

—*100 Edible Mushrooms*. Ann Arbor: The University of Michigan Press, 2007.

Lincoff, Gary H. *National Audubon Society® Field Guide to North American Mushrooms*. New York: Alfred A. Knopf, 2011 (24th printing).

—*The Complete Mushroom Hunter*. Beverly, MA: Quarry Books (Quayside Publishing Group), 2010.

Miller, Dr. Orson K. Jr. and Hope H. Miller. *North American Mushrooms: A Field Guide To Edible And Inedible Fungi*. Guilford, CT: Falcon Guides (Globe Pequot), 2006.

Marrone, Teresa and Kathy Yerich. *Mushrooms of the Upper Midwest*. Cambridge, MN: Adventure Publications, 2014.

Siegel, Noah and Christian Schwarz. *Mushrooms of the Redwood Coast*. Berkeley: Ten Speed Press, 2016.

Trudell, Steve and Joe Ammirati. *Mushrooms of the Pacific Northwest*. Portland: Timber Press, Inc., 2009.

ACKNOWLEDGMENT

The authors would like to thank the Pacific Northwest Key Council for the online resources they provide, specifically the MatchMaker mushroom identification program, and the Pictorial Key to Mushrooms of the Pacific Northwest, without which the making of this book would have been far more difficult. Special thanks go to the principal creators of these programs, Ian Gibson (Matchmaker) and Danny Miller (Pictorial Key), whose work and communications have been most helpful.

Mushroom Observer

The Mushroom Observer website, mushroomobserver.org, is owned and operated by the Massachusetts-based nonprofit, Mushroom Observer, Inc. The website's purpose is to record information about mushrooms—their location, appearance and other information—by allowing members to post photos of their fungal finds and to discuss them with other enthusiasts. It can be used as an aid in identifying unfamiliar mushrooms, a research tool to study photos of mushrooms in various stages and locations, and a record of dates and locations of various species. This site currently has over 10,000 members, ranging from amateurs to professional mycologists. According to the site's owners, it is "a living field guide for mushrooms or a collaborative mushroom field journal."

Many photos in this book, as well as in the previous two books in this series, were originally posted on Mushroom Observer; the names (or Mushroom Observer handles) of the contributing photographers for photos used in this book are listed below. The publisher, and authors, wish to acknowledge the importance of the website, and the generosity of its contributing members.

INTRODUCTION: 13, **Velvety**: I.G. Safonov. **Notched gills**: Hugh Smith. **19**, **Basidiomycetes**: Linas Kudzma, Ph.D. **Ascomycetes**: Tom Bruns. **23**, **Toxic**: Martin Livezey.

TOP EDIBLES/TOP TOXICS: 27, **American Yellow Morel**: Sava Krstic. **29**, **Natural Black Morel**: Jason Hollinger; **Northwest Landscape Morel**, Tim Sage; **Immature Landscape Morel**, Andrew Heath. **32**, **B. fibrillosus**: Eric Badeau. **34**, **dripping inky cap**: Tim Sage. **36**, **L. gilbertsonii**: Steve Ness. **38**, **P. pulmonarius**: Drew T. Henderson. **39**, **P. ostreatus**: Ed Barge. **40**, **Veiled Oyster**: Thomas Tao Laxton. **41**, **Stalkless Paxillus**: Sava Krstic. **59**, **Toxic**: Martin Livezey. **60**, **Egg stage**: Andrew Standeven, Ph.D.; **Emerging from veil**: Yevgeny Nyden. **62**, **Death Cap**: David Rust; **Destroying Angel**: Ron Pastorino. **63**, **Smith's Amanita, left**: Maynard James Keenan. **65**, **Common Volvariella**: Jacob Kalichman. **66**, **Satan's Bolete**: Ron Pastorino. **67**, **Red-Pored Bolete**: Hugh Smith. **68**, **Slender Red-Pored Bolete**, Britt A. Bunyard, Ph.D. **70**, **main shot**: Drew Henderson. **71**, Dave Wasilewski. **72**, Eva Skific. **73**, **top:** Darvin DeShazer; **bottom:** Eva Skific. **74**, **both:** Hunter S.

CAP & STEM WITH GILLS: 81, **March Mushroom**: Dan Molter. **83**, **Common Agrocybe** and **Mulch Mushroom**: Tim Sage. **85**, **Meadow Mushroom**: Drew T. Henderson; **Horse Mushroom**: Tim Sage. **87**, **C. brunneum:** Ben Anderson; **C. olivieri:** Caleb Brown. **89, Funnel Clitocybe:** Mike McIvor. **95**, **Pitted Milk Cap:** Ron Pastorino; **Pitted Milk Cap stem detail:** Geoff Balme; **Coconut Milk Cap:** Britt A. Bunyard, Ph.D. **99**, **Clustered Collybia:** Ron Pastorino; **G. peronatus:** Caleb Brown; **G. fuscopurpureus:** Jacob Kalichman. **105**, **A. solidipes:** Christian Herrera, Lacey, WA. **109**, **Smoky-Gilled Woodlover:** Ed Barge; **Smoky-Gilled Woodlover:** Jason Hollinger; **H. dispersum:** www.mushroomobserver.org; **P. alnicola:** Julie Jones. **111**, **Questionable Stropharia** and **Wine Cap, faded:** Tim Sage; **Wine Cap, fresh Wine Cap, faded:** Ann F. Berger. **113**, **G. sapineus:** Britney Wharton-Ramsey; **G. punctifolius:** Erin Page Blanchard. **115**, **Hygrocybe coccinea:** Sava Krstic; **Hygrocybe flavescens:** Ron Pastorino. **117**, **L. 'deliciosus' group, left:** Ron Pastorino. **119**, **Western Amethyst Laccaria:** Britney Wharton-Ramsey; **Two-Colored Laccaria:** Christian Herrera, Lacey, WA. **123**, **Wooly Pine Spike:** Caleb Brown. **127**, **Willow Shield:** Caleb Brown. **133**, **Bitter Brown Leucopax:** Joceyn Gwynn. **137**,

L. necator (as L. turpis): Ron Pastorino. **141**, **C. subfoetidus:** Drew T. Henderson. **143**, **Colorful Young Blewit with Basal Mycelium:** Eva Skific; **Grass Blewit:** Dave Wasilewski; **L. glaucocana:** Darvin DeShazer. **151**, Tim Sage. **153**, Ron Pastorino. **156**, **left inset:** Britney Wharton-Ramsey. **164**, Kingman Bond Graham. **165**, Caleb Brown.

CAP & STEM WITH PORES/ATYPICAL CAPS: 177, **Big Black Foot:** Douglas Smith; **Little Black Foot:** Britney Wharton-Ramsey. **183**, **A. avellaneus:** Ron Pastorino. **190**, **left:** Trent Pearce. **195**, **Fluted Brown Elfin Saddle:** Ron Pastorino. **197**, **both:** Kevin Trim.

SHELF WITH PORES/SHELF: 203, **Hairy Turkey Tail:** Hunter S. **207**, **Conifer-Base Polypore:** Drew T. Henderson. **209**, **Young Lacquered Polypore:** Courtney and Patrick Roach; **Old Lacquered Polypore:** Tim Sage. **211**, **Young Blushing Rosette:** Rocky Houghtby; **Wooly Velvet Polypore:** Sava Krstic. **217**, **Mature Rosy Polypore:** Cindy Trubovitz. **218**, **left:** Tim Sage; **right:** Stephanie S. Jarvis, M.Sc. **219**, **both:** Ron Pastorino. **227**, **right:** Ron Pastorino.

SPHERICAL/CUP-SHAPED: 229, **Common Earthball:** Erlon Bailey; **Smooth Earthball:** Claude Kaufholtz-Couture, www.fungiquebec.ca. **235**, **Rounded Earthstar:** Trent Pearce; **Giant Hygroscopic Earthstar:** Ron Pastorino. **239**, **Scarlet Cup Fungus:** Sava Krstic.

CORAL & CLUB FUNGI/MISC: 247, **Wrinkled Coral:** Darvin DeShazer. **255**, **Witches' Butter:** Sava Krstic. **265**, Sava Krstic.

The following Mushroom Observer (mushroomobserver.org) images are used in this book. Individual photographers are listed in the credits above: 1422, 10728 ,13335, 31224, 31447, 42956, 55646, 56653, 61473, 64908, 65819, 65829, 67555, 98742, 109170, 117580, 117586, 117898, 119313, 123660, 130842, 135022, 141212, 141754, 162865, 169821, 174020, 179874, 183478, 197399, 201523, 201523, 208153, 216688, 264928, 271792, 273026, 275501, 284652, 286214, 288167, 298841, 298844, 308890, 311807, 311808, 316520, 328292, 330082, 330238, 330255, 330728, 339137, 350222, 354600, 369735, 370305, 370643, 375789, 382782, 385285, 386810, 387117, 413095, 422647, 451475, 453507, 465244, 472035, 480029, 481539, 483579, 486968, 490780, 498288, 511912, 515555, 542234, 575626, 576452, 577547, 581361, 597379, 608754, 642899, 653617, 667126, 673118, 673302, 674195, 681124, 681401, 681413, 682918, 691170, 695924, 738456, 772127, 793381, 807996, 840379, 842344, 843281, 858833

14, **473701**, Daniel B. Wheeler; **30**, **142252**, Hamilton; **33**, **285134**, BakerSt10; **35**, **30538**, Ken Stavropoulos; **51**, **66702**, John Harlan; **53**, **72990**, Ryane Snow; **67**, **183606**, BakerSt10; **70**, **182053**, BakerSt10; **85**, **704**, Nathan Wilson; **89**, **105143**, Paul Derbyshire; **93**, **296993**, John Kirkpatrick; **97**, **183776**, Jeff Riedenauer; **99**, **126**, Nathan Wilson; **103**, **662698**, Rand Workman; **105**, **387190**, Christopher Hodge; **117**, **72665**, John Kirkpatrick; **377417**, Jeff Hitchcock; **133**, **25484**, Paul Derbyshire; **137**, **111155**, Ryane Snow; **139**, **177659**, Rory Pease; **150**, **248446**, Richard Kneal; **152**, **568312**, Richard Kneal; **156**, **227121**, BlueCanoe; **695012**, Josh Grefe; **190**, **62937**, Ryane Snow, **201**, **211970**, BlueCanoe; **211**, **289397**, Randy Longnecker; **227**, **505537**, Robin Hudson.

63, **391905**, Noah Seigel, USFS; **68**, **390403**, Wendy Boes, USFS; **79**, **330255**, Noah Siegel, USFS.

Glossary

Agarics: A large family of mushrooms (both edible and poisonous) with gills. Sometimes used as a general term for multiple species of mushrooms growing in this form.

Amatoxins: Lethal toxins present in some species of mushrooms, including some *Amanita, Galerina, Lepiota* and *Conocybe* species. Ingestion causes extreme sickness and may cause death.

Annual: A mushroom whose fruitbody appears once a year in a particular season. (*Compare:* Perennial)

Ascomycete: Scientific name for a group of mushrooms whose spores develop in a sac-like container called an ascus. When the spores are ripe, the end of the sac opens to eject them. (*Compare:* Basidiomycete)

Ascus: The sac-like container that produces spores on the group of mushrooms called ascomycetes. (*Plural:* asci)

Attached gills: Gills that are attached to both the underside of the cap and to the stem. (*Compare:* Free gills)

Basidiomycete: Scientific name for a group of mushrooms whose spores develop on microscopic club-shaped appendages called basidia. This includes most mushrooms with gills and pores, as well as puffballs. (*Compare:* Ascomycete)

Basidium: Microscopic club-shaped appendage with tiny prongs that carry spores. (*Plural*: basidia) *See also* Basidiomycete.

Bolete: General name used for mushrooms that have a cap and stem with a pore surface under the cap rather than gills or teeth. Many are in the *Boletus* genera; others are not but are still commonly referred to as "boletes."

Bracket: Term used to describe mushrooms that grow laterally (sideways) from a tree or another object, usually without an obvious stem. (*Synonym:* Shelf)

Branching: The growth habit of a mushroom or part of a mushroom that has multiple stems or limbs, resembling the branches of a tree. (*Compare:* Unbranching)

Brown rot: A condition where a fungal organism breaks down and consumes the cellulose of a tree and replaces it with lignin, leaving a brown, corky material behind. (*Compare:* White rot)

Bruise/bruising: A color transformation, usually in the cut flesh, gills or pore surface of a mushroom.

Bulbous: Abruptly swollen or rounded; generally refers to the base of a mushroom stem. (*Compare:* Club-shaped)

Button: An immature or newly emerging mushroom on which the gills or pores underneath the cap are not visible yet. Usually spherical or egg-shaped.

Canker: A sore or tumor-like growth, derived from the Latin word *cancer.*

Cap: The top or head of the mushroom, usually used in reference to mushrooms with a stem. In forms with lateral (sideways) or less prominent stem growth, the cap may be more shelf-like. Called the pileus in some sources.

Chambered: A cavity that is broken into multiple enclosed spaces. In mushrooms, it may occur in the stem or inside the entire fungus.

Close gills: Numerous gills that are closely spaced but still have slight separation from one another.

Club-shaped: Gradually swollen; refers to the base of a mushroom stem. (*Compare:* Bulbous)

Concentric: Usually refers to ridges, lines or other bands of texture or color that are circular and parallel, surrounding a central point. (*Compare:* Radiate)

Coniferous: A tree or shrub with needle-like or scale-like leaves (usually evergreen) whose seeds are contained in cones. (*Compare:* Deciduous, Hardwood)

Cortina: A partial veil over the gills that resembles cotton fibers or a spiderweb.

Cross-veins: Connecting ridges between the gills or gill-like folds of some mushrooms; appears as a net-like pattern.

Crowded gills: Numerous gills that are so tightly packed that the spaces between them are not visible.

Crust: Mushrooms growing as a thin layer covering a surface, usually on dead or decaying tree branches or logs.

Cup: Multiple meanings. Usually refers to the shape of a mushroom whose cap or entire body is concave, like a bowl. Also used to describe the sac-like structure found at the base of the stem on some species (especially Amanita). Cup Fungi is additionally used as a general term for members of the Ascomycete group, which have sac-like structures that produce spores. *See also* Ascus, Volva.

Deciduous: Trees and shrubs that lose their leaves each year, rather than being evergreen; also referred to as hardwoods. (*Compare:* Coniferous)

Decomposer: Something that hastens or facilitates decay or decomposition.

Decurrent gills: Attached gills that run down the stem. (*Compare:* Attached gills)

Deliquesce: To dissolve, turning to liquid.

Eccentric: Off-center; for mushrooms it is usually used in reference to the placement or the growth of the stem.

Egg: The immature stage of growth where a mushroom is entirely covered by a thin membrane called a universal veil.

Fairy ring: A group of mushrooms growing in a circle or an arc.

Fertile: Capable of reproduction; for mushrooms, "fertile surface" refers to the surface that holds and releases spores. (*Compare:* Sterile)

Filament: A thin, string-like piece of material.

Flesh: For mushrooms, a term describing the interior that is revealed when the mushroom is cut.

Folds: Gill-like ridges found under the cap of some mushrooms (notably Chanterelles); like gills, the folds contain the microscopic spore-bearing structures.

Forked gills: Gills that branch into two (or more) sections, often near the cap edge.

Free gills: Gills that are attached to the underside of the cap but are not attached to the stem. (*Compare:* Attached gills)

Fruit/fruiting body: The part of a fungal organism that is visible above the ground or other growing medium; another word for what we generally call a mushroom.

Fungus: The scientific Kingdom that is neither plant nor animal; includes yeasts and molds as well as the fleshy fruit bodies we commonly call mushrooms. (*Plural:* fungi) *See also* Kingdom.

Gastrointestinal: The lower digestive tract of the body. "Gastrointestinal problems" refers to a stomachache, cramps and/or diarrhea.

Genus: Scientific classification in biology; the second-to-last level of Latin naming for a living organism. Could be considered the Latin "last name" for a living organism but is listed before the species name. (*Plural:* genera. *Compare:* Phylum, Species) *See also* Kingdom.

Gills: Blade-like or plate-like structures attached to the cap underside of some mushrooms; the gills contain the microscopic spore-bearing structures. Some sources refer to gills as lamellae. (*Singular:* lamella)

Glandular dots: Textural markings that are minutely raised and usually of a different color than the background; found on the stem of some mushrooms. Glandular dots are smaller than scabers. *See also* Scabers.

Habitat: A term used to describe the area where a mushroom grows, including geography, type of soil or other substrate, and other species of plants (usually trees) nearby.

Hand lens: A small, hand-held magnifying glass, used to see minute but not microscopic features. (*Synonym:* Loupe)

Hardwood: A broad-leaved tree whose seeds are contained in fruits or nuts; also referred to as deciduous trees. (*Compare:* Coniferous)

Host: A term used to describe an organism on which a mushroom (or other organism) is growing; the host may be a tree, plant or another mushroom. *See also* Parasite.

Hygrophanous: An adjective that describes a type of mushroom whose tissue changes appearance (color or texture) based on the amount of moisture present.

Kingdom: Scientific classification in biology; the first level of Latin naming for a living organism. Fungi are called the third kingdom, after plants and animals. The 7 levels of this classification are: Kingdom, Phylum, Class, Order, Family, Genus, Species.

Latex: Thickened fluid that comes from slicing the flesh or gills of *Lactarius* and some other species of mushrooms.

Loupe: A small, hand-held magnifying glass, used to see minute but not microscopic features. (*Synonym:* Hand lens)

Macro fungi: The fruiting body or reproductive structure of a fungus that is visible to the naked eye.

Margin: The edge, usually referring to the outer portion of a mushroom's cap.

Marginate: To have a well-defined border; with mushrooms, usually in reference to the edge of the cap or the bottom edge of the gills.

Membrane: Skin-like tissue; with mushrooms, usually used in reference to a partial or universal veil.

Milky: A term used to refer to some species of mushrooms that ooze a fluid when cut or scored across the gills or flesh. *See also* Latex.

Mixed woods: An area that has both deciduous and coniferous trees.

Morphology: The study or categorization of an organism based on its physical structure or appearance. (*Compare:* Taxonomy)

Mushroom: The general term for the fleshy fruitbody of a fungal organism.

Mycelium: The collective name for the root-like filaments of a fungal organism.

Mycology: The study of mushrooms.

Mycorrhizal: An adjective that describes a mushroom that grows from the ground but has a symbiotic relationship with the roots of trees. (*Compare:* Saprobe)

Notched gills: Gills that are attached to the stem with a slight notch at the point of attachment.

Parasite: An organism that grows on another living organism in a relationship that benefits one organism to the detriment of the other; feeding off something while it is still alive with no benefit to the host. *See also* Host.

Partial veil: A membrane on the underside of the cap of some immature mushrooms; it stretches from the stem to the cap edge, covering the gills or pores. When the cap expands as the mushroom matures it breaks the partial veil, sometimes leaving fragments on the cap edge and a ring on the stem. (*Compare:* Universal veil) *See also* Ring, Ring zone.

Patches: Small to medium-size, irregularly shaped pieces of tissue attached to the surface of a mushroom cap; they are remnants of a universal veil. *See also* Warts.

Perennial: A mushroom whose fruitbody persists over several years; new growth layers are added to the existing fruitbody each year. (*Compare:* Annual)

Phylum: Scientific classification in biology; the second level of Latin naming for a living organism. (*Plural:* phyla. *Compare:* Genus, Species) *See also* Kingdom.

Polypore: Literally means "having many pores"; refers to a group of mushroom species that release their spores from a surface covered with minute holes.

Pores: Minute holes or openings. In mushrooms, usually part of the fertile, or spore-producing, surface. *See also* Polypore.

Pubescent: Having minute hairs.

Radiate: With mushrooms, refers to lines, ridges or grooves that emanate from a central point, like the spokes of a wheel. The lines, ridges or grooves are often faint and only the outer portions may be visible. (*Compare:* Concentric)

Resupinate: A stemless fruitbody that appears to grow upside-down, with its back fused onto the substrate and its fertile surface facing upward. Usually found growing on fallen logs or other horizontal surfaces. *See also* Crust.

Reticulation: A net-like pattern of raised ridges.

Ring: A band of tissue encircling the stem of mushrooms that have a partial veil. It may be large and skirt-like, or small and fragile; it may be firmly attached to the stem or free. Also called an annulus. (*Compare:* Ring zone) *See also* Partial veil.

Ring zone: The place on a mushroom stem where a partial veil was once attached. The ring (see pg. 13) may move or deteriorate with age, leaving a zone where the stem texture or color may be different. It may also collect the spores that have been released from above. *See also* Partial veil.

Rosette: Growing in a circular and layered pattern, like a flower; rose-like.

Saprobe: Mushrooms that get their nutrients from dead or decaying organic matter are called saprobic. (*Compare:* Mycorrhizal)

Scabers: Minute raised scales on the stems of some mushrooms; often a different color than the stem. Scabers are larger than glandular dots. They are a key ID feature for some mushrooms, especially the *Leccinum* species, which are called scaber stalks. *See also* Glandular dots.

Scales: Raised growths that are generally minute to small. There are various textures possible, from fibrous and tufted, to pointy and sharp. The nature of the scales is usually a key ID feature. May be called scabrous in some sources.

Serrate: Jagged in appearance, like the edge of a saw blade. Usually in reference to the edges of gills.

Shelf: Term used to describe mushrooms that grow laterally (sideways) from a tree or another object, usually without an obvious stem. (*Synonym:* Bracket)

Species: Scientific classification in biology; the final or last level of Latin naming for a living organism. Could be considered the Latin "first name" for a living organism but is listed after the genus name. (*Compare:* Genus, Phylum) *See also* Kingdom.

Spore deposit: Visible ripe spores that have been released by a mushroom; may be seen on nearby plants, objects or other mushrooms. *See also* Spore print.

Spore print: A spore deposit deliberately caught on a piece of paper; spore prints are made by mushroom enthusiasts for purposes of identification.

Spores: Microscopic reproductive structures, like the "seeds" of mushrooms. Spores are part of sexual reproduction in fungi, as opposed to the same organism growing and spreading to produce additional fruit bodies.

Stem: The part of the mushroom on some species that grows to support a cap. Referred to as the stipe in some sources.

Sterile: Incapable of reproduction; for mushrooms, "sterile surface" refers to the non-spore-producing surface. (*Compare:* Fertile)

Striate: Lines or ridges on a mushroom, usually visible on the cap surface or on the stem.

Substrate: The material or medium on which a mushroom is growing: wood, soil, leaves, straw, compost, wood chips, etc.

Symbiotic: A mutually beneficial relationship, where one organism provides benefits to another in exchange for something it needs. (*Compare:* Parasite) *See also* Mycorrhizal.

Tawny: A color that ranges from tan to light brown, sometimes having a yellowish or reddish hue.

Taxonomy: The science of classifying and naming living organisms based on biological characteristics and relationships. Groups such as genus and species are called taxa. (*Singular:* taxon. *Compare:* Morphology)

Terrestrial: Growing from the ground. *See also* Substrate, Habitat.

Toadstool: Synonym for mushroom; often used to refer to poisonous species.

Tomentose: Having a dense covering of fine, short hair.

Tubes: Hollow cylindrical structures on some mushrooms, especially boletes, that contain the spore-producing structures. The pores are packed tightly together under the cap; openings in the bottoms of the tubes create a spongy texture known as a pore surface.

Umbo: A bump, knob or nipple-like protrusion at the top of a mushroom cap; a cap with this feature is called umbonate.

Unbranching: The growth habit of a mushroom or part of a mushroom that has a single stem or member. (*Compare:* Branching)

Uniform: Even all over. Usually in reference to a color, texture, size or other growth pattern.

Universal veil: A thin membrane that completely surrounds an immature or developing mushroom. As the mushroom grows, it breaks the partial veil, sometimes leaving fragments on the cap surface and around the base of the stem. (*Compare:* Partial veil) *See also* Button, Egg, Patches, Volva, Warts.

Veil remnants: The remains of a partial or universal veil on a mature mushroom. Partial veil remnants are typically shaggy, tissue-like pieces hanging from the cap edges. Universal veil remnants may appear as warts or patches on the top of a cap.

Viscid: Having a sticky, but not slimy, surface. The caps of some mushroom species react to moisture in the air and are tacky when wet.

Volva: The fragile, sac-like structure that remains at the base of the stem on species that have a universal veil. As the mushroom grows, it breaks through the membrane, leaving this sac at the base of the stem. It is a common feature of *Amanita* and *Volvariella* species and is sometimes called a cup.

Warts: Small, irregularly shaped pieces of tissue attached to the surface of a mushroom cap; they are remnants of a universal veil. *See also* Patches.

White rot: A condition where a fungal organism uses the lignin of a tree and replaces it with cellulose, leaving a soft, white rotted material behind. (*Compare:* Brown rot)

Zonate: Having distinct stripes, bands or zones of color or texture.

Index

Note: **Bold text** indicates primary species description

C

Q

R

S

T

U

V